Developing Kaggle Notebooks

Pave your way to becoming a Kaggle Notebooks Grandmaster

Gabriel Preda

BIRMINGHAM—MUMBAI

Packt and this book are not officially connected with Kaggle. This book is an effort from the Kaggle community of experts to help more developers.

Developing Kaggle Notebooks

Lead Senior Publishing Product Manager: Tushar Gupta

Acquisition Editor – Peer Reviews: Gaurav Gavas

Project Editor: Amisha Vathare

Content Development Editor: Tanya D'cruz

Copy Editor: Safis Editing

Technical Editor: Aniket Shetty

Proofreader: Safis Editing

Indexer: Rekha Nair

Presentation Designer: Ganesh Bhadwalkar

Developer Relations Marketing Executive: Monika Sangwan

First published: December 2023

Production reference: 1191223

Published by Packt Publishing Ltd.

Grosvenor House

11 St Paul's Square

Birmingham

B3 1RB, UK.

ISBN 978-1-80512-851-9

www.packt.com

Forewords

When I entered the world of AI and ML over twenty years ago, it was hard to describe to the people in my life what this field was. The ideas of *finding patterns in data* made it sound like I was hunting around in the attic with a flashlight. Telling family members about *creating models that made useful predictions* seemed to bring to mind children's toys, or maybe some sort of fortune-telling. And the suggestion that machines might *learn* or be made to act with some form of observable *intelligence* was seen as the sort of thing that serious people left to the realm of science fiction.

Here we are in 2023, and the world has changed dramatically. The world of AI and ML has made stunning advances and has become – at least in my opinion – one of the most important technologies in existence. Predictive models are a tightly integrated part of nearly every computational platform, system, or application and impact business, trade, health, education, transportation, nearly every scientific field, and creative fields from visual art to music to writing. Indeed, AI and ML have become so important that the topics of governance, policy, and regulation are also emerging areas of rapid development themselves, and it seems that there is a new development almost every week.

Much of the most recent focus of attention has been on Generative AI, driven by LLMs and related methods, all of which draw on the last decade of advances in scaling up deep learning methods. For these models, it can feel like bigger is always better, and the scale of resources – computation, data, expertise – needed to contribute to this field makes it inaccessible to anyone outside of a small number of large players in the space. Personally, I reject this viewpoint.

I think that **what the world really needs in this moment of massive change and development is for as many people as possible to learn how AI and ML models and systems work.** We need as many people as possible to be able to train models, yes, but also to tweak and change them, to evaluate them, to understand their strengths and weaknesses, and to help identify ways that they can be more reliable, more efficient, less biased, more useful, and more accessible to everyone across the globe. Doing this within a broad, worldwide community helps to make sure that the things we learn together are shared broadly but are also stress-tested and re-evaluated by others.

This spirit of sharing is something that I think Gabriel Preda has embodied for many years, as a leading Kaggle Grandmaster. His dedication to our Kaggle community has been amazing, and his willingness to share his expertise serves as an example for all of us. This is one of the reasons why I think that this book itself is so important. Creating and sharing notebooks is the best way to make sure that the things we think are true can be checked, verified, and built upon by others.

So what does the world of AI and ML need right now, in this incredible moment of possibility? It needs you.

Welcome to Kaggle!

D. Sculley

Kaggle CEO
December 2023

My background is in econometrics, and I became interested in machine learning initially as an alternative approach to solving forecasting problems. My personal experience with the new field was not entirely positive at the start: I lacked familiarity with the techniques, terminology, and credentials that typically facilitate entry.

We created Kaggle with the hope that the platform would allow people like me the opportunity to break into this powerful new field much easier than it was for me. Perhaps the thing that makes me most proud is the extent to which Kaggle has made data science and machine learning more accessible for a wide audience. Kaggle has seen newcomers evolve into top machine learners, securing positions at renowned companies like NVIDIA, Google, Hugging Face, and OpenAI, and even launching their ventures such as DataRobot.

Started as a machine learning competition platform, Kaggle has evolved to host datasets, notebooks, and discussions. Through Kaggle Learn, it offers easy-to-follow learning modules for beginners and the advanced alike. Currently, over 300,000 of the 15 million Kaggle users are actively publishing and ranked in the notebooks tier. Notebooks are an excellent way to share knowledge through exploration and analysis of datasets, prototyping machine learning models, collecting dataset data, and preparing training and inference scripts for competition.

Gabriel's book will make Kaggle more accessible, especially for those interested in learning how to create detailed data analysis notebooks, refine their presentation skills, and create powerful narratives with data. It also offers examples of using notebooks to iteratively build models to prepare for competition submissions, and introduces users to the newest available features on Kaggle, including a chapter that shows how to leverage the power of Generative AI through Kaggle Models for prototyping applications with large language models to generate code, create chains of tasks, or build retrieval augmented generation systems.

Gabriel is a triple Kaggle Grandmaster, with a seven-year tenure on Kaggle. He ranked 2nd in Datasets and 3rd in Notebooks. Some of his notebooks and datasets are the most upvoted by the community in the past. With his immense expertise filled within the pages of this book, those who complete this book should be able to confidently create great notebooks with a high impact on the community and, therefore, share their knowledge and engage with the community.

Machine learning and artificial intelligence are moving extremely fast, especially in recent years. Being active on Kaggle keeps you connected with the community that filters from the vast number of publications, new technologies, libraries, frameworks, and models what is useful and applicable to solving real-world problems. Many of the tools that have become standard in the industry have spread through Kaggle, after being validated by the Kaggle community.

Moreover, Kaggle offers users a way to "learn by doing." Especially in notebooks, there is a lot of feedback from the community, and contributors are stimulated to continuously improve the content that they are sharing.

So, for those of you who are reading this book and are new to Kaggle, I hope it helps make Kaggle, and especially writing Kaggle notebooks, less intimidating. And for those who have been on Kaggle for a while and are looking to level up, I hope this book from one of Kaggle's most respected members helps you get more out of your time on the platform.

Anthony Goldbloom

Founder and former CEO of Kaggle

Contributors

About the author

Gabriel Preda has a PhD in computational electromagnetics and started his career in academic and private research. Twenty-five years ago, he authored his first paper that included the use of an AI technique – Neural Networks – to solve inverse problems in nondestructive testing and evaluation. Soon after, he moved from academia to private research and worked for a few years as a researcher for a high-tech company in Tokyo. After he moved back to Europe, he co-founded two technology start-ups and has worked for several product companies and software service corporations in software development for more than 20 years, holding development and management positions. Currently, Gabriel is a Principal Data Scientist at Endava, working for a range of industries from banking and insurance to telecom, logistics, and healthcare. He is a high-profile contributor in the world of competitive machine learning and currently one of the few triple Kaggle Grandmasters (in Datasets, Notebooks, and Discussions).

My warmest thanks go to my family, Midori and Cristina, for their support and patience while I prepared this book. I am grateful to Anthony Goldbloom, co-founder and former CEO, and to D. Sculley, current CEO of Kaggle, for their forewords to this book. Finally, I would like to thank Tushar Gupta, Amisha Vathare, Tanya D'cruz, Monika Sangwan, Aniket Shetty, and all the Packt Publishing editorial and production staff for their support on this writing effort.

About the reviewers

Konrad Banachewicz is a data science manager with experience stretching longer than he likes to ponder on. He holds a PhD in statistics from Vrije Universiteit Amsterdam, where he focused on problems of extreme dependency modeling in credit risk. He slowly moved from classic statistics toward machine learning and into the business applications world. He worked in a variety of financial institutions on an array of data problems and visited all the stages of a data product cycle: from translating business requirements ("What do they really need?"), through data acquisition ("Spreadsheets and flat files? Really?"), wrangling, modeling, and testing (the actually fun part), all the way to presenting the results to people allergic to mathematical terminology (which is most of the business). He is currently the principal data scientist at IKEA.

As a person who stood on the shoulders of giants, I believe in sharing knowledge with others: it is very important to know how to approach practical problems with data science methods, but also how not to do it.

Marília Prata is a retired dental doctor who worked for 28 years in her private clinic, provided dental audit services for Petrobras (Petróleo Brasilero S/A), and served as a public servant in the Civil Police of Rio de Janeiro. She also completed two specializations in dental prosthesis and occupational dentistry. She is currently a triple Kaggle Grandmaster at the time of publishing, ranking second in Notebooks.

I'm very grateful to the Kaggle platform and its users (Kagglers) because it's a perfect place to start learning programming languages hands-on. Special thanks to Gabriel Preda for trusting my ability to review his invaluable work in this riveting field of data science.

Dr. Firat Gonen, PhD, orchestrates the Data and Analytics division at Allianz, propelling a Fortune 50 company with pioneering machine learning initiatives. His expertise, built on a foundation laid during his academic tenure culminating in a PhD from the University of Houston, now guides Allianz's data-driven strategies. His role at Allianz was preceded by leadership positions at Getir – Turkish Decacorn App – and Vodafone, where he honed his prowess in managing adept data teams. Dr. Gonen's extensive educational background and academic diligence are reflected in multiple peer-reviewed publications and complemented by his status as a Kaggle Triple Grandmaster, further adorned with numerous international data competition accolades. As the Z by HP Global Data Science Ambassador, Dr. Gonen advocates for the transformative power of data, underscoring the symbiotic relationship between cutting-edge technology and industry-leading insights. He was recently awarded the title of LinkedIn Top Data Science and Artificial Intelligence Voice. He also reviewed the Kaggle Book.

I would like to thank Deniz for her help, guidance, love, and her constant support along the way.

Join our book's Discord space

Join our Discord community to meet like-minded people and learn alongside more than 5000 members at:

https://packt.link/kaggle

Table of Contents

Preface

More than six years ago, before I first discovered Kaggle, I was searching for a new path in my professional career. A few years later, I was firmly entrenched in a new job, which Kaggle helped me find. Before discovering this marvelous site, I was looking around on different sites, reading articles, downloading and analyzing datasets, trying out pieces of code from GitHub or other sites, doing online trainings, and reading books. With Kaggle, I found more than a source of information; I found a community sharing the same interest in machine learning, and, more generally, in data science, looking to learn, share knowledge, and solve difficult challenges. I also discovered that in this community, if you want, you can experience an accelerated learning curve, because you can learn from the best, sometimes competing against them, and other times collaborating with them. You can also learn from the less experienced; after all these years on the platform, I am still learning from both crowds.

This mix of continuous challenges and fruitful collaboration makes Kaggle a unique platform, where new and old contributors can feel equally welcome and find things to learn or share. In my first months on the platform, I mostly learned from the vast collections of datasets and notebooks, analyzing competition data and offering solutions for active or past competitions and on the discussion threads. I soon started to contribute, mostly to notebooks, and discovered how rewarding it is to share your own findings and get feedback from other people on the platform. This book is about sharing this joy and what I learned while sharing my findings, ideas, and solutions with the community.

This book is intended to introduce you to the wide world of data analysis, with a focus on how you can use Kaggle Notebooks resources to help you achieve mastery in this field. We will cover simple concepts to more advanced ones. The book is also a personal journey and will take you down a similar path to the one I took while experimenting and learning about analyzing datasets and preparing for competitions.

Who this book is for

The book is intended for a wide audience with a keen interest in data science and machine learning and who would like to use Kaggle Notebooks to improve their skills as well as raise their Kaggle Notebooks ranks. To be precise, this book caters to:

- Absolute beginners on their Kaggle journey
- Experienced contributors who would like to develop various data ingestion, preparation, exploration, and visualization skills
- Experts who want to learn from one of the early Kaggle Notebooks Grandmasters how to rise in the upper Kaggle rankings
- Professionals who already use Kaggle for learning and competing and would like to learn more about data analytics

What this book covers

Chapter 1, Introducing Kaggle and Its Basic Functions, is a quick introduction to Kaggle and its main features, including competitions, datasets, code (formerly known as kernels or notebooks), discussions and additional resources, models, and learning.

Chapter 2, Getting Ready for Your Kaggle Environment, contains more details about the code features on Kaggle, with information about computing environments, how to use the online editor, how to fork and modify an existing example, and how to use the source control facilities on Kaggle to either save or run a new notebook.

Chapter 3, Starting Our Travel – Surviving the Titanic Disaster, introduces a simple dataset that will help you to build a foundation for the skills that we will further develop in the book. Most Kagglers will start their journey on the platform with this competition. We introduce some tools for data analysis in Python (pandas and NumPy), data visualization (Matplotlib, Seaborn, and Plotly), and suggestions on how to create the visual identity of your notebook. We will perform univariate and bivariate analysis of the features, analyze missing data, and generate new features with various techniques. You will also receive your first look into deep diving into data and using analysis combined with model baselining and iterative improvement to go from exploration to preparation when building a model.

Chapter 4, Take a Break and Have a Beer or Coffee in London, combines multiple tabular and map datasets to explore geographical data. We start with two datasets: the first dataset contains the spatial distribution of pubs in the United Kingdom (*Every Pub in England*), and the second contains the distribution of Starbucks coffee shops across the world (*Starbucks Locations Worldwide*).

We start by analyzing them separately, investigating missing data and understanding how we can fill in missing data by using alternative data sources. Then we analyze the datasets together and focus on one small region, i.e., London, where we superpose the data. We will also discuss aligning data with different spatial resolutions. More insights into style, presentation organization, and storytelling will be provided.

Chapter 5, Get Back to Work and Optimize Microloans for Developing Countries, goes one step further and starts analyzing data from a Kaggle analytics competition, *Data Science for Good: Kiva Crowdfunding*. Here, we combine multiple loan history, demographics, country development, and map datasets to create a story about how to improve the allocation of microloans in developing countries. One of the focuses of this chapter will be on creating a unified and personal presentation style, including a color scheme, section decorations, and graphics style. Another focus will be on creating a coherent story about and based on the data that supports the thesis of the notebook. We end the chapter with a quick investigation into an alternative data analytics competition dataset, *Meta Kaggle*, where we disprove a hypothesis about a perceived trend in the community.

Chapter 6, Can You Predict Bee Subspecies?, teaches you how to explore a dataset of images. The dataset used for this analysis is *The BeeImage Dataset: Annotated Honeybee Images*. We combine techniques for image analysis with techniques for the analysis and visualization of tabular data to create a rich and insightful analysis and prepare for building a machine learning pipeline for multiclass image classification. You will learn how to input and display sets of images, how to analyze the images, metadata, how to perform image augmentation, and how to work with different resizing options. We will also show how to start with a baseline model and then, based on the training and validation error analysis, iteratively refine the model.

Chapter 7, Text Analysis Is All You Need, uses `Jigsaw Unintended Bias in Toxicity Classification`, a dataset from a text classification competition. The data is from online postings and, before we use it to build a model, we will need to perform data quality assessment and data cleaning for text data. We will then explore the data, analyze the frequency of words and vocabulary peculiarities, get a few insights into syntactic and semantic analysis, perform sentiment analysis and topic modeling, and start the preparation for training a model. We will check the coverage of the vocabulary available with our tokenization or embedding solution for the corpus in our dataset and apply data processing to improve this vocabulary coverage.

Chapter 8, Analyzing Acoustic Signals to Predict the Next Simulated Earthquake, will look at how to work with time series, while analyzing the dataset for the `LANL Earthquake EDA and Prediction` competition.

After performing an analysis of the features, using various types of modality analysis to reveal the hidden patterns in the signals, we will learn how to generate features using the fast Fourier transform, Hilbert transform, and other transformations for this time-series model. Then we will learn how to generate several features using the various signal processing functions. Readers will learn the basics about analyzing signal data, as well as how to generate features using various signal processing transformations to build a model.

Chapter 9, Can You Find Out Which Movie Is a Deepfake?, discusses how to perform image and video analysis on *Deepfake Detection Challenge*, a large video dataset from a famous Kaggle competition. Analysis will start with training and data exploration, and readers will learn how to manipulate the .mp4 format, extract images from video, check video metadata information, perform pre-processing of extracted images, and find objects, including body, upper body, face, eyes, or mouth, in the images using either computer vision techniques or pre-trained models. Finally, we will prepare to build a model to come up with a solution for this deep fake detection competition.

Chapter 10, Unleash the Power of Generative AI with Kaggle Models, will provide unique and expert insights into how we can use Kaggle models to combine the semantic power of **Large Language Models (LLMs)** with LangChain and vector databases to unleash the power of Generative AI and prototype the latest breed of AI applications using the Kaggle platform.

Chapter 11, Closing Our Journey: How to Stay Relevant and on Top, provides insights on how to not only become one of the top Kaggle Notebooks contributors but also maintain that position, while creating quality notebooks, with a good structure and a great impact.

To get the most out of this book

You should have a basic understanding of Python and familiarity with Jupyter Notebooks. Ideally, you will also need some basic knowledge of libraries like pandas and NumPy.

The chapters contain both theory and code. If you want to run the code in the book, the easiest way is to follow the links on the README.md introduction page in the GitHub project for each notebook, fork the notebook, and run it on Kaggle. The Kaggle environment is pre-installed with all the needed Python libraries. Alternatively, you can download the notebooks from the GitHub project, upload them on Kaggle, attach the dataset resources mentioned in the book for each specific example, and run them. Another alternative is to download the datasets on Kaggle, install your own local environment, and run the notebooks there. In this case, however, you will need more advanced knowledge about how to set up a conda environment locally and install Python libraries using pip install or conda install.

Requirements for the chapter exercises	Version no.
Python	3.9 or higher

All exercises developed on the Kaggle platform use the current Python version, which is 3.10 at the time of writing this book.

Download the example code files

The code bundle for the book is hosted on GitHub at https://github.com/PacktPublishing/ Developing-Kaggle-Notebooks. We also have other code bundles from our rich catalog of books and videos available at https://github.com/PacktPublishing/. Check them out!

Download the color images

We also provide a PDF file that has color images of the screenshots/diagrams used in this book. You can download it here: https://packt.link/gbp/9781805128519.

Conventions used

There are a number of text conventions used throughout this book.

CodeInText: Indicates code words in text, database table names, folder names, filenames, file extensions, pathnames, dummy URLs, user input, and Twitter handles. For example: "Run the info() function for each dataset."

A block of code is set as follows:

```
for sentence in selected_text["comment_text"].head(5):
    print("\n")
    doc = nlp(sentence)
    for ent in doc.ents:
        print(ent.text, ent.start_char, ent.end_char, ent.label_)
    displacy.render(doc, style="ent",jupyter=True)
```

Any command-line input or output is written as follows:

```
!pip install kaggle
```

Bold: Indicates a new term, an important word, or words that you see on the screen. For instance, words in menus or dialog boxes appear in the text like this. For example: "You will have to start a notebook and then choose the **Set as Utility Script** menu item from the **File** menu."

Warnings or important notes appear like this.

 Tips and tricks appear like this.

Get in touch

Feedback from our readers is always welcome.

General feedback: Email feedback@packtpub.com and mention the book's title in the subject of your message. If you have questions about any aspect of this book, please email us at questions@packtpub.com.

Errata: Although we have taken every care to ensure the accuracy of our content, mistakes do happen. If you have found a mistake in this book, we would be grateful if you reported this to us. Please visit http://www.packtpub.com/submit-errata, click Submit Errata, and fill in the form.

Piracy: If you come across any illegal copies of our works in any form on the internet, we would be grateful if you would provide us with the location address or website name. Please contact us at copyright@packtpub.com with a link to the material.

If you are interested in becoming an author: If there is a topic that you have expertise in and you are interested in either writing or contributing to a book, please visit http://authors.packtpub.com.

Share your thoughts

Once you've read *Developing Kaggle Notebooks*, we'd love to hear your thoughts! Scan the QR code below to go straight to the Amazon review page for this book and share your feedback.

https://packt.link/r/1805128515

Your review is important to us and the tech community and will help us make sure we're delivering excellent quality content.

Download a free PDF copy of this book

Thanks for purchasing this book!

Do you like to read on the go but are unable to carry your print books everywhere?

Is your eBook purchase not compatible with the device of your choice?

Don't worry, now with every Packt book you get a DRM-free PDF version of that book at no cost.

Read anywhere, any place, on any device. Search, copy, and paste code from your favorite technical books directly into your application.

The perks don't stop there, you can get exclusive access to discounts, newsletters, and great free content in your inbox daily

Follow these simple steps to get the benefits:

1. Scan the QR code or visit the link below

https://packt.link/free-ebook/9781805128519

2. Submit your proof of purchase
3. That's it! We'll send your free PDF and other benefits to your email directly

1

Introducing Kaggle and Its Basic Functions

Kaggle is currently the main platform for competitive predictive modeling. Here, those who are passionate about machine learning, both experts and beginners, have a collaborative and competitive environment to learn, win recognition, share knowledge, and give back to the community. The company was launched in 2010, offering only machine learning competitions. Currently, it is a data platform that includes sections titled **Competitions**, **Datasets**, **Code**, **Discussions**, **Learn**, and, most recently, **Models**.

In 2011, Kaggle went through an investment round, valuing the company above $25 million. In 2017, it was acquired by Google (now Alphabet Inc.), becoming associated with Google Cloud. The most notable key persons from Kaggle are co-founders Anthony Goldbloom (long-time CEO until 2022) and Ben Hammer (CTO). Recently, D. Sculley, the legendary Google engineer, became Kaggle's new CEO, after Anthony Goldbloom stepped down to become involved in the development of a new start-up.

In this first chapter, we'll explore the main sections that the Kaggle platform offers its members. We will also learn how to create an account, how the platform is organized, and what its main sections are. In short, this chapter will cover the following topics:

- The Kaggle platform
- Kaggle Competitions
- Kaggle Datasets
- Kaggle Code
- Kaggle Discussions

- Kaggle Learn
- Kaggle Models

If you are familiar with the Kaggle platform, you probably know about these features already. You can choose to continue reading the following sections to refresh your knowledge about the platform or you can skip them and go directly to the next chapter.

The Kaggle platform

To start using Kaggle, you will have to create an account. You can register with your email and password or authenticate using your Google account directly. Once registered, you can start by creating a profile with your name, picture, role, and current organization. You then can add your location, which is optional, and a short personal presentation as well. After you perform an SMS verification and add some minimal content on the platform (run one notebook or script, make one competition submission, make one comment, or give one upvote), you will also be promoted from **Novice** to **Contributor**. The following figure shows a checklist for how to become a contributor. As you can see, all items are checked, which means that the user has already been promoted to the **Contributor** tier.

Contributor

You've completed your profile, engaged with the community, and fully explored Kaggle's platform.

☑ Run 1 notebook or script
☑ Make 1 competition submission
☑ Make 1 comment
☑ Give 1 upvote

Figure 1.1: Checklist to become a contributor

With the entire **Contributor** checklist completed, you are ready to start your Kaggle journey.

The current platform contains multiple features. The most important are:

- **Competitions:** This is where Kagglers can take part in competitions and submit their solutions to be scored.
- **Datasets:** In this section, users can upload datasets.
- **Code:** This is one of the most complex features of Kaggle. Also known as Kernels or Notebooks, it allows users to add code (independently or connected to datasets and competitions), modify it, run it to perform analysis, prepare models, and generate submission files for competitions.

- **Discussions**: In this section, contributors on the platform can add topics and comments to competitions, Notebooks, or datasets. Topics can also be added independently and linked to themes such as *Getting Started*.

Each of these sections allows you to gain medals, according to Kaggle's progression system. Once you start to contribute to one of these sections, you can also be ranked in the overall Kaggle ranking system for the respective section. There are two main methods to gain medals: by winning top positions in competitions and by getting upvotes for your work in the **Datasets**, **Code**, and **Discussions** sections.

Besides **Competitions**, **Datasets**, **Code**, and **Discussions**, there are two more sections with content on Kaggle:

- **Learn**: This is one of the coolest features of Kaggle. It contains a series of lectures and tutorials on various topics, from a basic introduction to programming languages to advanced topics like computer vision, model interpretability, and AI ethics. You can use all the other Kaggle resources as support materials for the lectures (Datasets, Competitions, Code, and Discussions).
- **Models**: This is the newest feature introduced on Kaggle. It allows you to load a model into your code, in the same way that you currently add datasets.

Now that we've had a quick overview of the various features of the Kaggle platform, the following sections will give you an in-depth view of Competitions, Datasets, Code, Discussions, Learn, and Models. Let's get started!

Kaggle Competitions

It all started with Competitions more than 12 years ago. The first competition had just a few participants. With the growing interest in machine learning and the increased community around Kaggle, the complexity of the competitions, the number of participants, and the interest around competitions increased significantly.

To start a competition, the competition host prepares a dataset, typically split between train and test. In the most common form, the train set has labeled data available, while the test set only contains the feature data. The host also adds information about the data and a presentation of the competition objective. This includes a description of the problem to set the background for the competitors. The host also adds information about the metrics used to evaluate the solutions to the competition. The terms and conditions of the competitions are also specified.

Competitors are allowed to submit a limited number of solutions per day and, at the end, the best two solutions (evaluated based on a portion of the test set used to calculate the public score) will be selected. Competitors also have the option to select two solutions themselves based on their own judgment. Then, these two selected solutions will be evaluated on the reserved subset of test data to generate the private score. This will be the final score used to rank the competitors.

There are several types of competitions:

- **Featured competitions**: The most important are the featured competitions. Currently, featured competitions might reunite several thousand teams, with tens or even hundreds of thousands of solutions submitted. Featured competitions are typically hosted by companies but also sometimes by research organizations or universities, and are usually aimed at solving a difficult problem related to a company or a research topic. The organizer turns to the large Kaggle community to bring their knowledge and skills, and the competitive aspect of the setup accelerates the development of a solution. Usually, a featured competition will also have a significant prize, which will be distributed according to the competition rules to the top competitors. Sometimes, the host will not include a prize but will offer a different incentive, such as recruiting the top competitors to work for them (with high-profile companies, this might be more interesting than a prize), vouchers for using cloud resources, or acceptance of the top solutions to be presented at high-profile conferences. Besides the Featured competitions, there are also Getting Started, Research, Community, Playground, Simulations, and Analytics competitions.

- **Getting Started competitions**: These are aimed at mostly beginners and tackle easily approachable machine learning problems to help build basic skills. These competitions are restarted periodically and the leaderboard is reset. The most notable ones are *Titanic – Machine Learning for Disaster*, *Digit Recognizer*, *House Prices – Advanced Regression Techniques*, and *Natural Language Processing with Disaster Tweets*.

- **Research competitions**: In Research competitions, the themes are related to finding the solution to a difficult scientific problem in various domains such as medicine, genetics, cell biology, and astronomy by applying a machine learning approach. Some of the most popular competitions in recent years were from this category and with the rising use of machine learning in many fields of fundamental and applied research, we can expect that this type of competition will be more and more frequent and popular.

- **Community competitions**: These are created by Kagglers and are either open to the public or private competitions, where only those invited can take part. For example, you can host a Community competition as a school or university project, where students are invited to join and compete to get the best grades.

Kaggle offers the infrastructure, which makes it very simple for you to define and start a new competition. You have to provide the training and test data, but this can be as simple as two files in CSV format. Additionally, you need to add a submission sample file, which gives the expected format for submissions. Participants in the competition have to replace the prediction in this file with their own prediction, save the file, and then submit it. Then, you have to choose a metric to assess the performance of a machine learning model (no need to define one, as you have a large collection of predefined metrics). At the same time, as the host, you will be required to upload a file with the correct, expected solution to the competition challenge, which will serve as reference against which all competitors' submissions will be checked. Once this is done, you just need to edit the terms and conditions, choose a start and end date for the competition, write the data description and objectives, and you are good to go. Other options that you can choose from are whether participants can team up or not, and whether joining the competition is open to everybody or just to people who receive the competition link.

- **Playground competitions**: Around three years ago, a new section of competitions was launched: Playground competitions. These are generally simple competitions, like the Getting Started ones, but will have a shorter lifespan (it was initially one month, but currently it is from one to four weeks). These competitions will be of low or medium difficulty and will help participants gain new skills. Such competitions are highly recommended to beginners but also to competitors with more experience who want to refine their skills in a certain domain.

- **Simulation competitions**: If the previous types are all supervised machine learning competitions, Simulations competitions are, in general, optimization competitions. The most well known are those around Christmas and New Year (Santa competitions) and also the Lux AI Challenge, which is currently in the third season. Some of the Simulation competitions are also recurrent and will qualify for an additional category: Annual competitions. Examples of such competitions that are of both the Simulations type and Annual are the Santa competitions.

- **Analytics competitions**: These are different in both the objective and the modality of scoring the solutions. The objective is to perform a detailed analysis of the competition dataset to get insights from the data. The score is based, in general, on the judgment of the organizers and, in some cases, on the popularity of the solutions that compete; in this case, the organizers will grant parts of the prizes to the most popular notebooks, based on the upvotes of Kagglers. In *Chapter 5*, we will analyze the data from one of the first Analytics competitions and also provide some insights into how to approach this type of competition.

For a long time, competitions required participants to prepare a submission file with the predictions for the test set. No other constraints were imposed on the method to prepare the submissions; the competitors were supposed to use their own computing resources to train models, validate them, and prepare the submission. Initially, there were no available resources on the platform to prepare a submission. After Kaggle started to provide computational resources, where you could prepare your model using Kaggle Kernels (later named Notebooks and now Code), you could submit directly from the platform, but there was no limitation imposed on this. Typically, the submission file will be evaluated on the fly and the result will be displayed almost instantly. The result (i.e., the score according to the competition metric) will be calculated only for a percentage of the test set. This percentage is announced at the start of the competition and is fixed. Also, the subset of test data used during the competition to calculate the displayed score (the public score) is fixed. After the end of the competition, the final score is calculated with the rest of the test data, and this final score (also known as the private score) is the final score for each competitor. The percentage of the test data used during the competition to evaluate the solution and provide the public score could be anything from a few percent to more than 50%. In most competitions, it tends to be less than 50%.

The reason Kaggle uses this approach is to prevent one unwanted phenomenon. Rather than improving their models for enhanced generalization, competitors might be inclined to optimize their solution to predict the test set as perfectly as possible, without considering the cross-validation score on their train data. In other words, the competitors might be inclined to overfit their solution on the test set. By splitting this data and only providing the score for a part of the test set – the public score – the organizers intend to prevent this.

With more and more complex competitions (sometimes with very large train and test sets), some participants with greater computational resources might gain an advantage, while others with limited resources may struggle to develop advanced models. Especially in featured competitions, the goal is often to create robust, production-compatible solutions. However, without setting restrictions on how solutions are obtained, achieving this goal may be difficult, especially if solutions with unrealistic resource use become prevalent. To limit the negative unwanted consequences of the "arms race" for better and better solutions, a few years ago, Kaggle introduced Code competitions. This kind of competition requires that all solutions be submitted from a running notebook on the Kaggle platform. In this way, the infrastructure to run the solution became fully controllable by Kaggle.

Also, not only are the computing resources limited in such competitions but there are also additional constraints: the duration of the run and internet access (to prevent the use of additional computing power through the use of external APIs or other remote computing resources).

Kagglers discovered quite fast that this was a limitation just for the inference part of the solution and an adaptation appeared: competitors started to train offline, large models that would not fit within the limits of computing power and time of run imposed by the Code competitions. Then, they uploaded the offline trained models (sometimes using very large computational resources) as datasets and loaded these models in the inference code that observed the limits for memory and computation time for the Code competitions.

In some cases, multiple models trained offline were loaded as datasets and inference combined these multiple models to create more precise solutions. Over time, Code competitions have become more refined. Some of them will only expose a few rows from the test set and not reveal the size of the real test set used for the public or future private test set. Therefore, Kagglers have to resort to clever probing techniques to estimate the limitations that might be incurred while running the final, private test set, to avoid a case where their code will fail due to surpassing memory or runtime limits.

Currently, there are also Code competitions that, after the active part of the competition (i.e., when competitors are allowed to continue to refine their solutions) ends, will not publish the private score, but will rerun the code with several new sets of test data, and reevaluate the set-wo selected solutions against these new datasets, which have never been seen before. Some of these competitions are about the stock market, cryptocurrency valuation, or credit performance predictions and they use real data. The evolution of Code competitions ran in parallel with the evolution of available computational resources on the platform, to provide users with the required computational power.

Some of the competitions (most notably the Featured competitions and the Research competitions) grant ranking points and medals to the participants. Ranking points are used to calculate the relative position of Kagglers in the general leaderboard of the platform. The formula to calculate the ranking points awarded for a competition hasn't changed since May 2015:

$$\left[\frac{100000}{\sqrt{N_{\text{teammates}}}}\right] \left[\text{Rank}^{-0.75}\right] \left[\log_{10}(1 + \log_{10}(N_{\text{teams}}))\right] \left[e^{-t/500}\right]$$

Figure 1.2: Formula for calculating ranking points

The number of points decreases with the square root of the number of teammates in the current competition team. More points are awarded for competitions with a larger number of teams. The number of points will also decrease over time, to keep the ranking up to date and competitive.

Medals are counted to get a promotion in the Kaggle progression system for competitions. Medals for competitions are obtained based on the position at the top of the competition leaderboard. The actual system is a bit more complicated but, generally, the top 10% will get a bronze medal, the top 5% will get a silver medal, and the top 1% will get a gold medal. The actual number of medals granted will be larger with an increased number of participants, but this is the basic principle.

With two bronze medals, you reach the Competition Expert tier. With two silver medals and one gold medal, you reach the Competition Master tier. And with one Solo gold medal (i.e., you obtained this medal without teaming up with others) and a total of five gold medals, you reach the most valuable Kaggle tier: the Competition Grandmaster. Currently, at the time of preparing this book, among the over 12 million users on Kaggle, there are 280 Kaggle Competition Grandmasters and 1,936 Masters.

The ranking system adds points depending on the position of users in the leaderboard, which grants ranking points. The points are not permanent, and, as we can see from *Figure 1.2*, there is a quite complex formula for points decreasing. If you do not continue to compete and get new points, your points will decrease quite fast and the only thing that will remind you of your past glory is the maximum rank you reached in the past. However, once you achieve a medal, you will always have that medal in your profile, even if your ranking position changes or your points decrease over time.

Kaggle Datasets

Kaggle Datasets were added only a few years back. Currently, there are more than 200,000 datasets available on the platform, contributed by the users. There were, of course, datasets in the past, associated with the competitions. With the new **Datasets** section, Kagglers can get medals and ranking based on the recognition of other users on the platform, in the form of upvotes for datasets contributed.

Everybody can contribute datasets and the process to add a dataset is quite simple. You first need to identify an interesting subject and a data source. This can be an external dataset that you are mirroring on Kaggle, provided that the right license is in place, or the data is collected by yourself. Datasets can also be authored collectively. There will be a main author, the one that initiates the dataset, but they can add other contributors with view or edit roles. There are a few compulsory steps to define a dataset on Kaggle.

First, you will have to upload one or multiple files and give a name to the dataset. Alternatively, you can set the dataset to be provided from a public link, which should point to a file or a public repository on GitHub. Another way to provision a dataset is from a Kaggle Notebook; in this case, the output of the notebook will be the content of the dataset. The dataset can also be created from a Google Cloud Storage resource. Before creating a dataset, you have the option to set it as public, and you can also check your current private quota. Each Kaggler has a limited private quota (which has been increasing slightly over time; currently, it is over 100 GB). If you decide to keep the dataset private, you will have to fit all your private datasets in this quota. If a dataset is kept private, you can decide at any time to delete it if you do not need it anymore. After the dataset is initialized, you can start improving it by adding additional information.

When creating a dataset, you have the option to add a subtitle, a description (with a minimum number of characters required), and information about each file in the dataset. For tabular datasets, you can also add titles and explanations for each column. Then, you can add tags to make the dataset easier to find through searching and clearly specify the topic, data type, and possible business or research domains, for those interested. You can also change the image associated with the dataset. It is advisable to use a public domain or personal picture. Adding metadata about authors, generating **DOI** (**Digital Object Identifier**) citations, and specifying provenance and expected update frequency are all helpful in boosting the visibility of your dataset. It will also improve the likelihood that your contribution will be correctly cited and used in other works. License information is also important, and you can select from a large list of frequently used licenses. With each element added in the description and metadata about the contributed dataset, you also increase the usability score, calculated automatically by Kaggle. It is not always possible to reach a 10/10 usability score (especially when you have a dataset with tens of thousands of files) but it is always preferable to try to improve the information associated with the dataset.

Once you publish your dataset, this will become visible in the **Datasets** section of the platform, and, depending on the usability and the quality perceived by the content moderators from Kaggle, you might get a special status of **Featured dataset**. Featured datasets get more visibility in searches and are included in the top section of recommended datasets when you select the **Datasets** section. Besides the **Featured** datasets, presented under a **Trending datasets** lane, you will see lanes with themes like **Sport**, **Health**, **Software**, **Food**, and **Travel**, as well as **Recently Viewed Datasets**.

The datasets can include all kinds of file formats. The most frequently used format is CSV. It is a very popular format outside Kaggle too and it is the best format choice for tabular data. When a file is in CSV format, Kaggle will display it, and you can choose to see the content in detail, by columns, or in a compact form. Other possible data formats used are JSON, SQLite, and archives. Although a ZIP archive is not a data format per se, it has full support on Kaggle and you can directly read the content of the archive, without unpacking it. Datasets also include modality-specific formats, various image formats (JPEG, PNG, and so on), audio signals formats (WAV, OGG, and MP3), and video formats. Domain-specific formats, like DICOM for medical imaging, are widely used. BigQuery, a dataset format specific to Google Cloud, is also used for datasets on Kaggle, and there is full support for accessing the content.

If you contribute to datasets, you can get ranking points and medals as well. The system is based on upvotes by other users, upvotes from yourself or from Novice Kagglers, or old upvotes not being included in the calculation for granting ranking points or medals. You can get to the Datasets Expert tier if you acquire three bronze medals, to Master if you get one gold medal and four silver medals, and to Datasets Grandmaster with five gold medals and five silver medals. Acquiring medals in Datasets is not easy, since upvotes in Datasets are not easily granted by users, and you will need 5 upvotes to get a bronze medal, 20 upvotes for a silver medal, and 50 upvotes for a gold medal. Once you get the medals, as these are based on votes, you can lose your medals over time, and even your status as Expert, Master, or Grandmaster can be lost if the users that upvoted you remove their upvote or if they are banned from the platform. This happens sometimes, and not so infrequently as you might think. So, if you want to secure your position, the best approach is to always create high-quality content; this will bring you more upvotes and medals than the minimum required.

Kaggle Code

Kaggle Code is one of the most active sections on the platform. Older names for Code are Kernels and Notebooks and you will frequently hear them used interchangeably. The number of current contributors, at the time of writing this book, exceeds 260,000 and is surpassed by only the **Discussions** section.

Code is used for the analysis of datasets or competition datasets, for preparing models for competition submissions, and for generating models and datasets. In the past, Code could use either R, Python, or Julia as programming languages; currently, you can only choose between Python (the default option) and R. You can set your editor as **Script** or **Notebook**. You can choose the computing resource to run your code, with **CPU** being the default.

Alternatively, you can choose between four options of accelerators if using Python as a programming language or two if using R. Accelerators are provided free of charge, but there is a quota, reset weekly. For high-demand accelerator resources, there might also be a waiting list.

Code is under source control and, when editing, you can choose to just save (and create a version) or save and run (and you create a code version and a run version). You can attach to Code datasets, Competitions datasets, and external utility scripts and models. As long as you are not rerunning the notebook, changes made in the resources used will not affect its visibility. If you try to rerun the code and refresh the datasets or utility script versions, you might need to account for changes in those data and code versions. The output of code can be used as input to other code, in the same way as you include datasets and models. By default, your code is private, and you do not need to make it public to submit the output to a competition.

If you make your code public, you can get upvotes, and these count for both the ranking in the Notebooks category as well as for getting medals. You need 5 bronze medals for the Expert tier in Notebooks, 10 silver medals for the Master tier, and 15 gold medals for the Grandmaster tier. One bronze medal needs 5 upvotes, a silver medal needs 20 upvotes, and a gold medal requires 50 upvotes. Upvotes in Notebooks can be revoked, and you can also make your public notebooks private again (or delete them). In such a case, all upvotes and medals associated with that Notebook are no longer counted for your ranking or performance tier. There are Code sections associated with Competitions, Datasets, and Models. At the time of writing this book, there were 125 Notebook Grandmasters and 472 Masters.

 Kaggle grows and changes continuously, both as a data and competitive machine learning platform and as a community. At the time of writing this book, starting with the new *2023 Kaggle AI Report*, Kaggle introduced a review system for Notebook competitions where all participants submitting an essay are also asked to provide a review for another three participants' essays. The final decision about which submission will win the competition is taken by a panel of experts from veteran Kaggle Grandmasters.

Kaggle Code's many features and options will be described in the next chapter in a more detailed manner.

Kaggle Discussions

Kaggle Discussions are either associated with other sections or independent. Competitions and Datasets both have Discussions sections. For Code, there is a Comments section. In the Discussions section, you can add topics for discussion or comments under a topic. For Code, you can add comments. Besides these contexts, you can add topics or comments under Forums, or you can follow discussions under Discussions from across the Kaggle section. Forums are grouped by subjects, and you can choose between **General**, **Getting Started**, **Product Feedback**, **Questions & Answers**, and **Competition Hosting**. Under Discussions, across Kaggle, you can search the content or focus on a tagged subtopic, like Your **Activity**, **Bookmarks**, **Beginner**, **Data Visualization**, **Computer Vision**, **NLP**, **Neural Networks**, and more.

Discussions also has a progression system and you can get ranking points and medals by accumulating upvotes. Unlike the other sections in which you can get upvotes, in Discussions, you can get downvotes as well. Ranking points can vanish over time and upvotes will count for medals only if from non-Novices and if new. You cannot upvote yourself in Discussions.

Performance tiers in Discussions start with Expert, and you can get this tier by accumulating 50 bronze medals. To get to the next tier, Master, you need 50 silver medals and 200 medals in total, and to reach the Grandmaster tier, you need 50 gold medals and 500 medals in total. Medals are easy to obtain in Discussions compared with other sections; you only need 1 upvote for a bronze medal, 5 upvotes for a silver medal, and a total of 10 upvotes for a gold medal. As with the Datasets and Code cases, the votes are not permanent. Users can decide to retract their upvotes; therefore, you can lose some of your upvotes, ranking points, medals, or even performance tier status.

At the time of writing this book, there were 62 Grandmasters in Discussions and 103 Masters.

Kaggle Learn

Kaggle Learn is one of the lesser-known gems on Kaggle. It contains compact learning modules, each centered on a certain subject related to data science or machine learning. Each learning module has several lessons, each one with a *Tutorial* section followed by an *Exercise* section. The *Tutorial* and *Exercise* sections are available in the form of interactive Kaggle Notebooks. To complete a learning module, you need to go through all the lessons. In each lesson, you will need to review the training material and successfully run the Exercise Notebook. Some of the cells in the Exercise Notebook have a verification associated with them. If you need help, there are also special cells in the notebook that reveal hints about how to solve the current exercise. Upon completing the entire learning module, you receive a certificate of completion from Kaggle.

Currently, Kaggle Learn is organized into three main sections:

- **Your Courses**, where you have the courses that you have completed and those that are now in progress (active).

- **Open courses** that you can explore further. The courses in this main section are from absolute beginner courses (such as *Intro to Programming, Python, Pandas, Intro to SQL*, and *Intro to Machine Learning*) to intermediate courses (such as *Data Cleaning, Intermediate Machine Learning, Feature Engineering*, and *Advanced SQL*). Also, it contains topic-specific courses like *Visualization, Geospatial Analysis, Computer Vision, Time Series*, and *Intro to Game AI and Reinforcement Learning*. Some courses touch on extremely interesting topics such as AI ethics and machine learning interpretability.

- **Guides**, which is dedicated to various learning guides for programs, frameworks, or domains of interest. This includes the *JAX Guide, TensorFlow Guide, Transfer Learning for Computer Vision Guide, Kaggle Competitions Guide, Natural Language Processing Guide*, and *R Guide*.

> Kaggle is also committed to supporting continuous learning and helping anyone benefit from the knowledge accumulated on the Kaggle platform and the Kaggle community. In the last two years, Kaggle has started to reach out and help professionals from underrepresented communities acquire skills and experience in data science and machine learning in the form of the KaggleX **BIPOC (Black, Indigenous, and People of Color)** Grant program, by pairing Kagglers, as mentors, with professionals from BIPOC communities, as mentees.

In the next section, we will familiarize ourselves with a rapidly evolving capability of the Kaggle platform: **Models**.

Kaggle Models

Models is the newest section introduced on the platform; at the time of writing this book, it is less than one month old. Models started to be contributed quite often by users in several ways and for a few purposes. Most frequently, models were saved as output of Notebooks (Code) after being trained using custom code, often in the context of a competition. Subsequently, these models can be optionally included in a dataset or used directly in code. Also, sometimes, models built outside the platform were uploaded as datasets and then included in the pipeline of users to prepare a solution for a competition. Meantime, model repositories were available either through a public cloud, like Google Cloud, AWS, or Azure, or from a company specialized in such a service, like Hugging Face.

With the concept of downloadable models ready to be used or easy to fine-tune for a custom task, Kaggle chose to include **Models** in this platform. Currently, you can search in several categories: *Text Classification, Image Feature Vector, Object Detection,* and *Image Segmentation.* Alternatively, you can use the *Model Finder* feature to explore models specialized in a certain modality: *Image, Text, Audio, Multimodal,* or *Video.* When searching the Models library, you can apply filters on *Task, Data Type, Framework, Language, License,* and *Size,* as well as functional criteria, like *Fine Tuneable.*

There are no ranking points or performance tiers related to models yet. Models can be upvoted and there is a Code and Discussions section associated with each model. In the future, it is possible that we will see evolution here as well and have models with ranking points as well as performance tiers if they make it possible to contribute models and get recognition for this. Currently, models are contributed by Google only.

We might see the Models feature evolving immensely in the near future, providing the community with a flexible and powerful tool for the creation of modular and scalable solutions to train and add inference to machine learning pipelines on the Kaggle platform.

Summary

In this chapter, we learned a little about the history of the Kaggle platform, its resources, and its capabilities. We then introduced the basics of how to create an account and start benefiting from the platform's resources and interaction with other users.

Initially a platform only for predictive modeling competitions, Kaggle has grown to become a complex data platform, with sections for Competitions, Datasets, Code (Notebooks), and Discussions. Hence, we learned how you can move up the ranks by accumulating ranking points and medals in Competitions and medals in Datasets, Notebooks, and Discussions. In the future, it is possible that Kaggle will also add ranking points for other sections besides Competitions, although this is a subject of debate in the Kaggle community. Additionally, Kaggle provides a learning platform (with **Learn**) and **Models** (which can be used in Notebooks).

It's now time to get ready for your trip around the data analysis world, using Kaggle resources. In the next chapter, you will learn how to use the full capacity of the platform to code, get familiar with the development environment, and learn how to use it to its maximum potential. Let's get ready!

Join our book's Discord space

Join our Discord community to meet like-minded people and learn alongside more than 5000 members at:

`https://packt.link/kaggle`

2

Getting Ready for Your Kaggle Environment

In the previous chapter, we learned how to create your Kaggle account, and what is most important to know about Competitions, Datasets, Code (Notebooks), Discussions, and Kaggle Learn and Models. In this chapter, we will explore the Kaggle Notebooks functionality. Kernels and Code are used as alternative names sometimes to refer to Notebooks, Kernels being the old name and Code being the new menu name for Notebooks. Both terms, the old one and the new one, illustrate something important about a notebook on Kaggle.

We will start by introducing what a Kaggle Notebook is and explaining the difference between Kaggle Scripts and Kaggle Notebooks. We will then show how we can create a notebook, either from scratch or derived from an existing one. After you start to edit a notebook, you have multiple options, and we will review each of them in this chapter, starting with the most common (editing data sources and models, changing computing resources, etc.) and then following with the remaining ones (setting a notebook as script, adding utility scripts to the notebook, adding and using secrets, etc.).

In a nutshell, the following main topics will be covered in this chapter:

- What is a Kaggle Notebook?
- How to create notebooks
- Exploring Notebook capabilities
- Using the Kaggle API

What is a Kaggle Notebook?

Kaggle Notebooks are integrated development environments that allow you to write code, version it, run it (using Kaggle platform computational resources), and produce the results in various forms. When you initiate work on a notebook, you start a coding editor. This, in turn, starts a Docker container, provisioned with the most used Python packages for data analysis and machine learning, running in a virtual machine allocated in Google Cloud. The code itself is linked to a code repository.

You can write code in one of two languages: Python or R. Currently, Python is used by most of the users on Kaggle, and all examples in this book will only be in Python.

The term **Notebooks** is used generically, but there are two types of Kaggle Notebooks: Scripts and Notebooks.

- **Kaggle Scripts**: Scripts are files that will execute all code sequentially. The output of the scripts' execution will be printed in the console. If you want, you can also execute a part of the script only, by selecting a few lines and pressing the **Run** button. If you are using the R language for development, you can use a special type of script, RMarkdown script. The environment to develop it is similar to the one for Python or R scripts, but you can use the syntax for RMarkdown, and the output will be a combination of the R code execution results and the RMarkdown syntax for text and graphical effects.

- **Kaggle Notebooks**: Notebooks have a similar look and feel as Jupyter Notebooks. They are similar but not identical. Kaggle Notebooks have multiple additional options to support integration with a Kaggle environment and a better user experience. Notebooks are composed of a succession of cells with either code or Markdown content, and each cell can be executed independently. You can code using either R or Python while using Notebooks. When running a cell, the output generated is displayed right under the cell in the case of code cells.

With a brief overview of Kaggle Notebooks and their essential components, let's see now how you can create a notebook.

How to create notebooks

There are several ways to start a notebook. You can start it from the main menu **Code** (*Figure 2.1*), from the context of a dataset (*Figure 2.2*), a Competition (*Figure 2.3*), or by forking (copying and editing) an existing notebook.

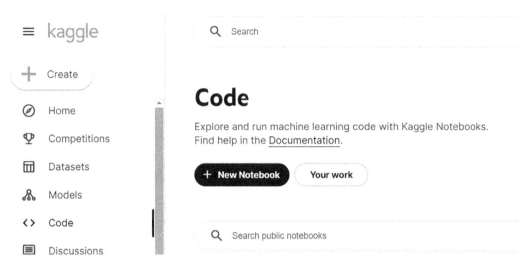

Figure 2.1: Create a new notebook from the Code menu

When you create a new notebook from the **Code** menu, this new notebook will appear in your list of notebooks but will not be added to any Dataset or Competition context.

If you choose to start it from a Kaggle Dataset, the dataset will be already added to the list of data associated with the notebook, and you will see it in the right-side panel (refer to *Figure 2.5*) when you edit the notebook.

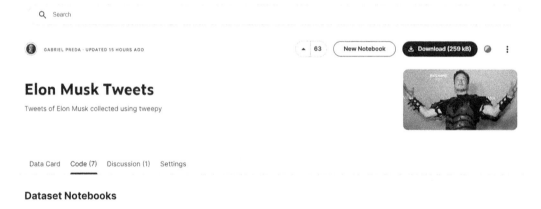

Figure 2.2: Create a new notebook in the context of a Dataset

The same is true in the case of a Competition. The Dataset associated with it will be already present in the list of datasets when you initialize the notebook.

Figure 2.3: Create a new notebook in the context of a Competition

To fork (copy and edit) an existing notebook, press the three vertical dots next to the **Edit** button of that notebook, and then select the **Copy & edit notebook** menu item from the drop-down list.

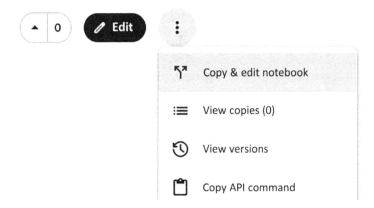

Figure 2.4: Fork a notebook from an existing one

Once created, the notebook will be open for editing, as you can see in the following screenshot. On the upper-left side, there is a regular menu (**File**, **Edit**, **View**, **Run**, **Add-ons**, and **Help**), with quick-action icons for editing and running under it. On the right-hand side, there is a retractable panel with more quick actions.

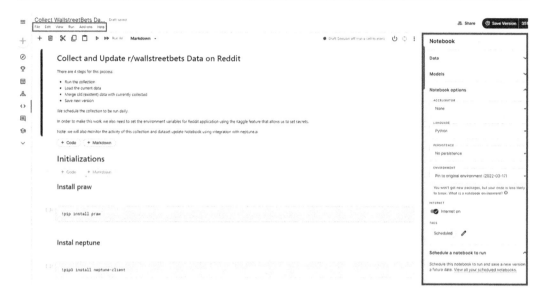

Figure 2.5: Main edit window for Kaggle Notebooks with the right-side panel with quick menus

The **File** menu is complex and offers options for input and output, as well as various settings for interactions with other resources on the platform (Models, Utility Scripts, and Notebooks). It has menu items to import an external notebook or export your current notebook, and to even add data or models to the notebook. You can also either save the current notebook as a utility script or add a utility script to the notebook. You can choose to set the language (to R or Python; by default, is set to Python). There is an option to set the current notebook as a script or a notebook (notebook is the default).

Additional options are for publishing and sharing the notebook on GitHub. To publish the notebook on GitHub, you will have to link your Kaggle account with the GitHub account by authorizing Kaggle to access your GitHub account. Once you perform this operation, updates of the notebook will be mirrored on GitHub as well. Using the **Share menu** item, you can set who can view or edit the notebook. Initially, you will be the only user with read and write access, but once you add contributors, they can also be assigned with both read or write access, or only with read (view) access. If you publish your notebook, then everyone will have access to read it, be able to fork (copy and edit) it, and then edit the work.

The **Edit** menu allows you to move cells around (up and down) or delete a selected cell. In **View**, you have options to adjust the look and feel of the editor (adding or removing themes, line numbers, and setting the editor layout) and the resulting output HTML content (see or hide input or output for selected cells, or collapse or extend cells).

The **Run** menu item provides controls to run one cell, all cells, all cells before or after, and to start/stop a session. At the restart of the session, the Kernel (i.e., the Docker container in which the notebook is running) is restarted, and all context data initialized when we run some of the cells is reset. This is a very useful option when, while editing, you want to reset the environment with all the variables. Add-ons menu groups, secret management, Google Cloud services, and the Google Cloud SDK — each of those extends the functionality of notebooks and will be presented under the *Advanced capabilities* section later in this chapter.

Now that we've learned how to create, edit, and run notebooks, let's continue by exploring more notebook features.

Exploring notebook capabilities

Notebooks serve as powerful tools for data exploration, model training, and running inferences. In this section, we will examine the various capabilities that Kaggle Notebooks have to offer.

We will start off with the most frequently used features of notebooks. We will go through the options to add various resources to a notebook (data and models) and to modify the execution environment. Then, we continue with more advanced features, which will include setting up utility scripts, adding or using secrets, using Google Cloud services, or upgrading a notebook to a Google Cloud AI Notebook. Let's get started!

Basic capabilities

On the right-side panel, we have quick menu actions for access to frequently used features of notebooks. In the following screenshot, we take a more detailed look at these quick menu actions.

Figure 2.6: Zoomed-in view of the right-side panel with quick menus

As you can see, the first quick menu actions are grouped under the **Data** section. Here, you have buttons to add or remove datasets from the notebook. By clicking on the **Add Data** button, you can add one existing dataset. You have the search text box and quick buttons to select from your datasets, competition datasets, and notebooks. When you select your notebooks, you can include the output of notebooks as data sources for the current notebook. You also have an upload button next to the **Add Data** button, and you can use it to upload a new dataset before adding it to the notebook. In the same **Data** section on the panel, you have the input and output folder browser, and buttons next to each item so that you can copy the path to either folders or files.

Right under the **Data** section, we have the **Models** section (see *Figure 2.6*). Here, we can add models to the notebook. **Models** is a new feature on the platform, and it allows you to use powerful pretrained models in your notebook.

In the **Notebook options** section, we can configure the accelerator, the language, the persistence option, the environment, and internet access as per our preferences (see *Figure 2.6*). By default, the notebook will use a **Central Processing Unit** (**CPU**) only. See the following screenshot for the expanded view of **Add Data**, **Add Models**, and **Notebook options** in the right-hand side panel:

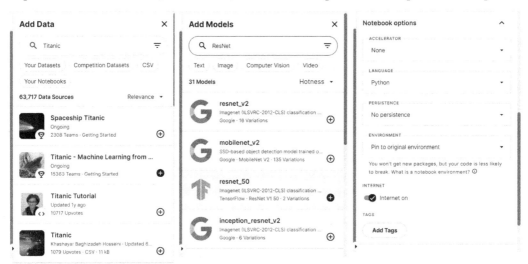

Figure 2.7: Right-side panel menus to add data and models and for Notebook options

You can search datasets by their name or path, and you have speed filters to search in competitions or the output of your notebooks. For **Models** as well, you can search by name and filter by type (text, image, computer vision, or video). **Notebook options** allows the selection of an accelerator type (**None** means CPU-only), the programming language, the persistence type, and the option for the environment.

By choosing the accelerator, you can switch to using one of the two hardware accelerator options for **Graphical Processing Unit** (**GPU**) or **Tensor Processing Unit** (**TPU**). The technical specifications for CPU configuration and accelerator configurations, at the time of writing, are given in *Table 2.1*. For all these specifications, either with CPU or GPU, you have a maximum of 12 hours of continuous execution time. In the case of TPUs, the execution time is limited to 9 hours. The input data size, however, is not limited. The output is limited to 20 GB. An additional 20 GB can be used only temporarily, during runtime, but it will not be saved after the run.

By default, your notebook is set to not use any persistence. You can opt to ensure persistence for files and variables, files only, or variables only.

Configuration	Cores	RAM
CPU	4 CPU cores	30 GB
P100 GPU	1 Nvidia Tesla P100 GPU 2 CPU cores	13 GB
T4 x 2 GPU	2 Nvidia Tesla T4 GPUs 2 CPU cores	13 GB
TPU	1 TPU 4 CPU cores	16 GB
TPU 1VM	96 CPU cores	330 GB

Table 2.1: Technical specification for CPU or accelerator specs

You can set your notebook to always use the original environment or to pin to the latest environment. Depending on what libraries you use and what data processing you perform, it might be useful to choose to work with the original environment or use the latest available environment. When you select the original environment, the settings of the original environment will be kept every time you run new versions of the notebook. With the alternative option to use the latest available environment, the environment (with predefined library versions) will be updated to the latest version.

The internet access is preset to "On," but in some cases, you would like to set it "Off." For certain code competitions, internet access is not allowed. In such cases, you will be able to download dynamic resources from the internet in your training notebook, but you will have to make sure that every needed resource is either internal to the notebook or in one of the attached models, utility scripts, or datasets, when running the inference notebook for that code competition.

We saw what the basic features of notebooks are and how to add data, models, and configure the running environment. Let's see now what the more advanced features are.

Advanced capabilities

Basic notebook functionality allows us to perform quick experiments, test ideas, and prototype solutions. If we want to build more complex functionalities, however, we will need to write reusable code, separate configurations (including secrets, like API keys) from code, and even integrate our code with external systems or components.

The Kaggle environment offers generous computational resources, but these are limited. We might want to combine Kaggle Notebooks with external resources, or we might want to integrate components from Kaggle (notebooks, datasets) with other components, Google Cloud, or our local environment. In the upcoming sections, we will learn how to achieve all these.

Setting a notebook as a utility script or adding utility scripts

In most cases, you will write all the code for your notebook in successive cells in the same file. For more complex code, and especially when you would like to reuse some of the code, without copying code between notebooks, you can choose to develop utility modules. Kaggle Notebooks offers a useful feature for this purpose, namely **Utility scripts**.

Utility scripts are created in the same way notebooks are. You will have to start a notebook and then choose the **Set as Utility Script** menu item from the **File** menu. If you want to use a utility script in your current notebook, you need to select the **Add utility script** menu item from the **File** menu. This will open a selector window for utility scripts on the right-side panel, and here, you can choose from your existing utility scripts and add one or more to your notebook. As you can see in the following screenshot, added utility scripts appear with the + button next to them (seen on the left panel) and are added to the notebook under a separate group, **usr/lib (Utility Scripts)**, just under the **Input** data section and before the **Output** data section (seen on the right panel):

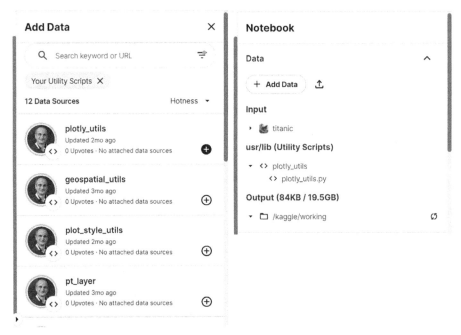

Figure 2.8: Selecting a utility script

To use the utility script within your code, you will have to import the module in the same way you import Python packages. In the following code snippet, we import the modules or functions included in one utility script:

```
from data_quality_stats import missing_data
```

As you can see, the function `missing_data` is defined in the utility script `data_quality_stats`.

Adding and using secrets

Sometimes, you might need to add environment variables in your notebook, and you would want to keep them secret, especially if you make the notebook public. Examples of such variables could be your connection token for an experiment tracking service, like Neptune.ai or Weights & Biases, or various API secret keys or tokens. In this case, you would most probably like to use one of the add-ons, **Kaggle Secrets**.

Upon selection of the **Kaggle Secrets** menu item, a window like the one in the following screenshot will appear. In this pop-up window, you can add new secrets by pressing the button **Add a new secret**. To include the secrets with the current notebook, just check the checkboxes near the secrets you want to include.

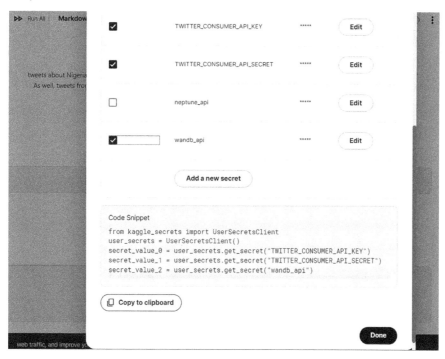

Figure 2.9: Add and select secrets

In the preceding screenshot, three secrets (two for a Twitter API connection and one for Weights & Biases experiment tracking) are selected. For each selected secret, there is an additional generated line like in the **Code Snippet** on the lower side of the window. You can copy all the generated lines to a clipboard to include in your notebook code. After you press **Done**, you will be able to paste the code into your notebook.

Once defined, the secret will be available to be included in any of your notebooks. You can modify the text of one secret using the **Edit** button next to its name. Note that when you fork one notebook that has secrets added, the secrets won't be associated anymore with the new notebook. To make available the secrets to a new or forked notebook, it is enough to enter the **Secrets** windows and press **Done**, in the context of editing that notebook. Of course, if someone else is copying your notebook, that Kaggler (Kaggle user) will have to set their own secrets. And if that Kaggler chooses to use different names for the variables associated with the secrets, they will also need to operate the change in the code. This feature allows you to not only manage useful environment variables but also easily configure your notebooks.

Using Google Cloud services in Kaggle Notebooks

To take advantage of Google Cloud services in your notebook, from the **Add-ons** menu, select **Google Cloud Services**. In the dialog window that opens, you can sync your Google account with your notebook by clicking on **Attach to Notebook**. You can also select which Google Cloud services you want to integrate with your Kaggle environment.

Currently, Kaggle offers integration with Google Cloud Storage, BigQuery, and AutoML. When using these services through Kaggle Notebooks, you need to know that this will incur charges, according to the plan you have. If you choose to use only public data with BigQuery, you will not incur any charges.

In the following figure, we show how you can select these services:

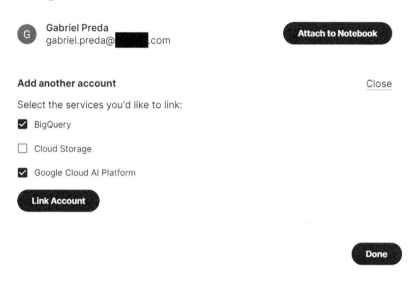

Figure 2.10: Kaggle integration options

Select what Google Cloud services to use in Kaggle Notebooks. As mentioned, you will need to link your Google Cloud account to Kaggle. In the selection screen, you can choose from **BigQuery**, **Cloud Storage**, and **Google Cloud AI Platform** (Vertex AI Workbench). In our example, two out of the three available services were selected.

Upgrading your Kaggle Notebook to Google Cloud AI Notebooks

If you reach the limit of resources available for Kaggle Notebooks (RAM, the number of cores, or execution time), you can choose to promote your notebook to Google Cloud AI Notebooks by exporting your notebook to Google Cloud. Google Cloud AI Notebooks is a paid service from Google Cloud, and it gives you access to computing resources in Google Cloud for machine learning, using a notebook as an **integrated development environment** (**IDE**). For this action, select **File | Upgrade to Google AI Notebooks**, and you will be directed to the following window:

Figure 2.11: Upgrade to Goole Cloud AI Platform Notebooks

Follow this three-step process: set up a billing-enabled Google Cloud project, set up your network instance, and run your code. Your code can run without the resource limits now.

Let's see now how we can use a notebook to automatize the update of a dataset.

Using a Notebook to automatically update a Dataset

You can automatize the generation of a Dataset using Kaggle Notebooks by combining two features: a scheduled rerun of notebooks and an update of a Dataset upon a Notebook run.

First, create the Notebook that will collect the data. It can be, for example, a Notebook that crawls pages of a certain site to retrieve RSS News feeds or connect to the Twitter API (as in the previous example) to download tweets. Set as the Notebook output the collected data.

After the notebook runs for the first time, initialize a Dataset with the output of the notebook by selecting **Output | Create Dataset**, and set the option for the Dataset to be updated every time the notebook is running.

Then, edit the notebook again, and schedule it to run with the frequency that you want your data to be refreshed, as you can see in the following screenshot. Once you set it like that, you will have the notebook running automatically, and because the Dataset has the setting to be updated when running the notebook, the update of the Dataset will happen automatically going forward.

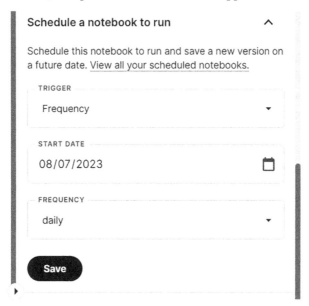

Figure 2.12: Scheduling a Notebook to run daily, starting from August 7, 2023

The mechanism described here allows you to perform the entire automatization process, using only Kaggle tools available from the user interface. For more complex processes, you can always use the Kaggle API to define and automatically perform your tasks. In the next subsection, we will describe the basic functionality available with the Kaggle API, with a focus on manipulating notebooks.

Using the Kaggle API to create, update, download, and monitor your notebooks

The Kaggle API is a powerful tool that extends the functionality available in the Kaggle user interface. You can use it for various tasks: define, update, and download datasets, submit to competitions, define new notebooks, push or pull versions of notebooks, or verify a run status.

There are just two simple steps for you to start using the Kaggle API. Let's get started:

1. First, you will need to create an authentication token. Navigate to your account, and from the right-side icon, select the menu item **Account**. Then go to the **API** section. Here, click on the **Create new API token** button to download your authentication token (it is a file named kaggle.json). If you will be using the Kaggle API from a Windows machine, its location is C:\Users\<your_name>\.kaggle\kaggle.json. On a Mac or Linux machine, the path to the file should be ~/.kaggle/kaggle.json.

2. Next, you will have to install the Kaggle API Python module. Run the following in your selected Python or conda environment:

```
!pip install kaggle
```

With these two steps, you are ready to start using the Kaggle API.

The API also provides multiple options to list notebooks in your account, check notebook status, download a copy, create the first version of a notebook, run it, and more. Let's look at each of these options:

- To list all notebooks based on a certain name pattern, run the following command:

```
Kaggle kernels list -s <name-pattern>
```

    The command will return a table with the {username}/{kernel-slug}, which matches the name pattern, the last runtime, the number of votes, the notebook title, and the author-readable name.

- To verify the status of a certain notebook in your environment, run the following command:

```
kaggle kernels status {username}/{kernel-slug}.
```

    Here, {username}/{kernel-slug} is not the entire path to the notebook on Kaggle but the part of the path that will follow the platform path https://www.kaggle.com.

- The preceding command will return the kernel status. For example, if the kernel execution was complete, it will return:

```
{username}/{kernel-slug} has status "complete"
```

- You can download a notebook by running the following command:

```
kaggle kernels pull {username}/{kernel-slug} /path/to/download
```

    In this case, a Jupyter Notebook with the name {kernel-slug}.ipynb will be downloaded in the folder specified by /path/to/download.

- To create the first version of a notebook and run it, first define a Kaggle metadata file with the command:

```
kaggle kernels init -p /path/to/kernel
```

Your generated Kaggle metadata file will look like this:

```
{
  "id": "{username}/INSERT_KERNEL_SLUG_HERE",
  "title": "INSERT_TITLE_HERE",
  "code_file": "INSERT_CODE_FILE_PATH_HERE",
  "language": "Pick one of: {python,r,rmarkdown}",
  "kernel_type": "Pick one of: {script,notebook}",
  "is_private": "true",
  "enable_gpu": "false",
  "enable_internet": "true",
  "dataset_sources": [],
  "competition_sources": [],
  "kernel_sources": [],
  "model_sources": []
}
```

For the purpose of this demonstration, I edited the metadata file to generate a notebook called Test Kaggle API, which uses Python. For your convenience, I replaced my own username with {username}. You need to take care to correlate the {kernel-slug} with the real title, since normally the {kernel-slug} is generated as the lowercase version, without special characters and replacing spaces with dashes. Here is the result:

```
{
  "id": "{username}/test-kaggle-api",
  "title": "Test Kaggle API",
  "code_file": "test_kaggle_api.ipynb",
  "language": "python",
  "kernel_type": "notebook",
  "is_private": "true",
  "enable_gpu": "false",
  "enable_internet": "true",
  "dataset_sources": [],
  "competition_sources": [],
  "kernel_sources": [],
  "model_sources": []
}
```

- After you edit the metadata file, you can initiate the notebook with the following command:

```
Kaggle kernels push -p /path/to/kernel
```

- If you also created the prototype of your notebook in the /path/to/kernel folder and it is named test_kaggle_api.ipynb, you will receive the following answer to your command:

```
Kernel version 1 successfully pushed. Please check progress at
https://www.kaggle.com/code/{username} /test-kaggle-api
```

- You can also use the API to download the output of an existing notebook. For this, use the following code:

```
Kaggle kernels output {username}/{kernel-slug}
```

This will download a file called {kernel-slug}.log in the current folder. Alternatively, you can specify the path to the following destination:

```
Kaggle kernels output {username}/{kernel-slug} - p /path/to/dest
```

The file contains the execution logs of the kernel's last run.

We have learned how to create an authentication token and install the Kaggle API. Then, we saw how to use the Kaggle API to create a notebook, update it, and download it.

More details about how to use the Kaggle API to boost your platform usage can be found in the Kaggle documentation section about the API at https://www.kaggle.com/docs/api.

Summary

In this chapter, we learned what Kaggle Notebooks are, what types we can use, and with what programming languages. We also learned how to create, run, and update notebooks. We then visited some of the basic features for using notebooks, which will allow you to start using notebooks in an effective way, to ingest and analyze data from datasets or competitions, to start training models, and to prepare submissions for competitions. Additionally, we also reviewed some of the advanced features and even introduced the use of the Kaggle API to further extend your usage of notebooks, allowing you to build external data and ML pipelines that integrate with your Kaggle environment.

The more advanced features give you more flexibility in using Kaggle Notebooks. With Utility scripts, you can create modular code, with specialized Python modules for ingesting data, performing statistical analysis on it, preparing visualizations, generating features, and building models. You can reuse these modules between notebooks, without the need to copy code from one notebook to another. With secrets, on the other hand, you can make public your notebooks that use API keys to access external services, without exposing your personal keys; it is the Kaggle equivalent of a password vault.

With the integration with Google Cloud, you can expand your compute or storage resources, and surpass the limitations for such resources on the Kaggle platform. We also learned the basics of the Kaggle API. You know now how to use the Kaggle API to search for an existing notebook, create a new notebook, or download the output of an existing notebook. This gives you the flexibility to define hybrid pipelines that integrate Kaggle, Google Cloud, and local resources. You can also control your Kaggle Notebooks from external scripts.

In the next chapter, we will start our journey around the data world with a first stop: a classical exploration of the *Titanic* competition dataset.

Join our book's Discord space

Join our Discord community to meet like-minded people and learn alongside more than 5000 members at:

```
https://packt.link/kaggle
```

3

Starting Our Travel — Surviving the Titanic Disaster

In this chapter, we will start our journey around the data world. The first dataset we will analyze is from the competition *Titanic - Machine Learning from Disaster* (refer *Reference 1* at the end of this chapter for a link to this dataset). It is a rather small dataset and, because it is related to a competition, it is split between train and test sets.

In this chapter, besides the competition approach, we will introduce our systematic approach to exploratory data analysis and apply it to get familiar with the data, understand it in more detail, and extract useful insights. We will also provide a short introduction to the process of using the results of data analysis to build model training pipelines. Before diving into the actual data, it is useful to understand the context, and, ideally, define the possible objectives of the analysis.

All the code snapshots and the figures in this chapter are extracted from the accompanying note-book, *Titanic - start of a journey around data world* (refer *Reference 2*). The notebook is also available in the Chapter-03 folder of the GitHub repository for the book (see *References 3* and *4*).

In a nutshell, we will do the following in this chapter:

- Find out the story behind the Titanic dataset. We will learn what happened on that fateful day in 1912 when the Titanic sank, and we will find out the size of the crew, how many passengers were aboard, and how many fatalities there were.
- Get familiar with the data, explain the meaning of the features, get a first view of the data quality, and explore some statistical information about the data.
- Continue the data exploration with univariate analysis after we introduce the graphical elements used through the analysis: a customized color palette and a derived color map.

- Add more insights into the data using multivariate analysis to capture complex interactions between the features.
- Perform a detailed analysis using the recorded passengers' names, from which we will extract multiple features.
- Explore the richness of features using an aggregated view of feature variation.
- Prepare a baseline model.

A closer look at the Titanic

The Titanic was a British passenger ship that sank on its first voyage in the North Atlantic in April 1912. The tragic event, caused by striking an iceberg, resulted in more than 1,500 fatalities (the estimate by US officials was 1,517 and by the British investigating committee, it was 1,503) from the 2,224 total number of crew and passengers. Most of the casualties were part of the crew, followed by third-class passengers.

How was this possible? The Titanic was considered an unsinkable vessel when it was built using state-of-the-art technology in the early 20th century. This confidence was the recipe for disaster. As we know, it did sink, as the contact with the iceberg damaged several water-tight compartments – enough to compromise its integrity. The ship was originally designed to carry 48 lifeboats but only 20 were present on board, and most of those were carrying less than 60% of their full capacity when they were lowered into the water.

The Titanic was 269 meters in length and had a maximum breadth of 28 meters. It had seven decks identified with letters from A to G (A and B were for first-class passengers, C was mostly reserved for crew, and D to G were for second- and third-class passengers). It also had two additional decks: the boat deck (from where the boats were lowered into the water) and the Orlop deck (below the waterline). Although third-class and second-class amenities were not as luxurious and comfortable as those in first-class, all classes had common leisure facilities, like a library, smoking rooms, and even a gymnasium. Passengers could also use open-air or indoor promenade areas. The Titanic was advanced in terms of comfort and amenities compared to other liners of the era.

The Titanic started its voyage from Southampton and had two other stops scheduled – one in Cherbourg, France, and one in Queenstown, Ireland. The passengers were shuttled with special trains from London and Paris to Southampton and Cherbourg, respectively. The crew on the Titanic consisted of around 885 people for this first trip. The majority of the crew were not sailors but stewards, who took care of the passengers, firemen, stockers, and engineers, who were in charge of the engines of the ship.

Conducting data inspection

The story of the Titanic is fascinating. For those interested in data exploration, the data about the tragedy is also captivating. Let's start with a short introduction to the competition data. The dataset from *Titanic - Machine Learning from Disaster* contains three **CSV (comma-separated values)** files, as in many Kaggle competitions that you will encounter:

- `train.csv`
- `test.csv`
- `sample_submission.csv`

We will start by loading these files into a new notebook. You learned how to do this in the previous chapter, in the *Basic capabilities* section. You can also create a notebook by forking one that already exists. In our case, we will start a new notebook from scratch.

Usually, notebooks start with a cell in which we import packages. We will do the same here. In one of the next cells, we would like to read train and test data. In general, the CSV files that you need have similar directories as in this example:

```
train_df = pd.read_csv("/kaggle/input/titanic/train.csv")
test_df = pd.read_csv("/kaggle/input/titanic/test.csv")
```

After we load the data, we will manually inspect it, looking at what each column contains – that is, samples of data. We will do this for each file in the dataset, but mostly, we will focus on the train and test files for now.

Understanding the data

In *Figures 3.1* and *3.2*, we get a glimpse of a selection of values. From this visual inspection, we can already see some characteristics of the data. Let's try to summarize them. The following columns are common to both train and test files:

- `PassengerId`: A unique identifier for each patient.
- `Pclass`: The class in which each passenger was traveling. We know from our background information that possible values are 1, 2, or 3. This can be considered a categorical data type. Because the order of the class conveys meaning and is ordered, we can consider it as ordinal or numerical.
- `Name`: This is a text type of field. It is the full name of the passenger, with their family name, first name, and, in some cases, their name before marriage, as well as a nickname. It also contains their title regarding social class, background, profession, or, in some cases, royalty.

- Sex: This is also a categorical field. We can assume that this was important information at the time, considering that they prioritized saving women and children first.
- Age: This is a numerical field. Also, their age was an important feature since children were prioritized for saving.
- SibSp: This field provides the siblings or the spouse of each passenger. It is an indicator of the size of the family or group with which the passenger was traveling. This is important information since we can safely assume that one would not board a lifeboat without their brothers, sisters, or partner.
- Parch: This is the number of parents (for child passengers) or children (for parent passengers). Considering that parents would wait for all their children before boarding a lifeboat, this is also an important feature. Together with SibSp, Parch can be used to calculate the size of the family for each passenger.
- Ticket: This is a code associated with the ticket. It is an alphanumerical field, neither categorical nor numerical.
- Fare: This is a numerical field. From the sample we see, we can observe that Fare values varied considerably (with one order of magnitude from class 3 to class 1) but we can also see that some of the passengers in the same class had quite different Fare values.
- Cabin: This is an alphanumerical field. From the small sample that we see in *Figures 3.1 and 3.2*, we can see that some of the values are missing. In other cases, there are multiple cabins reserved for the same passenger (presumably a well-to-do passenger traveling with their family). The name of a cabin starts with a letter (C, D, E, or F). We remember that there are multiple decks on the Titanic so we can guess that the letter represents the deck and then that is followed by the cabin number on that deck.
- Embarked: This is a categorical field. In the sample here, we only see the letters C, S, and Q, and we already know that the Titanic started from Southampton and had a stop at Cherbourg, France, and one at Queenstown (today, this is called Cobh, the port for Cork, Ireland). We can infer that S stands for Southampton (the starting port), C stands for Cherbourg, and Q for Queenstown.

The train file contains a Survived field as well, which is the target feature. This has either a value of 1 or 0, where 1 means the passenger survived and 0 means they sadly didn't.

	PassengerId	Survived	Pclass	Name	Sex	Age	SibSp	Parch	Ticket	Fare	Cabin	Embarked
187	188	1	1	Romaine, Mr. Charles Hallace ("Mr C Rolmane")	male	45.0	0	0	111428	26.55	NaN	S
120	121	0	2	Hickman, Mr. Stanley George	male	21.0	2	0	S.O.C. 14879	73.50	NaN	S
546	547	1	2	Beane, Mrs. Edward (Ethel Clarke)	female	19.0	1	0	2908	26.00	NaN	S
308	309	0	2	Abelson, Mr. Samuel	male	30.0	1	0	P/PP 3381	24.00	NaN	C
286	287	1	3	de Mulder, Mr. Theodore	male	30.0	0	0	345774	9.50	NaN	S

Figure 3.1: Sample of the train data file

The test file does not include the target feature, as you can see in the following sample:

	PassengerId	Pclass	Name	Sex	Age	SibSp	Parch	Ticket	Fare	Cabin	Embarked
19	911	3	Assaf Khalil, Mrs. Mariana (Miriam")"	female	45.0	0	0	2696	7.2250	NaN	C
69	961	1	Fortune, Mrs. Mark (Mary McDougald)	female	60.0	1	4	19950	263.0000	C23 C25 C27	S
350	1242	1	Greenfield, Mrs. Leo David (Blanche Strouse)	female	45.0	0	1	PC 17759	63.3583	D10 D12	C
196	1088	1	Spedden, Master. Robert Douglas	male	6.0	0	2	16966	134.5000	E34	C
322	1214	2	Nesson, Mr. Israel	male	26.0	0	0	244368	13.0000	F2	S

Figure 3.2: Sample of the test data file

Once we have had a look at the columns in the train and test files, we can continue with a few additional checks to find the dimensions of the datasets and the feature distribution:

1. Check the shape of each dataset (`train_df` and `test_df`), using the `shape()` function. This will give us the dimension of the train and test files (number of rows and columns).

2. Run the `info()` function for each dataset. This will give us more complex information, such as the amount of non-null data per column, and the type of the data.

3. Run the `describe()` function for each dataset. This only applies to numerical data and will create a statistic on the data distribution, including minimum, maximum, and first 25%, 50%, and 75% values, as well as the average value and standard deviation.

The preceding checks give us preliminary information on the data distribution for the numerical values in the train and test datasets. We can continue later in our analysis with more sophisticated and detailed tools, but for now, you may consider these steps a general preliminary approach for investigating any tabular dataset that you put your hands on.

Analyzing the data

By evaluating the shape of the dataset, the types of values, the number of null values, and the feature distribution, we will form a preliminary image of the dataset.

We can build our own tools for inspecting data statistics. I will introduce here three small scripts to get the missing value stats, the unique values, and the most frequent values.

First, the code to retrieve missing data:

```python
def missing_data(data):
    total = data.isnull().sum()
    percent = (data.isnull().sum()/data.isnull().count()*100)
    tt = pd.concat([total, percent], axis=1, keys=['Total', 'Percent'])
    types = []
    for col in data.columns:
        dtype = str(data[col].dtype)
        types.append(dtype)
    tt['Types'] = types
    return(np.transpose(tt))
```

Next, the code to display the most frequent values:

```python
def most_frequent_values(data):
    total = data.count()
    tt = pd.DataFrame(total)
    tt.columns = ['Total']
    items = []
    vals = []
```

```
        for col in data.columns:
            try:
                itm = data[col].value_counts().index[0]
                val = data[col].value_counts().values[0]
                items.append(itm)
                vals.append(val)
            except Exception as ex:
                print(ex)
                items.append(0)
                vals.append(0)
                continue
        tt['Most frequent item'] = items
        tt['Frequence'] = vals
        tt['Percent from total'] = np.round(vals / total * 100, 3)
        return(np.transpose(tt))
```

And finally, the code for unique values:

```
def unique_values(data):
    total = data.count()
    tt = pd.DataFrame(total)
    tt.columns = ['Total']
    uniques = []
    for col in data.columns:
        unique = data[col].nunique()
        uniques.append(unique)
    tt['Uniques'] = uniques
    return(np.transpose(tt))
```

In the next chapter, we will reuse these functions. On Kaggle, you can do this by implementing utility scripts. We will include these functions in a reusable utility script that will then be included in other notebooks as well.

In the following figure, we see the result of applying the `missing_data` function to the train (*a*) and test (*b*) datasets:

	PassengerId	Survived	Pclass	Name	Sex	Age	SibSp	Parch	Ticket	Fare	Cabin	Embarked
Total	0	0	0	0	0	177	0	0	0	0	687	2
Percent	0.0	0.0	0.0	0.0	0.0	19.86532	0.0	0.0	0.0	0.0	77.104377	0.224467
Types	int64	int64	int64	object	object	float64	int64	int64	object	float64	object	object

a

	PassengerId	Pclass	Name	Sex	Age	SibSp	Parch	Ticket	Fare	Cabin	Embarked
Total	0	0	0	0	86	0	0	0	1	327	0
Percent	0.0	0.0	0.0	0.0	20.574163	0.0	0.0	0.0	0.239234	78.229665	0.0
Types	int64	int64	object	object	float64	int64	int64	object	float64	object	object

b

Figure 3.3: Missing values in (a) train and (b) test sets, respectively

Some of the fields, like `Age` and `Cabin`, show a considerable percentage of missing data, both for train and test datasets. From the inspection of the missing data percentage, we can also preliminarily evaluate the quality of the data with respect to the train-test split. If the percentages of missing values for a certain feature are very different in train and test data, we can already suspect that the splitting did not capture the overall data distribution. In our case, the percentages of missing values have close values for each feature in the train and test datasets.

In the following figure, we can see the most frequent values for the features in the train (*a*) and test (*b*) datasets:

	PassengerId	Survived	Pclass	Name	Sex	Age	SibSp	Parch	Ticket	Fare	Cabin	Embarked
Total	891	891	891	891	891	714	891	891	891	891	204	889
Most frequent item	1	0	3	Braund, Mr. Owen Harris	male	24.0	0	0	347082	8.05	B96 B98	S
Frequence	1	549	491	1	577	30	608	678	7	43	4	644
Percent from total	0.112	61.616	55.107	0.112	64.759	4.202	68.238	76.094	0.786	4.826	1.961	72.441

a

	PassengerId	Pclass	Name	Sex	Age	SibSp	Parch	Ticket	Fare	Cabin	Embarked
Total	418	418	418	418	332	418	418	418	417	91	418
Most frequent item	892	3	Kelly, Mr. James	male	21.0	0	0	PC 17608	7.75	B57 B59 B63 B66	S
Frequence	1	218	1	266	17	283	324	5	21	3	270
Percent from total	0.239	52.153	0.239	63.636	5.12	67.703	77.512	1.196	5.036	3.297	64.593

b

Figure 3.4: Most frequent values in (a) train and (b) test sets, respectively.

We already can see from the preceding data that most of the people on the Titanic were male (and this majority is reflected in both the train and test datasets), and most of the passengers and crew embarked in Southampton (S). For features with more granular values, like Age, the most frequent value differs in train and test data, although the values with maximum frequency are close (Age value of 21 in train versus 24 in the test dataset). This hints at the limitations of using Age directly as a feature in a machine learning model since we can already observe that the overall distribution is different between train and test data.

The following figure shows the results of applying the unique_values function to obtain the unique values stats for train and test datasets:

	PassengerId	Survived	Pclass	Name	Sex	Age	SibSp	Parch	Ticket	Fare	Cabin	Embarked
Total	891	891	891	891	891	714	891	891	891	891	204	889
Uniques	891	2	3	891	2	88	7	7	681	248	147	3

a

	PassengerId	Pclass	Name	Sex	Age	SibSp	Parch	Ticket	Fare	Cabin	Embarked
Total	418	418	418	418	332	418	418	418	417	91	418
Uniques	418	3	418	2	79	7	8	363	169	76	3

b

Figure 3.5: Unique values in (a) train and (b) test sets, respectively

As you can see, for the categorical type of fields, all categories present in the train dataset are also present in the test dataset. Ideally, we would like the same results to show for numerical features such as SibSp or Parch. However, in the case of Parch, we can see that the number of unique values is 7 in train and 8 in test data.

In this section, we started with an initial data inspection to understand the dataset features, followed by checking the data quality to see whether we had missing values. We also conducted a statistical analysis of the features in both train and test datasets. Next in our data exploration, we will perform univariate analysis on the categorical and numerical features of the train and test datasets. The images with plots of various features provide more information and are easier to understand and interpret, even for a non-technical reader.

Performing univariate analysis

Before starting to build our first plots, we will set a unique color scheme for the notebook. Ensuring color and style unity across the entire notebook helps us to maintain the consistency of the presentation and ensures a well-balanced experience for the reader. The notebook will have a consistent presentation and the visuals will coherently support the notebook narrative.

Therefore, we will define the set of colors that we will use throughout the notebook in our graphics. We will select a palette that will create a visual identity specific to our work. This can be one of the already-defined palettes or color sets or we can define our own palette, based on a set of colors chosen to match the subject. For this sea-faring (or nautical) related notebook, I chose a set of marine colors with several shades of blue. Based on this set of colors, I also defined a palette. The code for defining and displaying the palette is:

```python
import matplotlib.pyplot as plt
from matplotlib.colors import ListedColormap
import seaborn as sns

def set_color_map(color_list):
    cmap_custom = ListedColormap(color_list)
    print("Notebook Color Schema:")
    sns.palplot(sns.color_palette(color_list))
    plt.show()
    return cmap_custom

color_list = ["#A5D7E8", "#576CBC", "#19376D", "#0b2447"]
cmap_custom = set_color_map(color_list)
```

In the following figure, we show the reduced set of colors that compose our custom palette. The notebook color scheme uses shades of blue, from a pale clear-sky color to a dark ultramarine:

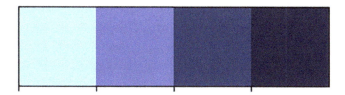

Figure 3.6: The notebook color scheme

We will define two plotting functions (one for categorical, and one for continuous/numerical values) to represent the distribution of one feature on the same image, grouped by survival or grouped by the train/test set.

We will concatenate train and test in a single dataset (and add a new column storing the original/ source dataset). The functions use two of the most common libraries for data plotting: matplotlib and seaborn. As we will plot these graphs for multiple features, it is preferable to define a few plotting functions, so that we don't repeat the code.

In the first function, we display two sets of values using the option hue of the countplot function from seaborn:

```
def plot_count_pairs(data_df, feature, title, hue="set"):
    f, ax = plt.subplots(1, 1, figsize=(8, 4))
    sns.countplot(x=feature, data=data_df, hue=hue, palette= color_list)
    plt.grid(color="black", linestyle="-.", linewidth=0.5, axis="y",
which="major")
    ax.set_title(f"Number of passengers / {title}")
    plt.show()
```

In the second function, to display feature distribution, we call histplot from seaborn twice – once for each feature:

```
def plot_distribution_pairs(data_df, feature, title, hue="set"):
    f, ax = plt.subplots(1, 1, figsize=(8, 4))
    for i, h in enumerate(data_df[hue].unique()):
        g = sns.histplot(data_df.loc[data_df[hue]==h, feature],
color=color_list[i], ax=ax, label=h)
    #plt.grid(color="black", linestyle="-.", linewidth=0.5, axis="y",
which="major")
    ax.set_title(f"Number of passengers / {title}")
    g.legend()
    plt.show()
```

To see the complete list of images, go to the book repository and check the *Titanic - start of a journey around data world* notebook (*Reference 3*). Alternatively, you can access the same content on Kaggle, by following this path: `https://www.kaggle.com/code/gpreda/titanic-start-of-a-journey-around-data-world` (*Reference 2*).

Here, we only show a small selection of images, for only two features – one for a categorical value and one for a numerical value. In the notebook, we represent the graphs for `Sex`, `Pclass`, `SibSp`, `Parch`, and `Embark`, as well as `Age` and `Fare`.

We will represent each of these features in two graphs: one shows the distribution of the feature for all passengers, grouped by train/test. The other shows, for the same feature, the distribution only for train data, and the split between `Survived`/`Not Survived`.

We start with `Pclass` (which is a categorical feature), showing the distribution of the feature for all passengers, grouped by train/test datasets. Notice in the following screenshot, there are three classes, 1, 2, and 3:

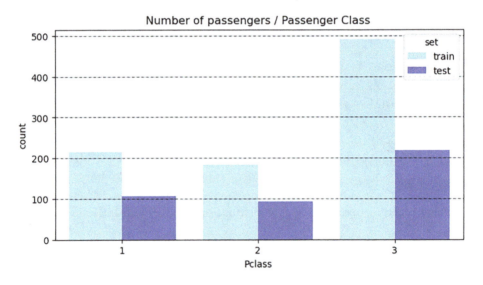

Figure 3.7: Number of passengers per passenger class, grouped by train and test

For the same `Pclass` feature, but only from the train set, we represent the data grouped by `Survived`:

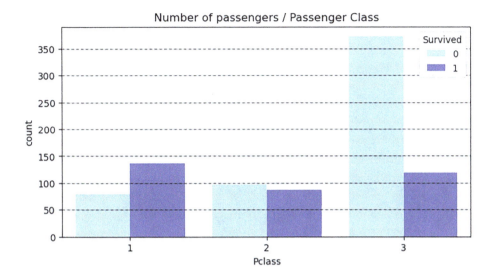

Figure 3.8: Number of passengers per passenger class in the train set, grouped by Survived

We follow with Age (which is a numerical value). In *Figure 3.9*, we show the histogram of Age in all the data (train and test), grouped by train/test. We are using a histogram here because this feature, although not a continuous number (is still discrete), has many values (from the stats we ran, it appears that there are at least 88 unique Age values), and is, from the point of view of our analysis, just like a continuous number.

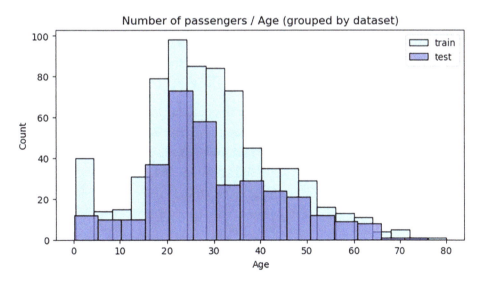

Figure 3.9: Number of passengers per Age, grouped by train and test

Figure 3.10 shows the histogram of Age in the train set, grouped by survival status.

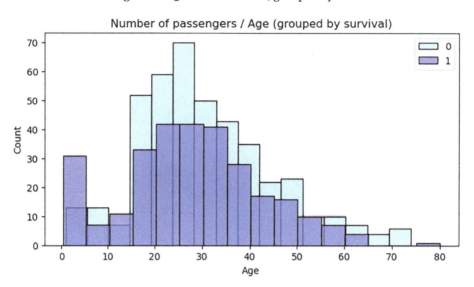

Figure 3.10: Number of passengers per Age in the train set, grouped by survival status

By simple inspection of these univariate distributions for either categorical or continuous (numerical) data, we can already understand some interesting facts from the data. For example, in *Figures 3.7* and *3.8*, we can see that the ratio between data in the train and test sets is quite similar with respect to the distribution in the three classes (1, 2, and 3). At the same time, from the Survived/Not Survived distribution, we can see that while around 60% of first-class passengers survived, the split of Survived/Not Survived in second class was around 50-50%, while in third class, only around 25% of the passengers survived. Similarly, we can extract useful insights from the univariate distributions of Sex, SibSp (siblings or spouses), or Parch (number of parents or children).

In some cases, we would like to build new features from existing features – in other words, perform feature engineering. Feature engineering involves the extraction and transformation of useful information from raw data. One technique for feature engineering is to define a new feature as a function of other features. We saw that Parch and SibSp together give information about families that were present on the Titanic. By summing up Parch and SibSp and adding 1 (for the actual passenger), for each passenger, we get the size of their family onboard the Titanic.

In *Figure 3.11*, we can see the graph for family size, from all passengers, grouped by train/test datasets:

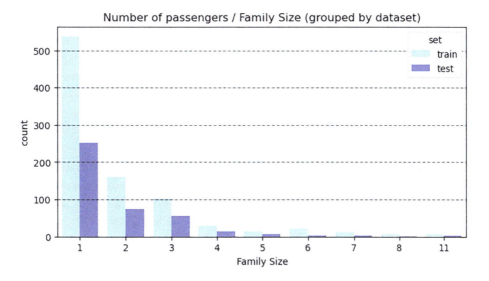

Figure 3.11: Number of passengers per family size, grouped by train and test

In the next figure, we see the graph for train data, for the same family size, grouped by Survived/ Not Survived:

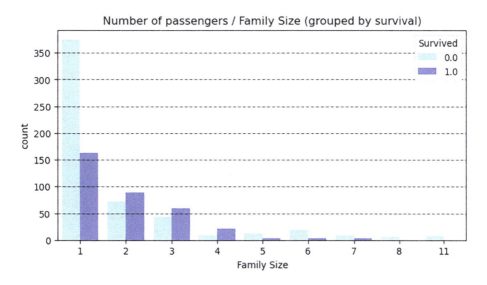

Figure 3.12: Number of passengers per family size, grouped by survival status

We can observe that prevalent is the number of single passengers (and the large number also highlights the high frequency of this type of passenger in third class). This number is then followed by families without children and single parents, followed by small and large families of up to 8 and even 11 members. As you can see, this pattern came from data analysis using an exploratory approach before modeling.

If we look then at the survival rate, we can see that single passengers had a small survival rate (around 30%) while small families (with 2, 3, or 4 members) had a survival rate above 50%. As the size of the family became larger than 4, we can see that the survival rate decreased severely, with families with 8 or 11 members having a zero survival rate.

This might be because they were traveling in cheaper classes (we know that survival in third class was inferior to survival in first class) or because they spent too much time trying to gather all their family members before heading to the lifeboats. We will investigate these details a bit later in this chapter.

We can observe that Age and Fare are distributed values. While it is useful to know the exact age of a certain passenger, there is not much value when we build a model to include the exact age. Actually, by learning a large variety of ages, the model risks overfitting the training data, and its generalization will degrade. For analysis and modeling purposes, it makes sense to aggregate the age (or fare) in value intervals.

The next code snippet shows the calculation of a new feature called Age Interval, to form five classes, from 0 to 4, corresponding to Age intervals between 0 and 16, 16 and 32, 32 and 48, 48 and 64, and above 64, respectively:

```
all_df["Age Interval"] = 0.0
all_df.loc[ all_df['Age'] <= 16, 'Age Interval']  = 0
all_df.loc[(all_df['Age'] > 16) & (all_df['Age'] <= 32), 'Age Interval'] =
1
all_df.loc[(all_df['Age'] > 32) & (all_df['Age'] <= 48), 'Age Interval'] =
2
all_df.loc[(all_df['Age'] > 48) & (all_df['Age'] <= 64), 'Age Interval'] =
3
all_df.loc[ all_df['Age'] > 64, 'Age Interval'] = 4
```

The following code block calculates a new feature called Fare Interval, where the values from 0 to 3 (four classes) are obtained from values of Fare between 0 and 7.91, 7.91 and 14.454, 14.454 and 31, and above 31, respectively:

```
all_df['Fare Interval'] = 0.0
all_df.loc[ all_df['Fare'] <= 7.91, 'Fare Interval'] = 0
all_df.loc[(all_df['Fare'] > 7.91) & (all_df['Fare'] <= 14.454), 'Fare
Interval'] = 1
all_df.loc[(all_df['Fare'] > 14.454) & (all_df['Fare'] <= 31), 'Fare
Interval']   = 2
all_df.loc[ all_df['Fare'] > 31, 'Fare Interval'] = 3
```

The feature transformations for Age and Fare described above have the effect of regularization. In the following graph, we show the Age Intervals for all passengers, separated by train and test:

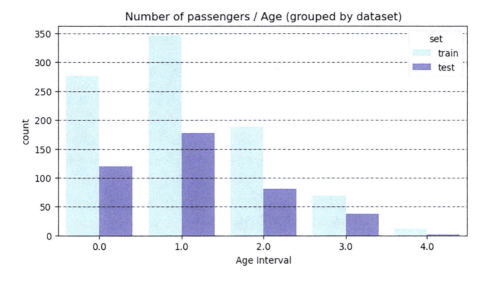

Figure 3.13: Number of passengers per Age intervals, grouped by train and test

The following figure shows the distribution of Age intervals for Survived versus Not Survived passengers:

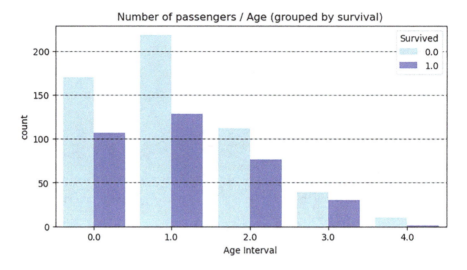

Figure 3.14: Number of passengers per Age intervals, grouped by Survived status

So far, we have analyzed individual features. We merged train and test and represented, on the same graph, the data split between train and test. We also showed the train data only for one feature, split between Survived and Not Survived, and we visualized a few engineered features. In the next section, we will follow by representing multiple features on the same graph using multivariate analysis.

Performing multivariate analysis

We saw how, by using graphs for the distribution of each feature, we can get very interesting insights into the data. Then, we experimented with feature engineering to get useful, more relevant features. While observing variables separately can help us get an initial image of the data distribution, grouping values and looking at more than one feature at a time can reveal correlations and more insights into how different features interact.

Now, we will use various graphics to explore correlations of features while we also explore the visualization options. We will continue for now with our initial option of using a combination of the matplotlib and seaborn graphical libraries.

Figure 3.15 shows the number of passengers per Age Interval, grouped by passenger class. We can see from this image that in third class, the majority of passengers were in the first and second Age interval (that is, between 0–16 and 16–32 years old), while in first class, we have the most well-balanced age groups. The most balanced age interval between the three classes is the third age interval.

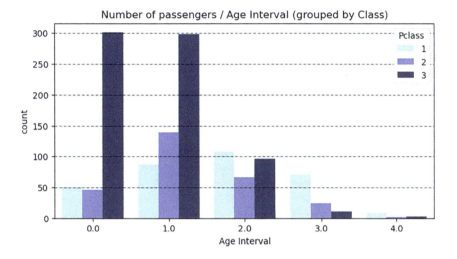

Figure 3.15: Number of passengers per Age Interval, grouped by class

As we can see in the next graph in *Figure 3.16*, most passengers embarked at Southampton (identified by the initial **S**). Also, most of these passengers were of a young age, under 32 (age intervals **0** and **1**). For people embarking in Cherbourg (identified by the initial **C**), the age groups are more balanced. The passengers who embarked in Queensland (identified by the initial **Q**) were mostly in the first age group.

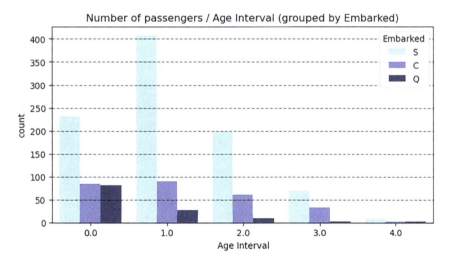

Figure 3.16: Number of passengers per Age Interval, grouped by embarked port

From the following figure, we can see that with increased family size and lower passenger class, the likelihood of surviving decreased. The worst survival rate was for large families in third class, where almost no one survived. Even for small families, being in third class drastically reduced their likelihood of survival.

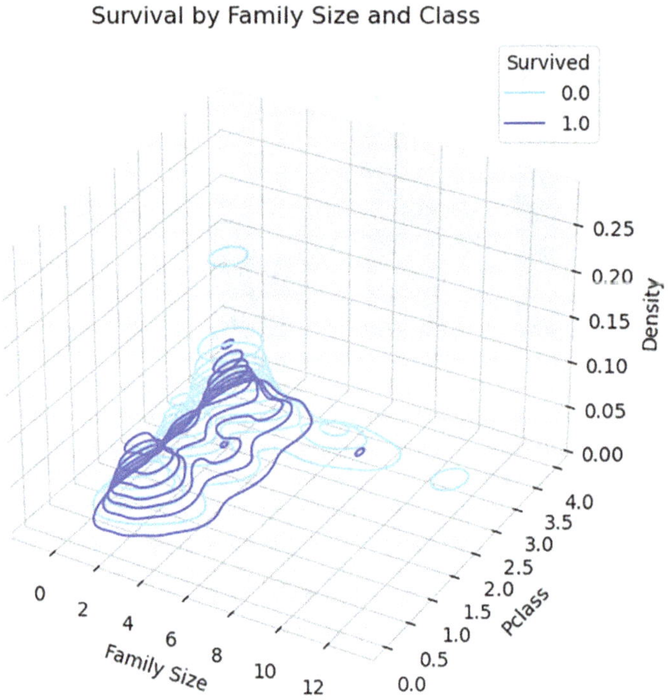

Figure 3.17: Distribution of family size and passenger class (Pclass), grouped by Survived status

We can also create composed features – for example, we can merge Sex and Pclass, two of the most predictive factors, into one single feature; let's call it Sex_Pclass. The following figure shows the distribution of this new feature when we split the values based on survival status. Females in first and second class had a survival rate above 90%. In third class, females had around a 50% survival rate. Males in first and second class had survival rates of around 30% and 20%, respectively. Most of the males in third class died.

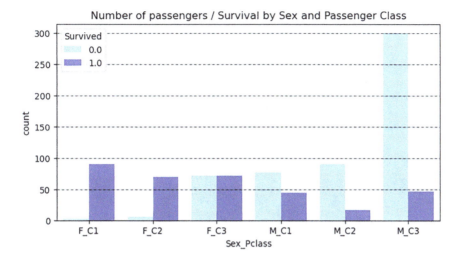

Figure 3.18: Distribution composed feature Sex_Pclass, grouped by Survived status

After the data quality assessment, we demonstrated how to perform univariate analysis. Then, we gave a few examples of feature engineering for numerical data, and performed multivariate analysis. Next, we will explore the richness of information we can find in the passengers' names. Let's see *what is in a name*.

Extracting meaningful information from passenger names

We continue now with our analysis, including analyzing the passengers' names to extract meaningful information. As you will remember from the beginning of this chapter, the Name column also contains some additional information. After our preliminary visual analysis, it became apparent that all names follow a similar structure. They begin with a Family Name, followed by a comma, then a Title (short version, followed by a period), then a Given Name, and, in cases where a new name was acquired through marriage, the previous or Maiden Name. Let's process the data to extract this information. The code to extract this information will be:

```
def parse_names(row):
    try:
        text = row["Name"]
        split_text = text.split(",")
        family_name = split_text[0]
        next_text = split_text[1]
```

```
        split_text = next_text.split(".")
        title =  (split_text[0] + ".").lstrip().rstrip()
        next_text = split_text[1]
        if "(" in next_text:
            split_text = next_text.split("(")
            given_name = split_text[0]
            maiden_name = split_text[1].rstrip(")")
            return pd.Series([family_name, title, given_name, maiden_
name])
        else:
            given_name = next_text
            return pd.Series([family_name, title, given_name, None])
    except Exception as ex:
        print(f"Exception: {ex}")


all_df[["Family Name", "Title", "Given Name", "Maiden Name"]] = all_
df.apply(lambda row: parse_names(row), axis=1)
```

As you might've noticed, we opted to use the split function to implement the extraction of Family Name, Title, Given Name, and Maiden Name. We can also use a more compact implementation, with regex.

Let's inspect the results, by looking first at the distribution of Title and Sex in parallel:

Title	Capt.	Col.	Don.	Dona.	Dr.	Jonkheer.	Lady.	Major.	Master.	Miss.	Mlle.	Mme.	Mr.	Mrs.	Ms.	Rev.	Sir.	the Countess.
Sex																		
female	0	0	0	1	1	0	1	0	0	260	2	1	0	197	2	0	0	1
male	1	4	1	0	7	1	0	2	61	0	0	0	757	0	0	8	1	0

Figure 3.19: Distribution of Title by Sex

We can see that most of the titles are gender-specific, with the most frequent being Miss (with a Mlle. version) and Mrs. (with Mme. and Dona. versions) for females, and Mr. (and Ms. or Don. versions) and Master for males. Some titles are rare, like military (Capt., Col., Major, and Jonkheer), occupational (Dr. and Rev.), or nobility (Sir, Lady, and Countess). Dr. is the only title that is used by both genders, and we will take a closer look at it a bit later in this chapter.

Let's look now at the distribution of Title by Age Interval:

Title / Age Interval	Capt.	Col.	Don.	Dona.	Dr.	Jonkheer.	Lady.	Major.	Master.	Miss.	Mlle.	Mme.	Mr.	Mrs.	Ms.	Rev.	Sir.	the Countess.
0.0	0	0	0	0	1	0	0	0	61	111	0	0	193	30	1	0	0	0
1.0	0	0	0	0	2	0	0	0	0	113	2	1	334	68	1	3	0	0
2.0	0	1	1	1	1	1	1	1	0	29	0	0	163	67	0	2	0	1
3.0	0	3	0	0	4	0	0	1	0	7	0	0	56	31	0	3	1	0
4.0	1	0	0	0	0	0	0	0	0	0	0	0	11	1	0	0	0	0

Figure 3.20: Distribution of Title by Age Interval

From this new view, we can see that some of the titles are reserved for certain age intervals, while others are distributed across all age intervals. Master appears to be used only for males under 18 years of age, but Mr. is also used for this age interval. From what we have seen, the Master title was only used for male children traveling with their families, whereas males of a young age with the title Mr. were traveling alone and, because independent already, were considered young adults. The title Miss doesn't respect the same pattern, since it is attributed equally to female children, young, or unmarried women (but less frequently for advanced ages). It is interesting to see that Dr. is a title well distributed in a wide range of ages.

Let's look now at a few of the large families from third class. If we sort the data by Family Name, Family Size, Ticket (to keep together those who traveled with the same ticket), and Age, we will obtain sequences of passengers from the same real family. The Family Name values with the highest occurrence are Andersson (11 entries), Sage (11 entries), Goodwin (8 entries), Asplund (8 entries) and Davies (7 entries). We don't yet know whether they are also from the same family or just share the same family name. Let's look at the data for the passengers who share the Andersson family name.

From *Figure 3.21*, we see that there is one family called Andersson with a father called Anders Johan and a mother called Alfrida Konstantia, accompanied by their five children (four daughters and one son) with ages between 2 and 11 years. The married women in the family are registered with their title followed by their husband's name, and their maiden name added within brackets. No one from this family traveling in third class survived.

	Name	Sex	Age	Title	Family Name	Given Name	Maiden Name	SibSp	Parch	Family Size	Ticket	Pclass	Survived
214	Andersson, Miss. Ida Augusta Margareta	female	38.0	Miss.	Andersson	Ida Augusta Margareta	None	4	2	7	347091	3	NaN
13	Andersson, Mr. Anders Johan	male	39.0	Mr.	Andersson	Anders Johan	None	1	5	7	347082	3	0.0
610	Andersson, Mrs. Anders Johan (Alfrida Konstant...	female	39.0	Mrs.	Andersson	Anders Johan	Alfrida Konstantia Brogren	1	5	7	347082	3	0.0
542	Andersson, Miss. Sigrid Elisabeth	female	11.0	Miss.	Andersson	Sigrid Elisabeth	None	4	2	7	347082	3	0.0
541	Andersson, Miss. Ingeborg Constanzia	female	9.0	Miss.	Andersson	Ingeborg Constanzia	None	4	2	7	347082	3	0.0
813	Andersson, Miss. Ebba Iris Alfrida	female	6.0	Miss.	Andersson	Ebba Iris Alfrida	None	4	2	7	347082	3	0.0
850	Andersson, Master. Sigvard Harald Elias	male	4.0	Master.	Andersson	Sigvard Harald Elias	None	4	2	7	347082	3	0.0
119	Andersson, Miss. Ellis Anna Maria	female	2.0	Miss.	Andersson	Ellis Anna Maria	None	4	2	7	347082	3	0.0
68	Andersson, Miss. Erna Alexandra	female	17.0	Miss.	Andersson	Erna Alexandra	None	4	2	7	3101281	3	1.0
146	Andersson, Mr. August Edvard ("Wennerstrom")	male	27.0	Mr.	Andersson	August Edvard	"Wennerstrom"	0	0	1	350043	3	1.0
320	Andersson, Mr. Johan Samuel	male	26.0	Mr.	Andersson	Johan Samuel	None	0	0	1	347075	3	NaN

Figure 3.21: Passengers sharing the Andersson family name

Only those who traveled on the same ticket were part of the same family. This means that only those traveling with ticket number 347082 were part of the Andersson family, while the others were traveling separately. The data seems to not be very accurate in their cases since some of them appear to be part of a larger family but we cannot find their relatives.

The next largest family is Sage, as we can see from *Figure 3.22*. This was an 11-member family (two parents and nine children). We do not know their ages (apart from one of the boys' who was 14.5 years old); we just know their names and the fact that there were five boys and four girls. We suppose that three of the boys were grown-up since their titles were Mr.. We only know that 9 out of the 11 did not survive (the other family members, for which **Survived** has no assigned value, are part of the test set).

	Name	Sex	Age	Title	Family Name	Given Name	Maiden Name	SibSp	Parch	Family Size	Ticket	Pclass	Survived
360	Sage, Master. William Henry	male	14.5	Master.	Sage	William Henry	None	8	2	11	CA. 2343	3	NaN
159	Sage, Master. Thomas Henry	male	NaN	Master.	Sage	Thomas Henry	None	8	2	11	CA. 2343	3	0.0
180	Sage, Miss. Constance Gladys	female	NaN	Miss.	Sage	Constance Gladys	None	8	2	11	CA. 2343	3	0.0
201	Sage, Mr. Frederick	male	NaN	Mr.	Sage	Frederick	None	8	2	11	CA. 2343	3	0.0
324	Sage, Mr. George John Jr	male	NaN	Mr.	Sage	George John Jr	None	8	2	11	CA. 2343	3	0.0
792	Sage, Miss. Stella Anna	female	NaN	Miss.	Sage	Stella Anna	None	8	2	11	CA. 2343	3	0.0
846	Sage, Mr. Douglas Bullen	male	NaN	Mr.	Sage	Douglas Bullen	None	8	2	11	CA. 2343	3	0.0
863	Sage, Miss. Dorothy Edith 'Dolly'	female	NaN	Miss.	Sage	Dorothy Edith 'Dolly'	None	8	2	11	CA. 2343	3	0.0
188	Sage, Miss. Ada	female	NaN	Miss.	Sage	Ada	None	8	2	11	CA. 2343	3	NaN
342	Sage, Mr. John George	male	NaN	Mr.	Sage	John George	None	1	9	11	CA. 2343	3	NaN
365	Sage, Mrs. John (Annie Bullen)	female	NaN	Mrs.	Sage	John	Annie Bullen	1	9	11	CA. 2343	3	NaN

Figure 3.22: Passengers sharing the Sage family name

The stories of these families who were looking for a better life in the New World are moving, especially when we realize that, sadly, these large families with lots of children didn't manage to save themselves. We don't know what the decisive factor was: they might have waited too long until they headed for the boat deck, hoping to reunite, or maybe they were struggling to keep together on their way to the lifeboats. Either way, adding the family size information into the model might give us a useful feature to predict survival, since we can see that people in larger families had a lower chance of survival.

There are also other interesting analyses we can make, with fewer predictive values for survival, but which can give us some more insights into the data distribution. The following figure shows the Given Name distribution (grouped by sex) for the overall data:

Girls and Young Women Names on Titanic   Boys and Men Names on Titanic

Figure 3.23: Passengers' given names (girls/unmarried women and boys/men)

The following figure shows the Family Name distribution overall and according to embarking port. We saw that most passengers embarked in Southampton (identified with **S**); therefore, the distribution of embarked passengers' names in this port will dominate the overall case. The other two embarking ports were Cherbourg, France (identified with **C**) and Queenstown, Ireland (identified with **Q**). We can observe the prevalence of ethnic names in various embarkment ports, with Scandinavian in Southampton; French, Italian, Greek, and North African in Cherbourg; and Irish and Scottish in Queenstown.

Figure 3.24: Family names grouped by embarking port

In *Figure 3.25*, we see the two passengers sharing cabin **D17**. One of them had the title `Dr.` and was also a female. She was traveling with another female companion, Mrs. Swift, in first class. Both of them survived.

We created an engineered feature, `Title`, because Dr. Leader was both a `Mrs.` (we know she was married because her maiden name is also mentioned) and a `Dr.`; we had to choose which title to assign to her. `Dr.` was a title associated mostly with males (with lower survival likelihood) at that time. As a female, she would have had a higher survival probability. While that is matter of debate, of course, I mention it here just to give you a better image of the depth we can get while engineering the candidate features for a predictive model.

	PassengerId	Survived	Pclass	Name	Sex	Age	SibSp	Parch	Ticket	Fare	Cabin	Embarked	Title
796	797	1	1	Leader, Dr. Alice (Farnham)	female	49.0	0	0	17465	25.9292	D17	S	Mrs
862	863	1	1	Swift, Mrs. Frederick Joel (Margaret Welles Ba...	female	48.0	0	0	17466	25.9292	D17	S	Mrs

Figure 3.25: Passengers sharing cabin D17 – one of them was a female and had the Dr. title

After introducing univariate and multivariate analysis and a few types of feature engineering, including the processing of names to extract titles, we also performed some detailed analysis of large families and some rare cases: very large families and passengers with unusual titles. In the next section, we will create a dashboard figure with multiple plots, each with univariate or bivariate analysis. We can use such complex figures to better capture the complex feature interactions, without loading one graph with too many features.

Creating a dashboard showing multiple plots

We have explored categorical and numerical data, as well as text data. We have learned how to extract various features from text data, and we built aggregated features from some of the numerical ones. Let's now build two more features by grouping **Title** and **Family Size**. We will create two new features:

- **Titles:** By clustering together similar titles (like `Miss` with `Mlle.`, or `Mrs.` and `Mme.`) or rare (like `Dona.`, `Don.`, `Capt.`, `Jonkheer`, `Rev.`, and `Countess`) and keeping the most frequent ones – `Mr.`, `Mrs.`, `Master`, and `Miss`

- **Family Type:** By creating three clusters from the **Family Size** values – **Single** for a family size of 1, **Small** for families made of up to 4 members, and **Large** for families with more than 4 members

Then, we will represent, on a single graph, several simple or derived features that we learned have an important predictive value. We show the passengers' survival rates for Sex, Passenger Class (Pclass), Age Interval, Fare Interval, Family Type, and Title (clustered). The graphs also show the percentage that the subset (given by both the category and survived status) represents from all passengers:

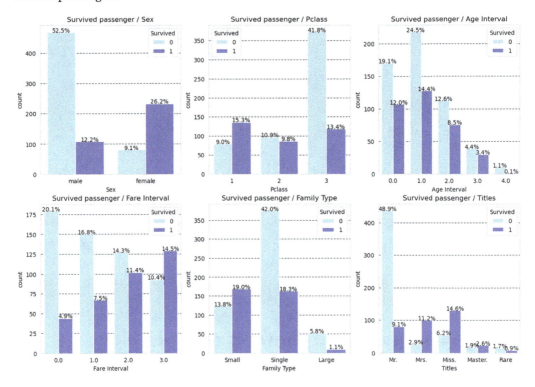

Figure 3.26: Passenger survival rates for different features (original or derived)

With that, we have performed a step-by-step exploratory data analysis of the *Titanic - Machine Learning from Disaster* competition dataset. Now, with the knowledge we gathered about data distribution, the relationship between features, and the correlation between various features and the target feature (the Survived field), we will create a baseline model.

Building a baseline model

As a result of our data analysis, we were able to identify some of the features with predictive value. We can now build a model by using this knowledge to select relevant features. We will start with a model that will use just two out of the many features we investigated. This is called a baseline model and it is used as a starting point for the incremental refinement of the solution.

For the baseline model, we chose a `RandomForestClassifier` model. The model is simple to use, gives good results with the default parameters, and can be interpreted easily, using feature importance.

Let's begin with the following code block to implement the model. First, we import a few libraries that are needed to prepare the model. Then, we convert the categorical data to numerical. We need to do this since the model we chose deals with numbers only. The operation of converting the categorical feature values to numbers is called label encoding. Then, we split the train dataset into train and validation subsets, using an 80-20% split. The model is then fitted using the train subset and we use the validation subset to evaluate the trained (fitted) model:

```python
from sklearn.model_selection import train_test_split
from sklearn import metrics
from sklearn.ensemble import RandomForestClassifier

# convert categorical data in numerical
for dataset in [train_df, test_df]:
    dataset['Sex'] = dataset['Sex'].map( {'female': 1, 'male': 0}
).astype(int)

# train-validation split (20% validation)
VALID_SIZE = 0.2
train, valid = train_test_split(train_df, test_size=VALID_SIZE, random_
state=42, shuffle=True)

# define predictors and target feature (labels)
predictors = ["Sex", "Pclass"]
target = 'Survived'

# train and validation data and labels
train_X = train[predictors]
train_Y = train[target].values
valid_X = valid[predictors]
valid_Y = valid[target].values

# define the classification model (Random Forest)
clf = RandomForestClassifier(n_jobs=-1,
                             random_state=42,
```

```
                                criterion="gini",
                                n_estimators=100,
                                verbose=False)
# fit the model with training data and labels
clf.fit(train_X, train_Y)


# predict the survival status for the validation set
preds = clf.predict(valid_X)
```

In *Figure 3.27*, we show the precision, recall, and f1-score for the validation set (values obtained using the classification_report function from the sklearn.metrics module).

```
                 precision    recall  f1-score   support

Not Survived          0.73      0.96      0.83       105
    Survived          0.90      0.49      0.63        74

    accuracy                              0.77       179
   Macro avg          0.81      0.72      0.73       179
weighted avg          0.80      0.77      0.75       179
```

Figure 3.27: Classification report for the validation data for the baseline model trained with
Sex and Pclass features

The preceding results obtained with this baseline model are still poor. We will have to refine the model using the techniques for model refinement, starting with the observations on training and validation errors. Based on these observations, we might want to improve the training first before focusing on improving model generalization. We might, therefore, opt for adding more features (with predictive values), either by selecting from existing features or creating new features via feature engineering, performing hyperparameter optimization, choosing a better classification algorithm, or combining different algorithms.

Summary

In this chapter, we started our journey around the data world on board the Titanic. We started with a preliminary statistical analysis of each feature and then continued with univariate analysis and feature engineering to create derived or aggregated features. We extracted multiple features from text, and we also created complex graphs to visualize multiple features at the same time and reveal their predictive value. We then learned how to assign a uniform visual identity for our analysis by using a custom color map across the notebook.

For some of the features – most notably, those derived from names – we performed a deep-dive exploration to learn about the fate of large families on the Titanic and about name distribution according to the embarking port. Some of the analysis and visualization tools are easily reusable and, in the next chapter, we will see how to extract them to be used as utility scripts in other notebooks as well.

In the next chapter, we will perform a detailed exploratory data analysis on two datasets with geospatial data. For each of the datasets, we will start with a data quality assessment, and then continue with data exploration, introducing analysis methods, tools, and libraries specific for geographical data analysis. We will learn how to manipulate polygon data, and how to merge, fusion, and clip sets of geographical data stored as collections of polygons. We will also introduce various libraries for the visualization of geospatial data. After performing the individual analyses on both datasets, we will combine the information from the two datasets to build advanced maps with several layers of information from the two datasets.

References

1. Titanic - Machine Learning from Disaster, Kaggle competition: `https://www.kaggle.com/competitions/titanic`

2. Gabriel Preda, Titanic – start of a journey around data world, Kaggle notebook: `https://www.kaggle.com/code/gpreda/titanic-start-of-a-journey-around-data-world`

3. Developing-Kaggle-Notebooks, Packt Publishing GitHub repository: `https://github.com/PacktPublishing/Developing-Kaggle-Notebooks/`

4. Developing-Kaggle-Notebooks, Packt Publishing GitHub repository, Chapter 3: `https://github.com/PacktPublishing/Developing-Kaggle-Notebooks/tree/main/Chapter-03`

Join our book's Discord space

Join our Discord community to meet like-minded people and learn alongside more than 5000 members at:

`https://packt.link/kaggle`

4

Take a Break and Have a Beer or Coffee in London

We continue our journey around the world using data by exploring two datasets in this chapter with geographically distributed information. The first dataset is *Every Pub in England* (see *Reference 1*). This dataset contains the unique ID, name, address, postcode, and information regarding the geographical position of almost every pub in England. The second dataset is called *Starbucks Locations Worldwide* (see *Reference 3*) which contains store number, name, and ownership details, as well as street address, city, and geographical information (latitude and longitude) for all Starbucks stores in the world.

Apart from combining these two datasets, we will also add additional geographical support data. We will learn how to work with missing data, how to perform imputation if needed, how to visualize geographical data, how to clip and merge polygon data, how to generate custom maps, and how to create multiple layers over them. These are just a few tricks that we will learn in this chapter, but in a nutshell, the following topics will be covered:

- Detailed data analysis for pubs in England and Starbucks across the world
- Combined geospatial analysis of pubs and Starbucks in London

The pretext for this chapter's exploration of geospatial analysis tools and techniques is to analyze how the pubs and Starbucks coffee shops geographically interwind, answering such questions as "If somebody had enjoyed a few pints of ale in a pub in downtown London and then fancied a coffee, how far would they have to go to the nearest Starbucks coffee shop?" Or, to give another example, "For the current Starbucks shop, which pubs are closer to this one than to any other Starbucks coffee shop?" Of course, these are not the only questions we will try to answer, but we wanted to give you a glimpse of what we will achieve by the end of this chapter.

Pubs in England

The *Every Pub in England* dataset (*Reference 1*) contains data about 51,566 pubs in England, including the pub name, the address, the postal code, the geographical position (both by easting and northing and by latitude and longitude), and the local authority. I created a notebook, *Every Pub in England – Data Exploration* (*Reference 2*) to investigate this data. The code snippets in the current section are mainly from this notebook. It might be easier for you to follow the notebook in parallel with the explanations in the book.

Data quality check

For the data quality check, we will use the info() and describe() functions to get a first glimpse. These two can be considered the first place to start. Then, we can also use our custom data quality statistics functions defined in the previous chapter. Because we will keep using them, we will group them in a utility script. I call this utility script data_quality_stats, and I defined in this module the functions missing_data, most_frequent_values, and unique_values.

To use the functions defined in this utility script, we need to first add it to the notebook. From the **File** menu, we will select the **Add utility script** menu item, and then add the utility script by selecting it in the **Add Data** panel on the right-hand side of the editor window:

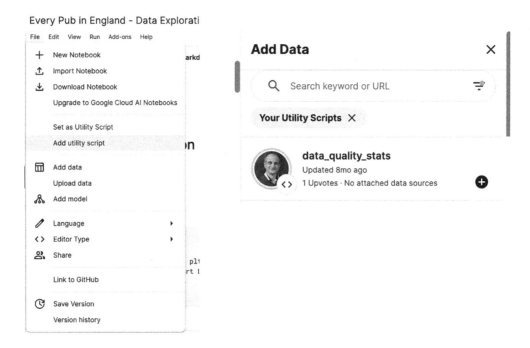

Figure 4.1: Adding a utility script to the notebook

Then, we will add `import` to one of the first notebook cells:

```
from data_quality_stats import missing_data, most_frequent_values, unique_
values
```

Let's check the results after applying this function to our `pub_df` dataframe. *Figure.4.2* shows the missing values:

	fas_id	name	address	postcode	easting	northing	latitude	longitude	local_authority
Total	0	0	0	0	0	0	0	0	2
Percent	0.0	0.0	0.0	0.0	0.0	0.0	0.0	0.0	0.003879
Types	int64	object	object	object	int64	float64	object	object	object

Figure 4.2: Missing values

We can see that there are two missing values for local authorities. Other than that, it appears that there are no others. We need to be alert with regard to the missing values, as some might be hidden; for instance, a missing value could be replaced according to a convention with a specific value (like using "-1" to indicate null values for positive numbers or "NA" for categorical cases).

Figure 4.3 depicts the most frequent values:

	fas_id	name	address	postcode	easting	northing	latitude	longitude	local_authority
Total	51566	51566	51566	51566	51566	51566	51566	51566	51564
Most frequent item	24	The Red Lion	Lancaster University, Bailrigg Lane, Lancaster...	L2 6RE	622675	-5527598.0	\N	\N	County Durham
Frequence	1	193	8	10	70	70	70	70	679
Percent from total	0.002	0.374	0.016	0.019	0.136	0.136	0.136	0.136	1.317

Figure 4.3: Most frequent values

If we look now at the most frequent values, we can observe that for both **latitude** and **longitude**, there are 70 items with the value **\N**. It's interesting that, there are **70** most frequent values for **easting** and **northing**. Easting and northing are geographic Cartesian coordinates: easting refers to the eastward-measured distance, while northing refers to the northward-measured distance. According to the **Universal Transverse Mercator (UTM)** coordinate system, northing is the distance to the Equator; Easting, in the same coordinate system, is the distance to the "false easting," which is uniquely defined in each UTM zone. We can also observe that the most frequently used name for a pub is **The Red Lion**, and that there are **8** pubs in **Lancaster University**. As for the unique values, we can observe that there are more addresses than postcodes and more latitudes and longitudes than postcodes.

Figure 4.4 depicts the unique values:

	fas_id	name	address	postcode	easting	northing	latitude	longitude	local_authority
Total	51566	51566	51566	51566	51566	51566	51566	51566	51564
Uniques	51566	35636	50162	46625	43172	43945	46655	46735	376

Figure 4.4: Unique values

The number of unique values for **address** is larger than the one for **postcode** (more addresses on the same postcode). The total number of different local authorities is **376**. Additionally, notice that the number of unique names is smaller than the number of unique addresses (presumably, there are several popular pub names).

Let's check a bit more about the two missing local authority values. It is odd, since there are only two missing values, which is not expected. We also know that we have 70 missing values for both **latitude** and **longitude**, and those are marked with **\N**. Look at the rows containing this missing local authority information:

	fas_id	name	address	postcode	easting	northing	latitude	longitude	local_authority
768	7499	J D Wetherspoon \"The Star\","105 High Street,...	EN11 8TN	537293	208856	51.761556	-0.012036	Broxbourne	NaN
43212	412676	\"Rory's Bar\","57 Market Place, Malton, North...	YO17 7LX	478582	471715	54.135281	-0.798783	Ryedale	NaN

Figure 4.5: Rows with local authority information missing

It appears that the information is missing because when the parser used by pandas to read the CSV file encountered the sequence \"," it was not able to distinguish the comma separator (,). Therefore, for those two lines, it merged **name** with **address** and then shifted left every column by one position, thus corrupting every column, from **address** to **local_authority**.

We have two options to address this issue:

- One option is to try and give a list of separators to the parser. In our case, it will be a bit tricky, since we have only a comma separator. Also, if we try to use a multi-character separator, we will need to switch to a different engine, Python, because the default engine does not work with multi-character separators.

- The second option, and the preferred one, is to write a small piece of code to fix the issue in the two rows where we spotted it.

Here is the piece of code to fix the issue with the two rows. We use the indexes of the two rows (we can see them in *Figure 4.5* – the first column, without a name) to identify them and perform the correction only on these rows:

```
columns = ['local_authority', 'longitude', 'latitude', 'northing',
'easting', 'postcode', 'address']
# use the rows indexes to locate the rows
for index in [768, 43212]:
    for idx in range(len(columns) - 1):
        # we use `at` to make sure the changes are done on the actual
dataframe, not on a copy of it
        pub_df.at[index, columns[idx]] = pub_df.loc[index][columns[idx +
1]]


    # split the corrupted name and assign the name and address
    name_and_addresse = pub_df.loc[index]['name'].split("\",\"")
    pub_df.at[index, 'name'] = name_and_addresse[0]
    pub_df.at[index, 'address'] = name_and_addresse[1]
```

In *Figure 4.6*, we can see that the name and address are now split and assigned to the correct column, and the rest of the columns were shifted to the right:

	fas_id	name	address	postcode	easting	northing	latitude	longitude	local_authority
768	7499	J D Wetherspoon \"The Star\	105 High Street, Hoddesdon, Hertfordshire	EN11 8TN	537293	208856.0	51.761556	-0.012036	Broxbourne
43212	412676	\"Rory's Bar\	57 Market Place, Malton, North Yorkshire	YO17 7LX	478582	471715.0	54.135281	-0.798783	Ryedale

Figure 4.6: Rows with local authority information after correction

If we check the missing data again, it will appear that no other data is missing. We already know that, in fact, there are 70 missing latitudes and longitudes; they are just marked with \N. If we check separately the latitude or longitude columns that have this value and then the rows where both columns have the same value, we can conclude that there are only 70 rows in total with this anomaly. For the same rows, we see that **northing** and **easting** have unique values, and these values are not correct.

Consequently, we will not be able to reconstruct the latitude and longitude from **easting** and **northing**. When checking the corresponding postcode, address, and local authority for these rows, we can see that there are multiple locations, in multiple local authority regions. There are 65 different postcodes in these 70 rows. Since we do have the postcodes, we will be able to use them to reconstruct the latitude and longitude.

For this purpose, we will include the **Open Postcode Geo** dataset (see *Reference 4*) in our analysis. This dataset contains more than 2.5 million rows and many other columns, besides the postcode, latitude, and longitude. We read the CSV file from the **Open Postcode Geo** dataset, select only four columns (**postcode**, **country**, **latitude**, and **longitude**), and filter out any rows with post-codes that are not included in the list of postcodes, from the 70 rows we targeted in our original dataset with pubs. We set as None the values of longitude and latitude for the 70 rows with missing geographical data:

```
post_code_df = pd.read_csv("/kaggle/input/open-postcode-geo/open_postcode_
geo.csv", header=None, low_memory=False)


post_code_df = post_code_df[[0, 6, 7, 8]]
post_code_df.columns = ['postcode', 'country', 'latitude', 'longitude']
```

We merge the two resulting datasets (the one with pubs and the one with postcodes), and we fill in the missing values for **latitude** and **longitude** in the *left* columns with the values from the *right* columns:

```
pub_df = pub_df.merge(post_code_df, on="postcode", how="left")
pub_df['latitude'] = pub_df['latitude_x'].fillna(pub_df['latitude_y'])
pub_df['longitude'] = pub_df['longitude_x'].fillna(pub_df['longitude_y'])
pub_df = pub_df.drop(["country", "latitude_x", "latitude_y",
"longitude_x", "longitude_y"], axis=1)
```

Now, we've replaced all the missing data in the targeted rows with valid latitude and longitude values. *Figure 4.7* is a snapshot of what the combined dataset looks like.

	fas_id	name	address	postcode	easting	northing	local_authority	latitude	longitude
0	24	Anchor Inn	Upper Street, Stratford St Mary, COLCHESTER, E...	CO7 6LW	604748	234405.0	Babergh	51.97039	0.979328
1	30	Angel Inn	Egremont Street, Glemsford, SUDBURY, Suffolk	CO10 7SA	582888	247368.0	Babergh	52.094427	0.668408
2	63	Black Boy Hotel	7 Market Hill, SUDBURY, Suffolk	CO10 2EA	587356	241327.0	Babergh	52.038683	0.730226
3	64	Black Horse	Lower Street, Stratford St Mary, COLCHESTER, E...	CO7 6JS	604270	233920.0	Babergh	51.966211	0.972091
4	65	Black Lion	Lion Road, Glemsford, SUDBURY, Suffolk	CO10 7RF	582750	248298.0	Babergh	52.102815	0.666893

Figure 4.7: Combined dataset snapshot (every pub in England and Open Postcode)

Now with imputation done, we can continue with data exploration.

Data exploration

We will start by exploring the frequency of each pub name and local authority. To represent this information, we will reuse the `colormap` and `plot` functions developed in the previous chapter. I created a utility script that is imported in the same way as the data statistics utility script:

```
from plot_utils import set_color_map, plot_count, show_wordcloud
```

After importing, we will extract the county and the city (if the address line contains more than two commas) and analyze the word frequency for those. The city is extracted with the simple code shown here:

```
def get_city(text):
    try:
        split_text = text.split(",")
        if len(split_text) > 3:
            return split_text[-2]
    except:
        return None
pub_df["address_city"] = pub_df["address"].apply(lambda x: get_city(x))
```

In *Figure 4.8*, we show the top 10 pubs per local authority:

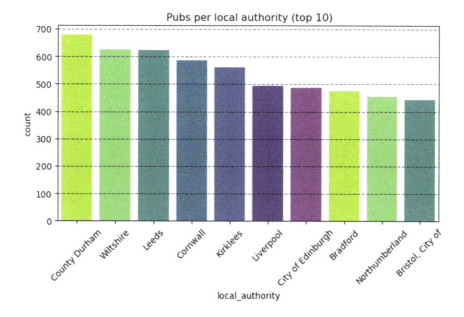

Figure 4.8: Pubs per local authority (top 10)

Figure 4.9 shows the top 10 pubs per county. We extract the county by retrieving the last substring after the comma from the address. In some cases, it is not a county but a large municipality, like London:

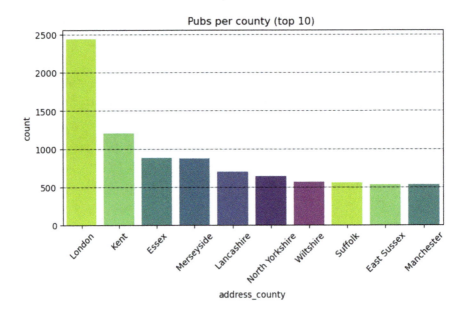

Figure 4.9: Pubs per county (top 10)

Figure 4.10 shows the distribution of words in pub names and addresses:

Figure 4.10: Distribution of words in the pub names (left) and addresses (right)

Because we have the geographical position of pubs, we would like to visualize this information. We can represent the positions of the pubs using the folium Python library and folium plugin MarkerCluster. Folium (which wraps some of the most popular Leaflet external plugins) is an excellent way to display geographically distributed information.

The code to show the UK map is given here:

```
import folium
from folium.plugins import MarkerCluster


uk_coords = [55, -3]


uk_map = folium.Map(location = uk_coords, zoom_start = 6)


uk_map
```

To add markers, we can add the following code (the code to initialize the folium map layer is not included):

```
locations_data = np.array(pub_map_df[["latitude", "longitude"]].
astype(float))
marker_cluster = MarkerCluster(locations = locations_data)
marker_cluster.add_to(uk_map)
uk_map
```

We can also add, besides locations, pop-up information for the MarkerCluster, as well as custom icons.

Figure 4.11 shows the folium (leaflet) map for the British Isles based on OpenStreetMap, without the pub information layer:

Figure 4.11: Map of the British Isles without the pub information layer

Figure 4.12 shows a map of the British Isles with the pub information layer added, using the MarkerCluster plugin. With MarkerCluster, the markers are replaced dynamically, with a widget showing the number of markers in a certain area. When zooming in on an area, the MarkerCluster display changes dynamically, showing a more detailed view of the markers' distribution:

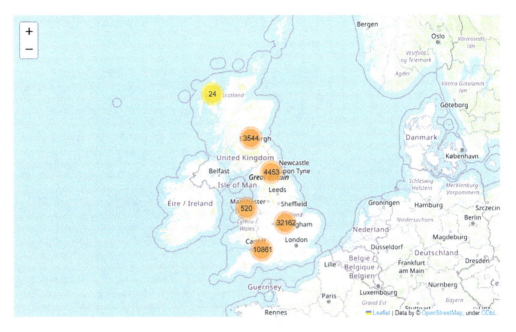

Figure 4.12: Map of the British Isles with the pub information layer added

Figure 4.13 shows a zoomed-in version of the previous map. The region that we zoom in on is the southern part of the British mainland:

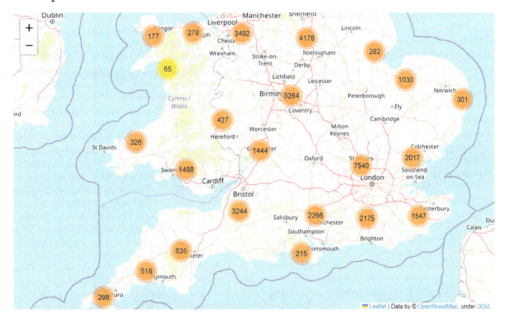

Figure 4.13: Map of the British Isles with the pub information layer added, zoomed in on the southern region, including the London area

Figure 4.14 zooms in on the London area. The clusters are broken into smaller groups, which appear as individual markers as we zoom in:

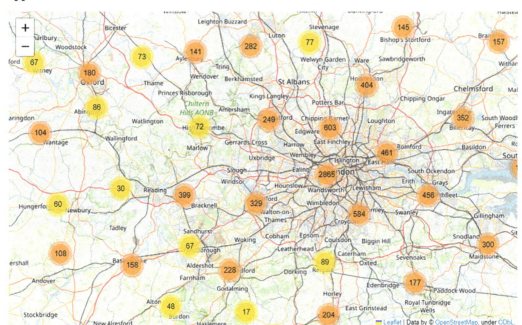

Figure 4.14: Zooming in on the London area

An alternative way to visualize the pub concentration is by using a heatmap. Heatmaps can create a very good intuition of the spatial distribution of data. They show distribution density with color shades, as shown in *Figure 4.15*. Heatmaps are useful to show the density of data points continuously, and it is also easier to evaluate their intensity at different locations using heatmaps. Because heatmaps use interpolation techniques to create a smooth transition between data points, they can provide a more visually appealing representation of the data distribution. You can see two zoom levels with a heatmap view of the pub distribution for all of Great Britain (left) and for the southwest tip of the mainland (right):

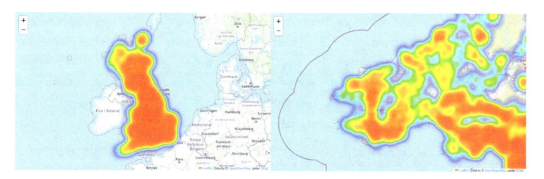

Figure 4.15: Maps using folium and Heatmap to show location density distribution

Notice that there are no pubs from Northern Ireland included. This is because the collection of the pub data excluded it as it isn't part of Great Britain.

Another way to represent the spatial distribution of the pub data is using the Voronoi polygons (or a Voronoi diagram) associated with the pubs' positions. **Voronoi polygons** represent the dual graph of a **Delaunay tessellation**. Let's explain these two concepts that we just introduced: Voronoi polygons and Delaunay tessellation.

If we have a distribution of points in a plane, we can use the Delaunay tessellation to generate the triangular tessellation for this set of points. This graph is a set of triangles whose edges connect all the points, without crossing over. If we draw the mediators of the edges in the Delaunay graph, the network generated from the intersection of those new lines' segments forms the Voronoi polygons mesh. In *Figure 4.16*, we show a set of points and then the Voronoi diagram associated with these points:

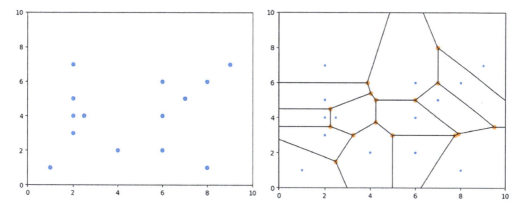

Figure 4.16: A set of points in a plane and the Voronoi polygons generated from this set of points

This Voronoi polygon graph has an interesting property. Inside a Voronoi polygon, all points are closer to the weight center of the polygon (which is one of the vertices of the original graph) than to any of the weight centers of any other neighboring polygon. Therefore, the Voronoi polygons drawn from our pubs' geographical position will accurately represent the pubs' concentration and will also show, with a good approximation, the area "covered" by a certain pub. We will use the Voronoi diagram, formed from the Voronoi polygons, to show the virtual area covered by each pub.

First, we extract the Voronoi polygons using the *Voronoi* function from `scipy.spatial`:

```
from scipy.spatial import Voronoi, voronoi_plot_2d

locations_data = np.array(pub_map_df[["longitude", "latitude"]].
astype(float))
pub_voronoi = Voronoi(locations_data)
```

We can represent the Voronoi polygons associated with the pubs (from `pub_voronoi`) using the `voronoi_plot_2d` function (see *Figure 4.17*). However, the graph has a few problems. First, there are many polygons that are very difficult to distinguish. Then, the pubs' locations (with dots in the graph) are not very legible. Another issue is that the polygons on the border are not aligned with the territory, creating unwanted artifacts that are not informative of the real area "covered" by a certain pub inside the Great Britain territory. We will apply a series of transformations to eliminate the aforementioned problems with the graph.

The following code creates an image of Voronoi polygons, as shown in *Figure 4.17*:

```
fig = voronoi_plot_2d(pub_voronoi,
                      show_vertices=False)
plt.xlim([-8, 3])
plt.ylim([49, 60])

plt.show()
```

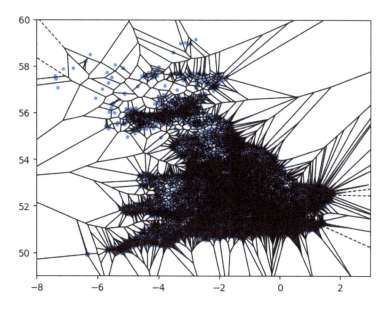

Figure 4.17: 2D plot of Voronoi polygons, extended outside the territory (not clipped)

If we want to represent the geographical area "covered" by each polygon only inside the territorial boundaries of Great Britain, we will have to clip the Voronoi polygons generated from the pubs' position with the polygons describing the territory boundary.

Fortunately, we have access to Kaggle for shapefile data file formats for various countries. For our purpose, we will import the UK ESRI shapefile data from the *GADM Data for UK* dataset (see *Reference 5*). This dataset provides incrementally detailed shapefile data, ranging from external boundaries (level 0) to country level (level 1) and county level (level 2) for the entire territory. Shapefiles can be read with several libraries; in this case, I preferred to use the geopandas library. This library has multiple useful features for our analysis. One of the advantages of selecting this library is that, while it adds functionality for manipulating and visualizing geospatial data, it keeps the user-friendliness and versatility of the pandas library. We load the files with incremental resolution for the territory information:

```python
import geopandas as gpd

uk_all = gpd.read_file("/kaggle/input/gadm-data-for-uk/GBR_adm0.shp")
uk_countries = gpd.read_file("/kaggle/input/gadm-data-for-uk/GBR_adm1.shp")
uk_counties = gpd.read_file("/kaggle/input/gadm-data-for-uk/GBR_adm2.shp")
```

The data is loaded using the geopandas read_file function. This returns a GeoDataFrame object, a special type of DataFrame. It's an extension of the DataFrame objects used with pandas and includes geospatial data. If a DataFrame typically includes columns of type integer, float, text, and date, a GeoDataFrame will also include columns with data specific for spatial analysis, for example, polygons associated with the representation of geospatial regions.

It is useful to inspect the geospatial data before using it to clip the Voronoi polygons. Let's visualize the three different resolution data. We can do this using the plot function associated with each **GeoDataFrame**:

```
fig, ax = plt.subplots(1, 3, figsize = (15, 6))
uk_all.plot(ax = ax[0], color = color_list[2], edgecolor = color_list[6])
uk_countries.plot(ax = ax[1], color = color_list[1], edgecolor = color_
list[6])
uk_counties.plot(ax = ax[2], color = color_list[0], edgecolor = color_
list[6])
plt.suptitle("United Kingdom territory (all, countries and counties
level)")
plt.show()
```

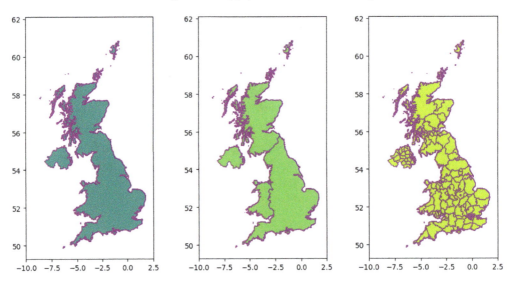

Figure 4.18: Shapefile data for the UK for the entire territory, country level, and county level (left to right)

We already observed that the pubs are only in England, Scotland, and Wales, not in Northern Ireland. If we clip the Voronoi polygons for the pubs using the UK-level data, we could encounter a situation where Voronoi polygons containing pubs from the western coast of England and Wales might spill over into the territory of Northern Ireland. This could result in an unwanted artifact. To avoid this, we can process the data as follows:

- Extract from the country-level shapefile only the data for England, Scotland, and Wales.
- Merge the polygon data from the three countries using the `dissolve` method from geopandas.

```
uk_countries_selected = uk_countries.loc[~uk_countries.NAME_1.
isin(["Northern Ireland"])]

uk_countries_dissolved = uk_countries_selected.dissolve()

fig, ax = plt.subplots(1, 1, figsize = (6, 6))
uk_countries_dissolved.plot(ax = ax, color = color_list[1], edgecolor =
color_list[6])
plt.suptitle("Great Britain territory (without Northern Ireland)")
plt.show()
```

The resulting content is shown here:

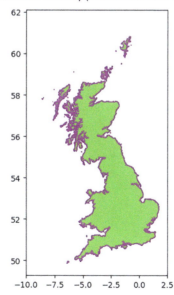

Figure 4.19: Shapefile data with England, Scotland, and Wales after filtering Northern Ireland and using dissolve to merge the polygons

Now, we have the right clipping polygon for the Voronoi polygons from the three countries. Before clipping the polygons, we need to extract them from the Voronoi object. The following code does just that:

```
def extract_voronoi_polygon_list(voronoi_polygons):
    voronoi_poly_list = []
    for region in voronoi_polygons.regions:
        if -1 in region:
            continue
        else:
            pass
        if len(region) != 0:
            voronoi_poly_region = Polygon(voronoi_polygons.
vertices[region])
            voronoi_poly_list.append(voronoi_poly_region)
        else:
            continue
    return voronoi_poly_list


voronoi_poly_list = extract_voronoi_polygon_list(pub_voronoi)
```

With that, we have everything we need to perform the clipping operation. We start by converting the list of Voronoi polygons into a GeoDataFrame object, similar to the uk_countries_dissolved object that we will use to clip them. We are clipping the polygons so that, when we represent them, the polygons will not extend over the boundary. For the clipping operation to be performed correctly, and without errors, we will have to use the same projection as for the clipping object. We use the clip function from the geopandas library. This operation is highly time- and CPU-intensive. On Kaggle infrastructure, running the entire operation (with the CPU) for the 45,000 polygons in our list takes 35 minutes:

```
voronoi_polygons = gpd.GeoDataFrame(voronoi_poly_list, columns =
['geometry'], crs=uk_countries_dissolved.crs)

start_time = time.time()
voronoi_polys_clipped = gpd.clip(voronoi_polygons, uk_countries_dissolved)
end_time = time.time()
print(f"Total time: {round(end_time - start_time, 4)} sec.")
```

The following code plots the entire collection of clipped polygons:

```python
fig, ax = plt.subplots(1, 1, figsize = (20, 20))
plt.style.use('bmh')
uk_all.plot(ax = ax, color = 'none', edgecolor = 'dimgray')
voronoi_polys_clipped.plot(ax = ax, cmap = cmap_custom, edgecolor =
'black', linewidth = 0.25)
plt.title("All pubs in England - Voronoi polygons with each pub area")
plt.show()
```

In *Figure 4.20*, we can see the resulting plot. There are areas with a larger concentration of pubs (smaller polygons) and areas where there is a large distance between two pubs (in certain areas of Scotland, for example).

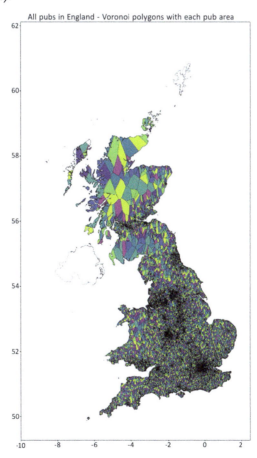

Figure 4.20: Voronoi polygons from the pub geospatial distribution, clipped using the dissolved country-level data from the three countries selected (England, Wales, and Scotland)

Another modality to show the spatial distribution of pubs is to aggregate the data at the local authority level and to build Voronoi polygons around the geospatial center of the pub distribution for that local authority. Each new Voronoi polygon center is the mean latitude/longitude coordinates for each pub in the current local authority. The resulting polygon mesh does not reconstruct the spatial distribution of the local authorities, but it represents with good accuracy the relative pub distribution. The resulting Voronoi polygon set is clipped using the same clipping polygons as before. To be more precise, before we used clipping polygons, the contours were obtained by dissolving the country-level shapefile data. We can use a graded colormap to represent the density of the pubs per area. Let's see the code to create and visualize this mesh.

First, we create a dataset that contains, for each local authority, the number of pubs and the average latitude and longitude of the pub locations:

```python
pub_df["latitude"] = pub_df["latitude"].apply(lambda x: float(x))
pub_df["longitude"] = pub_df["longitude"].apply(lambda x: float(x))

pubs_df = pub_df.groupby(["local_authority"])["name"].count().reset_
index()
pubs_df.columns = ["local_authority", "pubs"]

lat_df = pub_df.groupby(["local_authority"])["latitude"].mean().reset_
index()
lat_df.columns = ["local_authority", "latitude"]

long_df = pub_df.groupby(["local_authority"])["longitude"].mean().reset_
index()
long_df.columns = ["local_authority", "longitude"]


pubs_df = pubs_df.merge(lat_df)
pubs_df = pubs_df.merge(long_df)

mean_loc_data = np.array(pubs_df[["longitude", "latitude"]].astype(float))
```

Then, we calculate the Voronoi polygons associated with this distribution:

```
mean_loc_data = np.array(pubs_df[["longitude", "latitude"]].astype(float))
pub_mean_voronoi = Voronoi(mean_loc_data)


mean_pub_poly_list = extract_voronoi_polygon_list(pub_mean_voronoi)
mean_voronoi_polygons = gpd.GeoDataFrame(mean_pub_poly_list, columns =
['geometry'], crs=uk_countries_dissolved.crs)
```

We clip the resulting polygons with the same polygon used before for clipping (a result of selecting England, Wales, and Scotland and dissolving the shapefiles into one single shapefile):

```
mean_voronoi_polys_clipped = gpd.clip(mean_voronoi_polygons, uk_countries_
dissolved)
```

The following code plots the Voronoi polygons from the aggregated pub geospatial distribution at a local authority level (the center of a Voronoi polygon is the average latitude/longitude for all pubs in the local authority area), clipped using the dissolved country-level (three countries are selected: England, Scotland, and Wales) data. We use a green color gradient for the pub density per area (see *Figure 4.21*):

```
fig, ax = plt.subplots(1, 1, figsize = (10,10))
plt.style.use('bmh')
uk_all.plot(ax = ax, color = 'none', edgecolor = 'dimgray')
mean_voronoi_polys_clipped.plot(ax = ax, cmap = "Greens_r")
plt.title("All pubs in England\nPubs density per local authority\nVoronoi
polygons for mean of pubs positions")
plt.show()
```

We used Voronoi polygons to visualize the pubs' geographical distribution. In *Figure 4.20*, we show each polygon with a different color. Because the points inside a Voronoi polygon are closer to the polygon center than to any other neighboring polygon center, each polygon is approximately the area covered by the pub positioned in the center of the polygon. In *Figure 4.21*, we use Voronoi polygons to build around the geometrical center of the pubs' distribution inside each local authority. We then use a color gradient to represent the relative pub density for each local authority. By using these original visualization techniques, we were able to represent more intuitively the spatial distribution of the pubs.

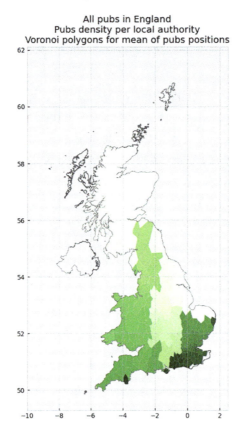

Figure 4.21: Voronoi polygons with a color intensity proportional to the pub density per local authority area

We will continue to investigate this data in the upcoming section, when we mix data from the pub dataset with the data from the Starbucks dataset. We intend to combine the information from the two datasets, using the Voronoi polygon areas to evaluate the relative distances between pubs and Starbucks in the London area.

By manipulating Voronoi polygons generated for pubs and Starbucks coffee shops, we will analyze the relative spatial distribution of pubs and Starbucks, generating maps where we can see, for example, a group of pubs that are closest to a Starbucks. The geometric properties of Voronoi polygons will prove to be extremely useful to do this.

With that in mind, let's proceed and explore the Starbucks dataset.

Starbucks around the world

We start the analysis for the *Starbucks Locations Worldwide* dataset with a detailed **Exploratory Data Analysis** (**EDA**) in the notebook *Starbucks Location Worldwide - Data Exploration*. (see *Reference 6*). You might want to follow the notebook in parallel with the text in the current section. The tools used in this dataset are imported from the `data_quality_stats` and `plot_style_utils` utility scripts. Before starting our analysis, it is important to explain that the dataset used for this analysis is from Kaggle and was collected 6 years ago.

Preliminary data analysis

The dataset has 25,600 rows. Some fields have just a few missing values. **Latitude** and **Longitude** have 1 value missing each, while there are 2 missing values for **Street Address** and 15 missing values for **City**. The fields that have the most missing data are **Postcode** (5.9%) and **Phone Number** (26.8%). In *Figure 4.22*, we can see a sample of the data:

	Brand	Store Number	Store Name	Ownership Type	Street Address	City	State/Province	Country	Postcode	Phone Number	Timezone	Longitude	Latitude
Total	25600	25600	25600	25600	25598	25585	25600	25600	24078	18739	25600	25599	25599
Most frequent item	Starbucks	19773-160973	Starbucks	Company Owned	Circular Building #6, Guard Post 8	上海市	CA	US	0	773-686-6180	GMT-05:00 America/New_York	-73.98	40.76
Frequence	25249	2	224	11932	11	542	2821	13608	101	17	4889	76	81
Percent from total	98.629	0.008	0.875	46.609	0.043	2.118	11.02	53.156	0.419	0.091	19.098	0.297	0.316

Figure 4.22: First rows of the Starbucks Locations Worldwide dataset

Looking at the most frequent values report, we can learn a few interesting things:

	Brand	Store Number	Store Name	Ownership Type	Street Address	City	State/Province	Country	Postcode	Phone Number	Timezone	Longitude	Latitude
Total	25600	25600	25600	25600	25598	25585	25600	25600	24078	18739	25600	25599	25599
Most frequent item	Starbucks	19773-160973	Starbucks	Company Owned	Circular Building #6, Guard Post 8	上海市	CA	US	0	773-686-6180	GMT-05:00 America/New_York	-73.98	40.76
Frequence	25249	2	224	11932	11	542	2821	13608	101	17	4889	76	81
Percent from total	98.629	0.008	0.875	46.609	0.043	2.118	11.02	53.156	0.419	0.091	19.098	0.297	0.316

Figure 4.23: The most frequent values for the Starbucks Locations Worldwide dataset

As expected, the state with the greatest number of Starbucks coffee shops is CA (USA). As per the city, the largest number of shops are in Shanghai. There is a unique address with up to 11 shops. Additionally, most of the shops per timezone are in the New York timezone .

Univariate and bivariate data analysis

For this dataset, I chose a color map blending the colors of Starbucks with green and shades of brown, like those of the high-quality roasted coffee they offer to their clients:

Figure 4.24: Notebook color map, blending Starbucks colors with the shades of roasted coffee

We will use the preceding custom colormap for the univariate analysis graphs. In the following figure, we show the distribution of coffee shops by country code. Most Starbucks are in the United States, with over 13,000 entries, followed by China, Canada and Japan:

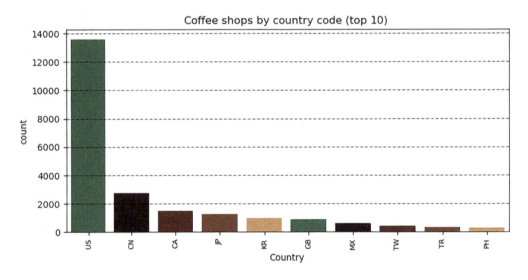

Figure 4.25: Coffee shops by country code. The US has the most, followed by China, Canada, and Japan

If we look at the distribution by state/province in *Figure 4.26*, we can see that in first place is California, with more than 25,000. In second place is Texas, with over 1,000 coffee shops, and in third place is England, with fewer than 1,000. Distribution by timezone shows that the most represented is the US East Coast timezone (the New York timezone).

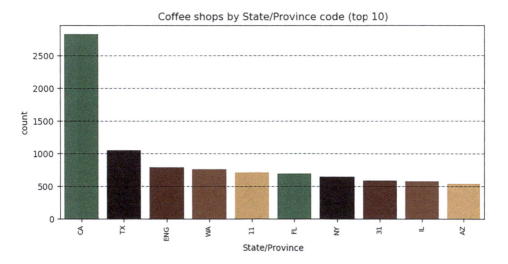

Figure 4.26: Coffee shops by State/Province code. California (CA) has the largest number of coffee shops, followed by Texas (TX)

Additionally, the majority of the coffee shops are in the New York (US East Coast) timezone:

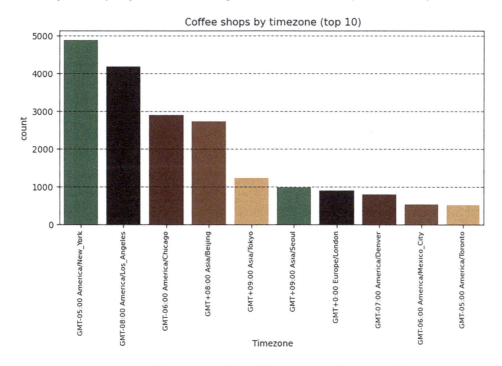

Figure 4.27: Coffee shops by timezone code, with the majority in the New York (US East Coast) timezone

Moving on, the ownership of Starbucks coffee shops is shown in *Figure 4.28*. We can observe that most of the coffee shops are company-owned (12,000), followed by licensed (more than 9,000), joint ventures (4,000), and franchises (fewer than 1,000):

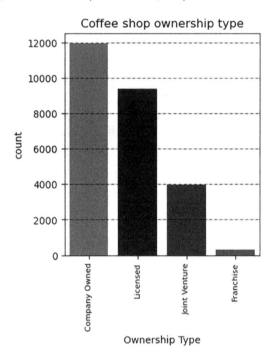

Figure 4.28: Coffee shop ownership types

It will be interesting to see next how the ownership type varies depending on the country. Let's represent the company ownership by country. The following figure shows the number of coffee shops per country for the top 10 countries. We use a logarithmic scale, due to data skewness (a measure of the asymmetry of the probability distribution). In other words, in a small number of countries, there are many coffee shops, while in the rest of the countries, there is a much smaller number. The United States has two types of ownership: company-owned and licensed. China has mostly joint ventures and company-owned, with a smaller number of licensed. In Japan, the majority of shops are joint ventures, with almost an equal amount of licensed and company-owned.

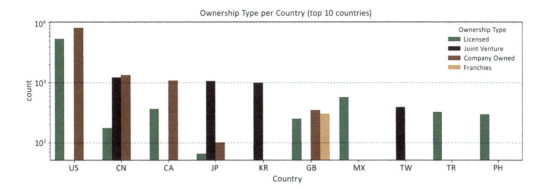

Figure 4.29: Coffee shops per country, grouped by ownership type

In the following figure, we show the number of coffee shops per city, grouped by ownership type. Because the city's names are written in multiple forms (with vernacular characters in lowercase and uppercase), I first unified the notation (and aligned all with an English name). The first cities are Shanghai, Seoul, and Beijing. Shanghai and Seoul have joint-venture coffee shops, while Beijing has only company-owned Starbucks coffee shops.

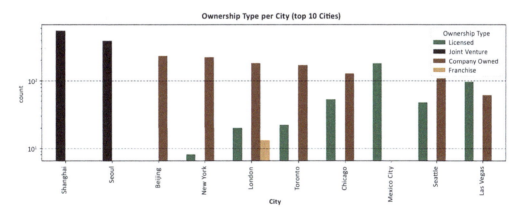

Figure 4.30: Coffee shops per city, grouped by ownership type

We performed univariate and bivariate analyses on the Starbucks coffee shops dataset. Now, we have a good understanding of the feature distribution and interactions. Moving on, let's perform another geospatial analysis, using and extending the tools that we already tested with the analysis of the pubs in England.

Geospatial analysis

We start by observing the distribution of Starbucks in the world. We use the folium library and MarkerCluster to represent on a dynamic map the geospatial distribution of coffee shops in the entire world. The code is shown here:

```python
coffee_df = coffee_df.loc[(~coffee_df.Latitude.isna()) & (~coffee_df.Longitude.isna())]
locations_data = np.array(coffee_df[["Latitude", "Longitude"]])
popups = coffee_df.apply(lambda row: f"Name: {row['Store Name']}", axis=1)
marker_cluster = MarkerCluster(
    locations = locations_data,
)
world_coords = [0., 0.]
world_map = folium.Map(location = world_coords, zoom_start = 1)
marker_cluster.add_to(world_map)
world_map
```

Folium/leaflet maps are browsable. We can pan, zoom in, and zoom out. In *Figure 4.31*, we show the entire world's distribution of coffee shops:

Figure 4.31: Worldwide Starbucks coffee shop distribution using folium over leaflets and MarkerCluster

In *Figure 4.32*, we show a zoom-in on the continental United States and Canada area. Clearly, the East and West coasts dominate Starbucks coffee shop distribution in the United States.

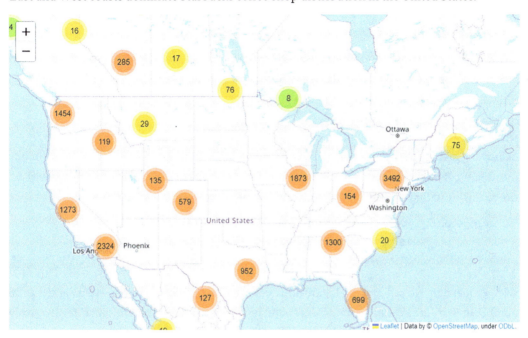

Figure 4.32: Starbucks coffee shop distribution in the United States

Another way to represent the spatial distribution of Starbucks coffee shops is to use the geopandas plot function. First, we will show the number of shops per country. For this, we aggregate the coffee shops per country:

```
coffee_agg_df = coffee_df.groupby(["Country"])["Brand"].count().reset_
index()
coffee_agg_df.columns = ["Country", "Shops"]
```

To represent the geospatial distribution with geopandas, we need to use the ISO3 country codes (country codes with three letters). In the Starbucks distribution dataset, we have only ISO2 (country codes with two letters). We can include a dataset that contains the equivalences, or we can import a Python package that will do the conversions for us. We will opt for the second solution and pip install, and then import the country-conversion Python package:

```
import geopandas as gpd
import matplotlib
import country_converter as cc
```

```
# convert ISO2 to ISO3 country codes - to be used with geopandas plot of
countries
coffee_agg_df["iso_a3"] = coffee_agg_df["Country"].apply(lambda x:
cc.convert(x, to='ISO3'))
```

Then, using geopandas, we load a dataset with polygon shapes for all countries, with low resolution. We then merge the two datasets (with shops and polygons):

```
world = gpd.read_file(gpd.datasets.get_path('naturalearth_lowres'))
world_shop = world.merge(coffee_agg_df, on="iso_a3", how="right")
```

Before displaying the country polygons, with the fill color adjusted to represent proportionally the number of Starbucks coffee shops in the current country, we will display a wireframe with all the countries so that we can also see on the map the countries without Starbucks:

```
world_shop.loc[world_shop.Shops.isna(), "Shops"] = 0
f, ax = plt.subplots(1, 1, figsize=(12, 5))
world_cp = world.copy()
```

With geopandas, we can apply a logarithmic colormap, which helps in representing the total number of Starbucks coffee shops across countries with a skewed distribution more effectively. It ensures a well-distributed color scheme, allowing us to differentiate between countries with a smaller number of coffee shops and those at the top in this regard. We also draw some of the latitude lines:

```
# transform, in the copied data, the projection in Cylindrical equal-area,
# which preserves the areas

world_cp= world_cp.to_crs({'proj':'cea'})
world_cp["area"] = world_cp['geometry'].area / 10**6 # km^2
world["area"] = world_cp["area"]='black', linewidth=0.25, ax=ax)
# draw countries polygons with log scale colormap
world_shop.plot(column='Shops', legend=True,\
            norm=matplotlib.colors.LogNorm(vmin=world_shop.Shops.min(),\
                                    vmax=world_shop.Shops.max()),
            cmap="rainbow",
            ax=ax)
plt.grid(color="black", linestyle=":", linewidth=0.1, axis="y",
which="major")
plt.xlabel("Longitude"); plt.ylabel("Latitude")
plt.title("Starbucks coffee shops distribution at country level")
plt.show()
```

This map is informative, but these countries have very different areas, populations, and population densities. To understand better the density of Starbucks coffee shops, we will also plot the number of shops per million citizens (for each country) and the number of shops per 1,000 square kilometers.

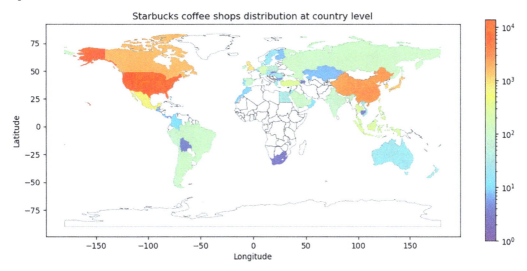

Figure 4.33: geopandas map showing the coffee shop density (the log scale) at the world level

For the preceding map, we chose geopandas precisely because it allows us to represent regions with color intensity on a logarithmic scale.

In the world dataset, we have the population estimate but we do not have the country area information. To calculate the Starbucks density per square kilometers, we need to also include the area. We can include a new dataset, with the country area, or we can use the features of geopandas to obtain the area from the polygons. With the current Mercator projection adapted to display the map in a way that is legible, the area is not calculated correctly.

We will copy the world dataset so that the transformation does not distort the polygons in the Mercator projection. We will then apply the transformation on the copy using the Cylindrical equal-area projection. This projection preserves the areas, and this is what we need for our calculations. After we perform the transformation, we concatenate the area to the world dataset:

```
world_cp = world.copy()
# transform, in the copied data, the projection in Cylindrical equal-area,
# which preserves the areas
world_cp= world_cp.to_crs({'proj':'cea'})
world_cp["area"] = world_cp['geometry'].area / 10**6 # km^2
world["area"] = world_cp["area"]
```

Let's verify that we have calculated the area correctly. We sample a few countries, and we verify that the areas match official records:

```
world.loc[world.iso_a3.isin(["GBR", "USA", "ROU"])]
```

	pop_est	continent	name	iso_a3	gdp_md_est	geometry	area
4	326625791	North America	United States of America	USA	18560000.0	MULTIPOLYGON (((-122.84000 49.00000, -120.0000...	9.509851e+06
117	21529967	Europe	Romania	ROU	441000.0	POLYGON ((28.23355 45.48828, 28.67978 45.30403...	2.383786e+05
143	64769452	Europe	United Kingdom	GBR	2788000.0	MULTIPOLYGON (((-6.19788 53.86757, -6.95373 54...	2.499296e+05

Figure 4.34: Area verification for the United States of America, Romania, and the UK

As you can see, for all the countries, the calculated area with the method used yielded correct surfaces that match the values in official records.

Now, we have all we need to prepare and display the maps with Starbucks densities per country, relative to area and population. The code for the calculation of the Starbucks densities is as follows:

```
world_shop = world.merge(coffee_agg_df, on="iso_a3", how="right")
world_shop["Shops / Population"] = world_shop["Shops"] / world_shop["pop_
est"] * 10**6  # shops/1 million population
world_shop["Shops / Area"] = world_shop["Shops"] / world_shop["area"] *
10**3. # shops / 1000 Km^2
```

Then, using the following code, we draw the distribution of Starbucks per 1 million people at the country level:

```
f, ax = plt.subplots(1, 1, figsize=(12, 5))
# show all countries contour with black and color while
world.plot(column=None, color="white", edgecolor='black', linewidth=0.25,
ax=ax)
# draw countries polygons
world_shop.plot(column='Shops / Population', legend=True,\
```

```
            cmap="rainbow",
            ax=ax)
plt.grid(color="black", linestyle=":", linewidth=0.1, axis="y",
which="major")
plt.xlabel("Longitude"); plt.ylabel("Latitude")
plt.title("Starbucks coffee shops / 1 million population - distribution at
country level")
plt.show()
```

We show the graph drawn with the preceding code in *Figure 4.35*. The countries with the highest number of Starbucks per million people are the United States, Canada, and the United Emirates, followed by Taiwan, South Korea, the UK, and Japan.

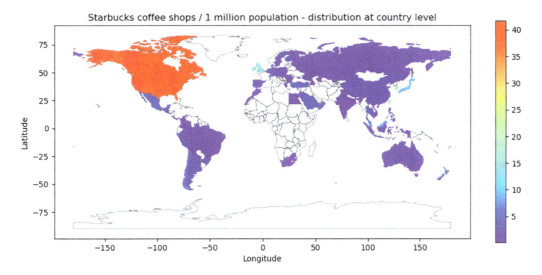

Figure 4.35: Starbucks per 1 million people – distribution per country

For each country, the number of Starbucks coffee shops per 1,000 square kilometers is displayed in the following figure:

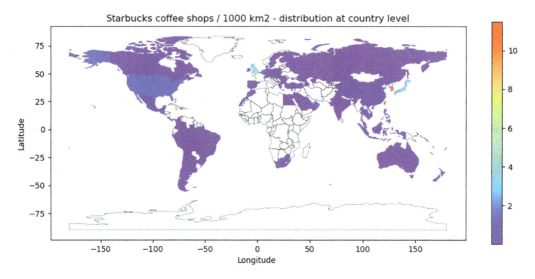

Figure 4.36: Starbucks per 1,000 square kilometers – distribution per country

We can see that the highest concentration of coffee shops is in countries like South Korea, Taiwan, Japan, and the UK.

Let's do a quick summary to wrap up this section. We analyzed the two datasets with pubs in England and Starbucks worldwide to get a good understanding of the data distribution in the two datasets. We also introduced several techniques and tools for geospatial data manipulation and analysis. We learned how to draw shapefile data, how to extract polygons from a shapefile, how to clip polygon sets using another set of polygons, and how to generate Voronoi polygons. This was all preparation for the main part of the analysis in this chapter, where we will combine the two datasets and learn how to generate multi-layer maps, where the information from the two datasets is combined creatively. Our goal is twofold: to introduce you to more advanced ways to analyze geospatial data, and to use creatively the methods introduced to see how we can get insights from both data sources, once combined.

Pubs and Starbucks in London

Until now, our analysis was focused on the individual datasets Every Pub in England and Starbucks Locations Worldwide. To support some of the data analysis tasks related to these two separate datasets, we have also added two more datasets, one with the geographical position of postal codes, replacing the missing latitude and longitude data, and one with shapefile data for the UK to clip the Voronoi polygons generated from pubs' positions, aligning them with the land contour of the island.

In the current section, we will combine the information from the two main data sources analyzed separately and apply methods developed during this preliminary analysis, supporting the objective of our study. This will focus on a smaller region, where we have both a high density of pubs and a concentration of Starbucks coffee shops, in London. We can already hypothesize that the geospatial concentration of Starbucks is smaller than the concentration of pubs.

We would like to see where the closest Starbucks is so that we can sober up with a coffee after we've had a few pints of ale. We already learned that Voronoi polygons have an interesting characteristic – any point inside a polygon is closer to its center than to any neighboring center. We will represent the pub locations in the London area, superposed over the Voronoi polygons generated from the Starbucks locations in the same area.

The notebook associated with this section is Coffee or Beer in London – Your Choice!, (see *Reference 11*). You might find it useful to follow the notebook along with the text in this section.

Data preparation

We start by reading the CSV files from the two datasets, Every Pub in England and Starbucks Locations Worldwide. We also now read the GBR_adm2.shp shapefile (with Great Britain local authorities' borders data) from GDM Data for the UK and the data from Open Postcode Geo. In this last file, we just filter four columns (postcode, country, latitude, and longitude).

From the pub data, we only select the entries that have as a local authority one of the 32 London boroughs. We add to this subset the City of London, which is not one of the boroughs. The City of London is in the center of London, and some of the pubs are located there, which we would like to include. We use the same list to filter the data in the shapefile data. To check that we have correctly selected all the shapefile data, we display the boroughs (and the City of London) polygons:

```
boroughs_df = counties_df.loc[counties_df.NAME_2.isin(london_boroughs)]
boroughs_df.plot(color=color_list[0], edgecolor=color_list[4])
plt.show()
```

In the following figure, observe that the City of London is missing (left). We have London in shapefile names, so we will just replace London with the City of London in the shapefile data. After the correction (right), we can see that by unifying the notation for the City of London, we now have all local authorities correctly represented on our map. Now, we have selected all areas that we want to include in our analysis of pubs and Starbucks coffee shops in the London area.

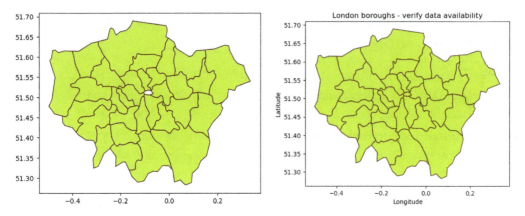

Figure 4.37: London boroughs (left) and the London boroughs and the City of London (right)

We also select Starbucks coffee shop data for the same sub-regions. For Starbucks data, the selection is shown in the following code:

```
coffee_df = coffee_df.loc[(coffee_df.City.isin(london_boroughs +
["London"])) &\
                (coffee_df.Country=="GB")]
```

We incorporate country information into the filtering criteria because London and the names of various other London boroughs are found across North America, where many cities borrow names from Great Britain.

We are aware, based on our previous analysis of the pub data, that some pubs have missing latitude and longitude, marked with \\N. Carry out the same transformations, including merging with the Open Postcode Geo data and cleaning, as discussed in the previous subsection for these pub rows. This process will involve assigning latitude and longitude data based on postcode matching.

Then, using the following code, we check that the pubs and Starbucks selected with the preceding criteria are all within the boundaries (or very close to those) of the London boroughs:

```
def verify_data_availability():
    f, ax = plt.subplots(1, 1, figsize=(10, 10))
    boroughs_df.plot(color="white", edgecolor=color_list[4], ax=ax)
    plt.scatter(x=pub_df["longitude"],y=pub_df["latitude"], color=color_
```

```
list[0], marker="+", label="Pubs")
    plt.scatter(x=coffee_df["Longitude"],y=coffee_df["Latitude"],
color=color_list[5], marker="o", label="Starbucks")
    plt.xlabel("Longitude"); plt.ylabel("Latitude"); plt.title("London
boroughs - verify data availability")
    plt.grid(color="black", linestyle=":", linewidth=0.1, axis="both",
which="major")
    plt.legend()
    plt.show()
```

We observe that there are two Starbucks that are quite remote from London. We set an additional condition for the selected Starbucks:

```
coffee_df = coffee_df.loc[coffee_df.Latitude<=51.7]
```

In the resulting figure, you'll see the pubs (cross) and Starbucks (points) in the London boroughs and the City of London, after filtering items outside these local authorities' zones and correcting the misattributions.

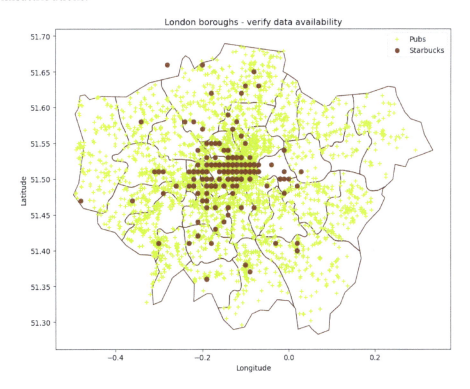

Figure 4.38: Pubs (cross) and Starbucks (points) in the London boroughs and the City of London after filtering items

There are still a few points outside the boundaries, but for now, we should be fine. These points will be filtered out once we use the local authority polygons to clip the Voronoi polygons associated with each pub and coffee shop. We observed a strange artifact regarding the alignment of Starbucks. All Starbucks shops seem to be aligned horizontally. This is because Starbucks positions are given with only two decimals (Starbucks coffee shops are from a global geolocation dataset, where the location is given with smaller precision), while the pubs are given six decimals. Consequently, the Starbucks shops appear to be aligned. Their positions are rounded to two decimals, and due to the close position of the coffee shops, they appear to be aligned, especially along the latitude lines.

Geospatial analysis

Now, let's represent the Voronoi polygons for pubs and Starbucks shops in London and its boroughs. We start by generating those polygons, using the same code we used before for our data analysis on `Every Pub in England`. First, let's do the pubs in the area. The code in the notebook is now more compact, since we are using the `geospatial_utils` utility script. The following code generates the object with the Voronoi polygons collection and then visualizes the collection:

```
pub_voronoi = get_voronoi_polygons(pub_df)
plot_voronoi_polygons(pub_voronoi,
                      title="Voronoi polygons from pubs locations in
London",
                      lat_limits=[51.2, 51.7],
                      long_limits=[-0.5, 0.3])
```

For this, the preceding code uses two functions defined in `geospatial_utils`.

The first function, `get_voronoi_polygons`, creates a list of Voronoi polygons from a list of points, with the *x* and *y* coordinates representing the longitude and latitude, respectively. To do this, it uses the Voronoi function in the `scipy.spatial` library:

```
def get_voronoi_polygons(data_df, latitude="latitude",
longitude="longitude"):
    """
    Create a list of Voronoi polygons from a list of points
    Args
        data_df: dataframe containing lat/long
        latitude: latitude feature
        longitude: longitude feature
```

```
    Returns
        Voronoi polygons graph (points, polygons) from the seed points in
data_df
        (a scipy.spatial.Voronoi object)
    """


    locations_data = np.array(data_df[[latitude, longitude]].
astype(float))
    data_voronoi = [[x[1], x[0]] for x in locations_data]
    voronoi_polygons = Voronoi(data_voronoi)
    print(f"Voronoi polygons: {len(voronoi_polygons.points)}")
    return voronoi_polygons
```

The second function, plot_voronoi_polygons, plots a spacy.spatial.Voronoi object, which is a collection of Voronoi polygons:

```
def plot_voronoi_polygons(voronoi_polygons, title, lat_limits, long_
limits):
    """
    Plot Voronoi polygons (visualization tool)
    Args
        voronoi_polygons: Voronoi polygons object (a scipy.spatial.Voronoi
object)
        title: graph title
        lat_limits: graph latitude (y) limits
        long_limits: graph longitude (x) limits
    Returns
        None
    """

    # do not show the vertices, only show edges and centers
    fig = voronoi_plot_2d(voronoi_polygons,
                    show_vertices=False)
    plt.xlim(long_limits)
    plt.ylim(lat_limits)
    plt.title(title)
    plt.show()
```

The collection of polygons generated is first extracted as a list of polygons, using the extract_voronoi_polygon_list function already defined in the previous section (and which was just moved to the new utility script). Then, the polygons are clipped using the external boundary of London boroughs, obtained by dissolving the borroughs_df GeoDataFrame:

```
boroughs_dissolved = boroughs_df.dissolve()
voronoi_polys_clipped = clip_polygons(voronoi_poly_list, boroughs_df)
```

The code for clip_polygons is defined as well in the geospatial_utils utility script. In the clip_polygons function, we use a list of polygons, poly_clipping, to clip polygons in another list, poly_list_origin. We transform the list with original polygons, poly_list_origin, in a geopandas DataFrame. We perform the clipping operation using the geopandas clip function. The resulting list of polygons clipped, polygons_clipped, is returned by the clip_polygons function:

```
def clip_polygons(poly_list_origin, poly_clipping):
    """

    Clip a list of polygons using an external polygon
    Args:
        poly_list_origin: list of polygons to clip
        poly_clipping: polygon used to clip the original list


    Returns:
        The original list of polygons, with the polygons clipped using the
clipping polygon
    """
```

```
    #convert the initial polygons list to a geodataframe
    polygons_gdf = gpd.GeoDataFrame(poly_list_origin, columns =
['geometry'], crs=poly_clipping.crs)
    start_time = time.time()
    polygons_clipped = gpd.clip(polygons_gdf, poly_clipping)
    end_time = time.time()
    print(f"Total time: {round(end_time - start_time, 4)} sec.")
    return polygons_clipped
```

The following figure shows the Voronoi polygons from pub locations in London (left) and the boroughs' boundary (right):

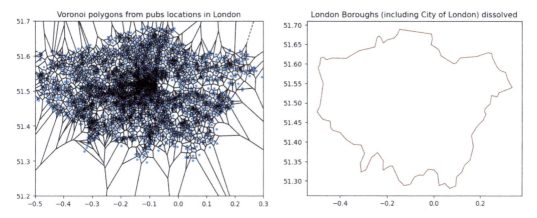

Figure 4.39: Pubs' Voronoi polygons in the London boroughs and the City of London (left) and the London boroughs' boundary (right). We use the boundary polygon to clip the Voronoi polygons

The following figure shows the boroughs' boundary and the pubs' position, as well as the Voronoi polygons associated with these locations. We can observe that the areas with the greatest pub density are in the City of London and its neighboring boroughs to the west, except for Tower Hamlets, which has only one pub.

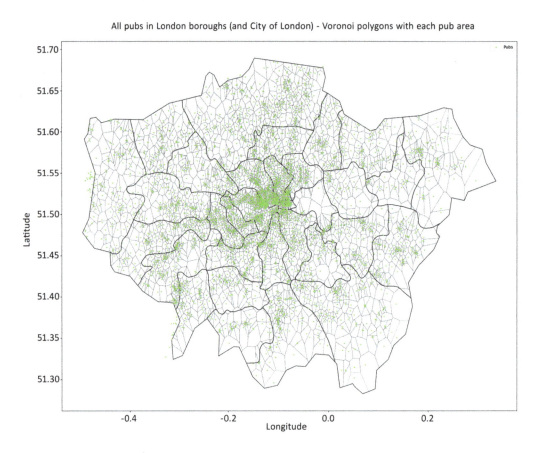

Figure 4.40: Pubs' Voronoi polygons in the London boroughs and the City of London (clipped),
showing pubs' locations and boroughs' boundaries

Next, we perform the same operations for the Starbucks coffee shop locations. We generate the Voronoi polygons and clip them with the same London borough border polygon, obtained by dissolving all the boroughs' polygons. The following figure shows the boroughs' boundaries and the Starbucks shops' positions, as well as the Voronoi polygons associated with these locations:

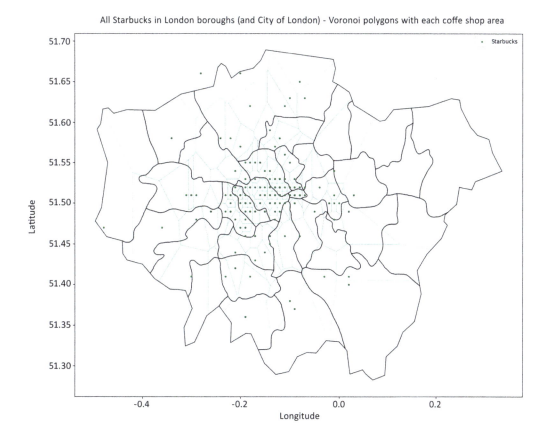

Figure 4.41: Starbucks' Voronoi polygons in the London boroughs and the City of London
(clipped), showing the shops' locations and boroughs' boundaries

The code for generating the Voronoi polygons object, visualizing it, extracting from it the list of polygons, and then clipping it is given here. First, let's see the code to generate the Voronoi polygons:

```
coffee_voronoi = get_voronoi_polygons(coffee_df, latitude="Latitude",
longitude="Longitude")
plot_voronoi_polygons(coffee_voronoi,
                    title="Voronoi polygons from Starbucks locations in
London",
                    lat_limits=[51.2, 51.7],
                    long_limits=[-0.5, 0.3])
```

Next is the code for extracting the list of polygons from the Voronoi polygons object and the code for clipping the polygons, using the borroughs' boundary:

```
coffee_voronoi_poly_list = extract_voronoi_polygon_list(coffee_voronoi)
coffee_voronoi_polys_clipped = clip_polygons(coffee_voronoi_poly_list,
boroughs_df)
```

Using the within_polygon function, we can identify the locations that are inside a polygon. The function is implemented in the geospatial_utils module. The function uses the within property of the Point object from the shapely.geometry library module. We apply the operation, for a given polygon, to all the points created from the longitude/latitude of all items (in our case, the pubs), getting the status (within, outside) of points relative to the reference polygon:

```
def within_polygon(data_original_df, polygon, latitude="latitude",
longitude="longitude"):
    """

    Args
        data_original_df: dataframe with latitude / longitude
        polygon: polygon (Polygon object)
        latitude: feature name for latitude n data_original_df
        longitude: feature name for longitude in data_original_df
    Returns
        coordinates of points inside polygon
        coordinates of points outside polygon
        polygon transformed into a geopandas dataframe
    """

    data_df = data_original_df.copy()
    data_df["in_poly"] = data_df.apply(lambda x: Point(x[longitude],
x[latitude]).within(polygon), axis=1)
    data_in_df = data_df[[longitude, latitude]].loc[data_df["in_
poly"]==True]
    data_out_df = data_df[[longitude, latitude]].loc[data_df["in_
poly"]==False]
    data_in_df.columns = ["long", "lat"]
    data_out_df.columns = ["long", "lat"]
    sel_polygon_gdf = gpd.GeoDataFrame([polygon], columns = ['geometry'])
    return data_in_df, data_out_df, sel_polygon_gdf
```

The following code applies the within_polygon function:

```
data_in_df, data_out_df, sel_polygon_gdf = within_polygon(pub_df, coffee_
voronoi_poly_list[6])
```

In the following figure, the pubs within the selected area (shown in the notebook associated with the book by a light brown and dark green fill color) are closer to the position of the Starbucks coffee shop centered on the selected area than to any other neighboring Starbucks coffee shop. The rest of the pubs are shown with a light green color. We can repeat the procedure for all polygons (and also for the boroughs' polygons).

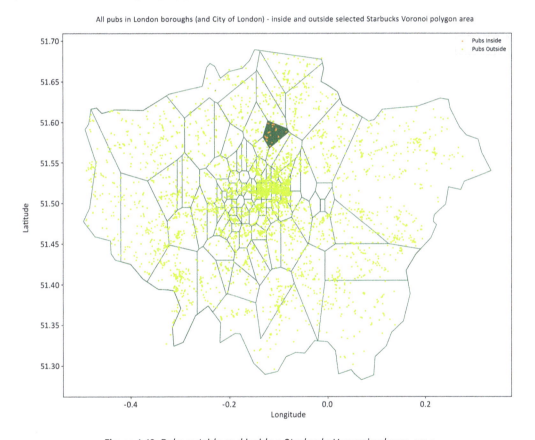

Figure 4.42: Pubs outside and inside a Starbucks Voronoi polygon area

We can represent the same items, pubs and Starbucks coffee shops, using folium maps too. These maps will allow interactions, including zooming in, zooming out, and panning. We can add multiple layers over a base map. Let's start by representing the London boroughs as the first layer of the map. On top of that, we will show the pubs in the London area. Each pub will have a popup as well, displaying the name of the pub and the address. We can select from multiple map tile providers.

Because I prefer to have a clearer background, I opted for two tile sources: "Stamen toner" and "CartoDB positron." For both options, the tiles are either black and white or pale colors, so the overlapping layers can be seen more easily. The following is the code to show the tiles (with "Stamen toner") in the London area, the contour of London boroughs (first layer of the map), and each pub location with `CircleMarker` (the second layer over the map). Each pub will have a popup, showing the pub name and address:

```python
# map with zoom on London area


m = folium.Map(location=[51.5, 0], zoom_start=10, tiles="Stamen Toner")
# London boroughs geo jsons
for _, r in boroughs_df.iterrows():
    simplified_geo = gpd.GeoSeries(r['geometry']).
simplify(tolerance=0.001)
    geo_json = simplified_geo.to_json()
    geo_json = folium.GeoJson(data=geo_json,
                        style_function=lambda x: {'fillColor': color_
list[1],
                                             'color': color_
list[2],
                                             'weight': 1})
    geo_json.add_to(m)
# pubs as CircleMarkers with popup with Name & Address info
for _, r in pub_df.iterrows():
    folium.CircleMarker(location=[r['latitude'], r['longitude']],
                        fill=True,
                        color=color_list[4],
                        fill_color=color_list[5],
                        weight=0.5,
                        radius=4,
                        popup="<strong>Name</strong>: <font
color='red'>{}</font> <br> <strong>Address</strong>: {}".format(r['name'],
r['address'])).add_to(m)
# display map
m
```

The following figure displays the map created with the preceding code. On this map, we show on superposed layers the following information:

- The London boroughs and City of London map areas, using "Stamen Toner" tiles
- The London boroughs and City of London boundaries
- The pubs in the preceding areas, shown with `CircleMarker`
- Optionally, for each pub, if selected, one popup showing the pub name and address

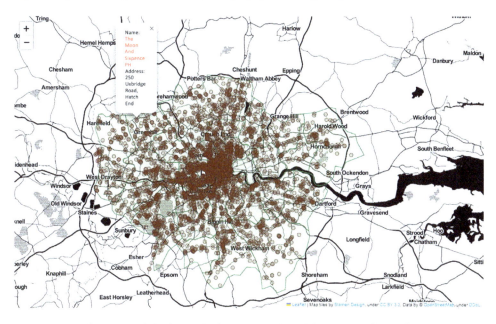

Figure 4.43: Leaflet map with the boroughs' borders and the pub locations in the London area

In the notebook, I show more images with Starbucks Voronoi polygons and locations, as well as maps with multiple layers of polygons and markers.

Another useful operation that we can perform is to calculate the area of polygons. The function to calculate areas for all polygons in a GeoDataFrame is `get_polygons_area`, which is also defined in `geospatial_utils`. It applies a transformation to the projection, in `cylindrical equal area`, on a copy of the GeoDataFrame. This projection will preserve the areas. We then add the area column to the original GeoDataFrame:

```
def get_polygons_area(data_gdf):
    """

    Add a column with polygons area to a GeoDataFrame
    A Cylindrical equal area projection is used to calculate
```

```
        polygons area

        Args
            data_gdf: a GeoDataFrame
        Returns
            the original data_gdf with an `area` column added
        """
        # copy the data, to not affect initial data projection
        data_cp = data_gdf.copy()
        # transform, in the copied data, the projection in Cylindrical equal-
area,
        # which preserves the areas
        data_cp = data_cp.to_crs({'proj':'cea'})
        data_cp["area"] = data_cp['geometry'].area / 10**6 # km^2
        data_gdf["area"] = data_cp["area"]
        # returns the initial data, with added area columns
        return data_gdf
```

We calculate the area for the boroughs, and then we count the number of pubs per borough. Then, we divide the number of pubs/boroughs by the borough area to obtain the pub density (in pubs per square kilometer):

```
boroughs_df = get_polygons_area(boroughs_df)
agg_pub_df = pub_df.groupby("local_authority")["name"].count().reset_
index()
agg_pub_df.columns = ["NAME_2", "pubs"]
boroughs_df = boroughs_df.merge(agg_pub_df)
```

We now need to represent the density with a continuous color scale, but we would like to use colors from our custom colormap. We can create our own continuous color map and use as seeds a few of the colors in our color list:

```
vmin = boroughs_df.pubs.min()
vmax = boroughs_df.pubs.max()
norm=plt.Normalize(vmin, vmax)
custom_cmap = matplotlib.colors.LinearSegmentedColormap.from_list("",
["white", color_list[0], color_list[2]])
```

For the pub density graph, we would like to use, with this custom colormap, a logarithmic scale. We can achieve this with the following code:

```python
fig, ax = plt.subplots(1, 1, figsize = (10, 5))
ax.set_facecolor("white")
boroughs_df.plot(ax = ax, column="pubs per sq.km",
                 norm=matplotlib.colors.LogNorm(vmin=boroughs_df["pubs per
sq.km"].min(),\
                                                vmax=boroughs_df["pubs per
sq.km"].max()),
                 cmap = custom_cmap, edgecolor = color_list[3],
                 linewidth = 1, legend=True),
plt.xlabel("Longitude"); plt.ylabel("Latitude");
plt.title("Pubs density (pubs / sq.km) in London")
plt.show()
```

The following figure shows the pub numbers in each borough (left) and the pub density per borough (right):

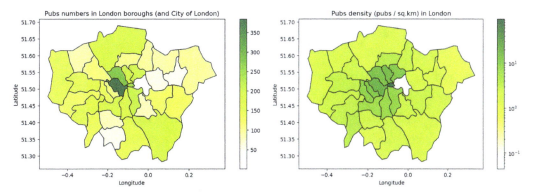

Figure 4.44: Pub numbers (left) and pub density on a logarithmic scale (right) per London borough

In the notebook associated with this section, *Coffee or Beer in London – Your Choice!* (see *Reference 11*), I also show the pub numbers and pub density per Starbucks Voronoi polygons area. The various techniques displayed in this section have hopefully equipped you with a starting toolset for the analysis and visualization of geospatial data.

Summary

In this chapter, we learned how to work with geographical information and maps, how to manipulate geometry data (clip and merge polygon data, cluster data to generate maps with fewer details, and remove subsets of geospatial data), and superpose several layers of data over maps. We also learned how to modify and extract information from a shapefile using geopandas and custom code, as well as creating or calculating geospatial features, like terrain area or geospatial object density. Additionally, we extracted reusable functions and grouped them in two utility scripts, which is Kaggle terminology for independent Python modules. These utility scripts can be imported like any other library and integrated with your notebook code.

In the next chapter, we are going to put to try out some of the tools and techniques for geospatial analysis, for a data analytics competition.

References

1. Every Pub in England, Kaggle Datasets: `https://www.kaggle.com/datasets/rtatman/every-pub-in-england`

2. Every Pub in England – Data Exploration, Kaggle Notebook: `https://github.com/PacktPublishing/Developing-Kaggle-Notebooks/blob/develop/Chapter-04/every-pub-in-england-data-exploration.ipynb`

3. Starbucks Locations Worldwide, Kaggle Datasets: `https://www.kaggle.com/datasets/starbucks/store-locations`

4. Open Postcode Geo, Kaggle Datasets: `https://www.kaggle.com/datasets/danwinchester/open-postcode-geo`

5. GADM Data for UK, Kaggle Datasets: `https://www.kaggle.com/datasets/gpreda/gadm-data-for-uk`

6. Starbucks Location Worldwide – Data Exploration, Kaggle Notebook: `https://github.com/PacktPublishing/Developing-Kaggle-Notebooks/blob/develop/Chapter-04/starbucks-location-worldwide-data-exploration.ipynb`

7. Polygon overlay in Leaflet Map: `https://stackoverflow.com/questions/59303421/polygon-overlay-in-leaflet-map`

8. Geopandas area: `https://geopandas.org/en/stable/docs/reference/api/geopandas.GeoSeries.area.html`

9. Scipy Spatial Voronoi – extract Voronoi polygons and represent them: `https://docs.scipy.org/doc/scipy/reference/generated/scipy.spatial.Voronoi.html`

10. Getting polygon areas using GeoPandas: `https://gis.stackexchange.com/questions/218450/getting-polygon-areas-using-geopandas`

11. Coffee or Beer in London – Your Choice!, Kaggle Notebook: `https://github.com/PacktPublishing/Developing-Kaggle-Notebooks/blob/develop/Chapter-04/coffee-or-beer-in-london-your-choice.ipynb`

Join our book's Discord space

Join our Discord community to meet like-minded people and learn alongside more than 5000 members at:

`https://packt.link/kaggle`

5

Get Back to Work and Optimize Microloans for Developing Countries

Approaching a new dataset resembles an archeological excavation and sometimes a police investigation. We proceed to unearth hidden pieces of insight from under a pile of data, or we try to uncover elusive evidence using a systematic, sometimes arid process, which resemble either the technical discipline of the archeologist or the method of the detective, respectively. All data can tell a story. It is the analyst's choice if this story is told in the style of a scientific report or the vivid, attractive form of a detective novel.

In this chapter, we will combine techniques we developed in previous chapters to analyze tabular (numerical and categorical), textual, and geospatial data. This involves combining data from multiple sources and showing you how to tell a story with that data. We will continue analyzing data from an early Kaggle competition, *Data Science for Good: Kiva Crowdfunding* (see *Reference 1*). You will learn how to tell a story using data in a way that is both informative and engaging for the reader. Then, we will go through a detailed analysis of a hypothesis from another competition dataset that specifically focuses on Kaggle metadata, Meta Kaggle (see *Reference 2*).

To sum up, the following topics will be covered in this chapter:

- An exploratory data analysis of the *Data Science for Good: Kiva Crowdfunding* analytics competition
- A solution for the same analytics competition, trying to understand what factors contribute to poverty

- An analysis of the *Meta Kaggle* dataset to validate (or invalidate) the perception that Kaggle competition team sizes increased suddenly a few years ago

Introducing the Kiva analytics competition

Kiva.org is an online crowdfunding platform that has the mission to extend to poor and financially excluded people around the world the benefits of financial services. These individuals can benefit from Kiva's services to borrow small amounts of money. These microloans are provided by Kiva through their partnerships with financial services institutions, in the countries where the receiver of the loans resides.

In the past, Kiva has provided over 1 billion US dollars in microloans to its targeted communities. To extend the reach of their assistance, and at the same time, to improve the understanding of the specific needs and factors that affect impoverished people in different parts of the world, Kiva wanted to better understand the conditions of each potential borrower. Due to the diversity of the problems in different parts of the world, the specificity of each case, and the multitude of influencing factors, Kiva's mission to identify the most demanding cases that need their financial assistance is quite difficult.

Kiva proposed to the data science community of Kaggle an analytics competition. The scope of the competition was to combine features from each loan into various poverty datasets and determine the actual welfare level of potential borrowers, categorizing them by region, gender, and sector. The evaluation of competitors' contributions in this competition was based on the granularity of the analysis, emphasizing adherence to local specifics, clarity of the explanation, and the originality of the approach. The competition organizers aimed to directly use the best analyses, hence the emphasis on localization and a clear explanation.

The *Data Science for Good: Kiva Crowdfunding* analytics competition requires the participants to identify or collect relevant data, besides the data provided by organizers. The data provided by the organizers includes loan information, the Kiva global **Multidimensional Poverty Index (MPI)** by region and location, loan theme, and loan themes by region.

The loan information includes the following:

- A unique ID
- A loan theme ID and type
- A local financial organization partner ID
- A funded amount (how much Kiva provided to the local partner)

- A loan amount (how much the local partner disbursed to the borrower)

- The activity of the borrower

- The use of the loan (how the loan will be used, or the loan purpose)

- The sector, country code, country name, region, and currency

- The posted time, disbursed time, funded time, and duration for which the loan was disbursed

- The total number of lenders that contributed to a loan

- The genders of the borrowers

- The repayment interval

Kiva MPI information by region and location includes the following:

- The region or country name

- The ISO-3 code for the country

- The world region

- The MPI value and the geolocation (latitude and longitude) of the current region

The loan theme includes:

- A unique ID

- A loan theme ID

- A loan theme type

- A corresponding partner ID

The loan theme by region dataset contains:

- A partner ID

- A field partner name

- The sector

- A loan theme ID and type

- The country and region

- The geocode (in four variants)

- The ISO-3 code

- The amount

- The location name

- The MPI region and MPI geocode (possibly duplicating the other geocodes)
- The rural percentage for the current region

There is a large amount of information in this competition dataset. Rather than performing a deep, detailed analysis of the data, we will target one data aspect.

What is a good solution to an analytics competition?

It is important to stress from the start that one good solution for an analytics competition is not necessarily a complete exploratory data analysis. From my experience with several analytics competitions and examining top-ranking solutions, I can say that sometimes the criteria for scoring in an analytics competition are quite the opposite. While the criteria may evolve over time, some are repeatedly adopted. For example, evaluators frequently prioritize the originality of the approach over the composition and the documentation.

 To obtain high scores on these criteria, authors will have to prepare themselves thoroughly. An extended exploration of the data is still necessary so that the results presented can be fully documented. While useful for research purposes, this approach doesn't need to be fully included in the narrative of the solution notebook. The author can select and discuss, in their story, a small part of the data, as long as the narrative is consistent and makes a strong, compelling case.

The author must select, from the rich data they explored, only those elements that will support their story. So composition is equally important, and the selected and interpreted data should offer hard evidence to support the narrative. The impact of the story will be higher if the narrative, structure, and content are original.

More data, more insights — analyzing the Kiva data competition

For this analysis, we preferred to include an additional data source, `Country Statistics - UNData` (see *Reference 3*). The data was gathered by one of the participants during the Kiva analytics competition, compiling essential statistical indicators for countries. This specific dataset is based on the **United Nations Statistics Division (UNSD)** of the **Department of Economic and Social Affairs (DESA)**. The key indicators can be grouped into four categories: general information, economic indicators, social indicators, and environmental and infrastructure indicators.

There are two CSV files in the `Country Statistics - UNData` dataset:

- One with the key indicators for all the countries in the `Country Statistics - UNData` dataset

- One covering only the countries present in the `Data Science for Good: Kiva Crowdfunding` dataset

There is a total of 50 columns in the `Country Statistics - UNData` dataset, starting with country and geographical region, population, population density, sex ratio, **Gross Domestic Product (GDP)**, GDP/capita, and GDP growth rate, and continuing with percentage of agriculture, industry, services from the economy, employment in the same sectors, agricultural production, trade indicators, urban population, and urban population growth rate. It also includes information such as the percentage of mobile subscriptions or seats held by women in national parliaments.

Some of the most interesting factors included are population percentages that use improved drinking water, population percentages that use improved sanitation facilities, infant mortality and fertility rates, and life expectancy. Many of these features included in UNData are relevant to how poverty is defined, and we will explore them in our journey.

Our main objective in this analysis is to understand how poverty can be measured so that we can provide the organizers with the necessary information to optimize their microloan allocation.

Understanding the borrower demographic

We start our exploration by focusing on who receives the loans, trying to answer the question, "Who are the borrowers?" In the Kiva dataset, there are 1,071,308 female borrowers and 274,904 male borrowers. Women seem to dominate not only in total but also in the number of associated borrowers for a loan. The number of women associated with a loan is 50, while the number of males associated is 44. There are multiple loans with both female and male borrowers, as well as only with men or only with women.

As you can see in the following graph, the majority of loans relate to female-only borrowers, with male-only borrowers in second place:

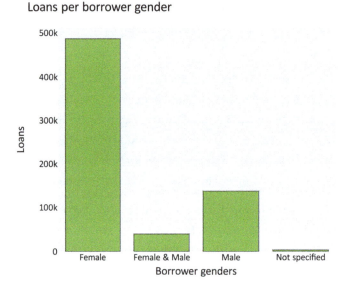

Figure 5.1: Borrower genders

In the following graphs, let's look at the distribution of female borrowers (left) and male borrowers (right), starting with the average number of female and male borrowers per sector:

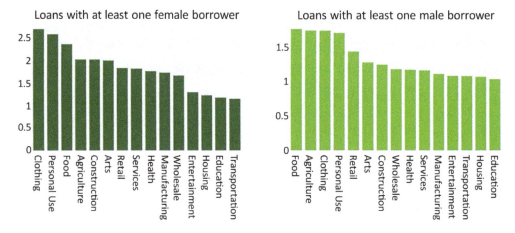

Figure 5.2: Average number of female/male borrowers per loan

As you can see, the average number of female borrowers per loan is broken down into 2.7 for **Clothing**, 2.6 for **Personal Use**, 2.4 for **Food**, and close to 2 for **Agriculture** and **Construction**. For the male borrowers, the average number of borrowers per loan is close to 1.75 for **Food**, **Agriculture**, **Clothing**, and **Personal Use**.

Next, we can see that the maximum number of female borrowers are for **Clothing**, **Food**, and **Retail**. For male borrowers, **Personal Use** and **Agriculture** have the maximum number of borrowers:

Maximum number of female/male borowers per loan

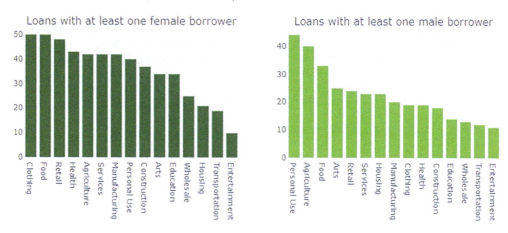

Figure 5.3: Maximum number of female/male borrowers per loan

These graphs were built using Plotly, a powerful and versatile graphical library that is open-source and Python-based. Through the *Kiva Microloans – A Data Exploration* notebook (see *Reference 4*), we will use Plotly extensively, for graphs with low or high complexity. The following code excerpt was used to build the graphs in *Figure 5.3*:

```
df = df.sort_values(by="max", ascending=False)
sectors_f = go.Bar(
        x = df['sector'],
        y = df['max'],
        name="Female borrowers",
        marker=dict(color=color_list[4]))
df2 = df2.sort_values(by="max", ascending=False)
sectors_m = go.Bar(
        x = df2['sector'],
        y = df2['max'],
        name="Male borrowers",
```

```
            marker=dict(color=color_list[3]))
fig = make_subplots(rows=1, cols=2, start_cell="top-left",
                    subplot_titles=("Loans with at least one female
borrower",
                                    "Loans with at least one male
borrower"))

fig.add_trace(sectors_f, row=1, col=1)
fig.add_trace(sectors_m, row=1, col=2)
layout = go.Layout(height=400, width=900, title="Maximum number of female/
male borowers/loan")
fig.update_layout(layout)
fig.update_layout(showlegend=False)
fig.show()
```

The code creates two bar graphs side by side, using Plotly's make_subplots function.

The borrowers repay the loans in multiple installments. The repayment scheme is diverse, and we can also see in *Figure 5.4* the differences between the distribution of repayment for females and males. The female-only borrower group has almost the same amount of loans with **monthly** and **irregular** repayment intervals, with only a small percentage of the loans being paid back in one installment (**bullet**). The male-only borrower group has the majority of repayments of the monthly type and a much larger percentage of the **bullet** repayment type than **irregular**. The **bullet** type is most probably characteristic of cyclic activities, like agriculture, when revenue is scarce, and repayment is possible only at harvest time (or when the harvest is paid).

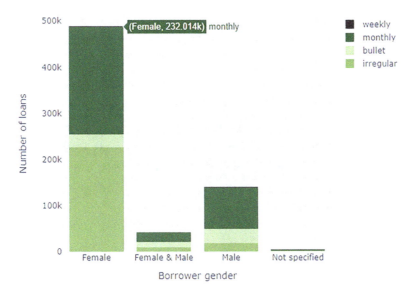

Figure 5.4: Repayment interval by borrower gender

Exploring MPI correlation with other factors

The United Nations Development Program has developed the **multidimensional poverty index**, or **MPI** for short (see *Reference 5* and *6*). The values used in our analysis are for 2017. The current report available is for 2022. In the current one, the UN highlights that 1.2 billion people are multidimensionally poor, 593 million being children under the age of 18. Among these 1.2 billion, 579 million live in Sub-Saharan Africa, followed by South Asia, with 385 million (see *Reference 3* at the end of the chapter).

MPI is a composite index, including three dimensions, multiple indicators, and poverty measures. The three dimensions are health, education, and standard of living. Indicators associated with the health dimension are nutrition and child mortality. Education is associated with two indicators: years of schooling and school attendance. Each of those has a 1/6 weight in the MPI value. Then, there are six indicators associated with the standard of living dimension: cooking fuel, sanitation, drinking water, electricity, housing, and assets. Each of those has a 1/18 weight (see *Reference 3*).

The value of MPI ranges between 0 and 1, the larger values meaning a higher exposure to poverty. The composition of this multidimensional factor created by the United Nations highlights the complexity of poverty. Indicators such as GDP or GDP per capita do not tell the entire story. We will try to understand the measures of poverty better and how several features in the Kiva and UNData datasets illustrate it.

Now, let's see where the borrowers live. For this, we will represent the Kiva regions' locations using a leaflet map. To build this map, we first remove the wrong latitude and longitude tuples (with values outside of real latitude/longitude values, for example, with a latitude larger than 90 or smaller than -90). Then, we will also remove data with wrong attributes. On the map, we also represent markers for each region with a size proportional to the MPI, which, as mentioned earlier, is a poverty index used by Kiva. In the next section, we will discuss this indicator in detail. The code to show the map is given here:

```python
# map with entire World
m = folium.Map(location=[0, 0], zoom_start=2, tiles="CartoDB Positron")


for _, r in region_df.iterrows():
    folium.CircleMarker(location=[r['lat'], r['lon']],
        fill=True,
        color=color_list[3],
        fill_color=color_list[3],
        weight=0.9,
        radius= 10 * (0.1 + r['MPI']),
        popup=folium.Popup("<strong>Region</strong>: {}<br>\
            <strong>Country</strong>: {}<br>\
            <strong>Location Name</strong>: {}<br>\
            <strong>World Region</strong>: {}<br>\
            <strong>MPI</strong>: {}".format(r['region'], r['country'],
r['LocationName'],\
                r['world_region'], r['MPI']), min_width=100, max_
width=300)).add_to(m)
m
```

In *Figure 5.5*, we show the distribution of MPI per region. The map contains some wrongly assigned locations as well, based on erroneous latitude/longitude pairs. These will be corrected when we represent the aggregated data at the country or larger world region level.

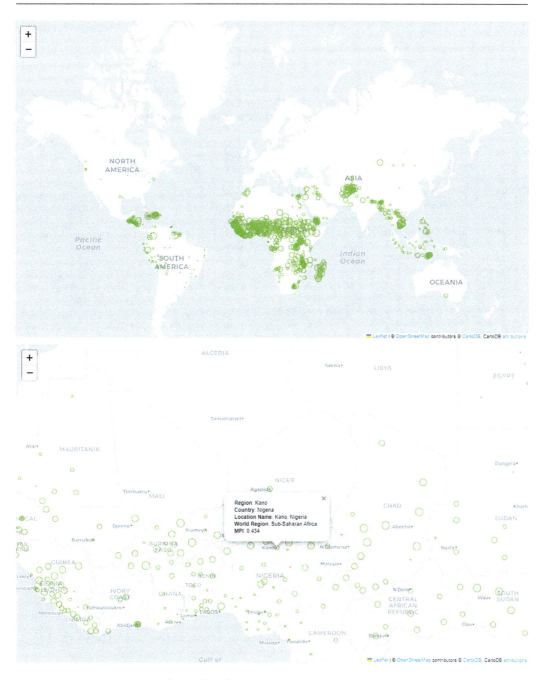

Figure 5.5: Regions in the world with the MPI poverty index. The full world map (top) and a zoom-in on Sub-Saharan Africa (bottom)

Let's also look at the distribution of MPI at the country and continent levels. In the analysis notebook associated with the current chapter, we will look at the minimum, maximum, and average values of MPI. Here, we only show the average values due to space constraints.

In *Figure 5.6*, we can see the MPI values at the country level. Notice that the largest concentration of high MPI values is in Sub-Saharan countries, followed by South-East Asia.

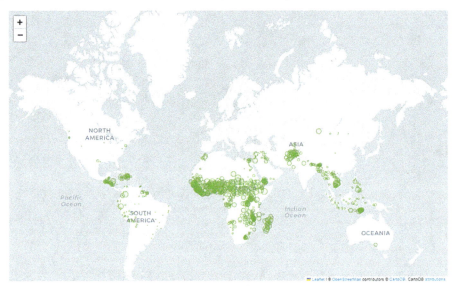

Distribution of average MPI per countries

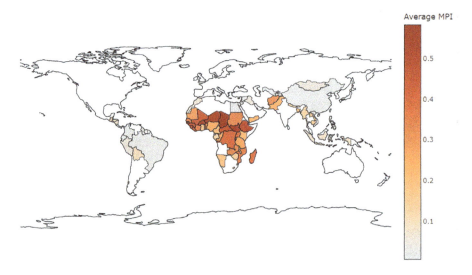

Figure 5.6: Countries with an averaged MPI poverty index. The largest values of the MPI average are in Sub-Saharan Africa

Similarly, *Figure 5.7* shows the MPI values at a world region level. Again, the largest average MPIs are in Sub-Saharan Africa, South Asia, East Asia, and the Pacific, followed by the Arab States.

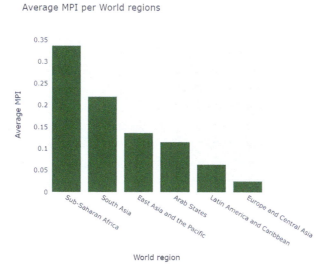

Figure 5.7: Countries with an averaged MPI poverty index

Let's see also what the average MPI per loan sector is. In *Figure 5.8*, we can see the distribution of the average MPI value per sector. The sector associated with the largest average MPI is **Agriculture**, followed by **Personal Use**, **Education**, **Retail** and **Construction**:

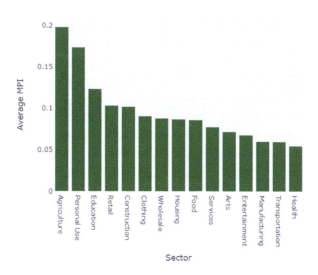

Figure 5.8: Average MPI per loan sector

As you can see, loans in the **Agriculture** sector show an average MPI of **0.2**, followed by **Personal Use** with approximately **0.18**, and **Education** with **0.12**.

We looked separately at the relationship of MPI with **World Region, Sector**, and **Borrower Gender**. Let's look now at the relationship between all these features. We will look at the number of loans and amount per loan distributed across these features' categories. Because the loan amounts are in various currencies, we will only look at them in USD. See *Figure 5.9* for the number of loans:

Number of loans / World Region / Sector / Borrower Gender / Repayment Interval

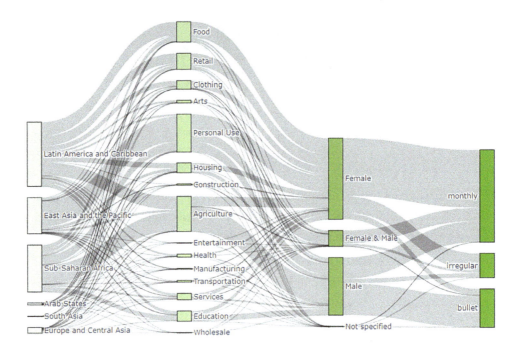

Figure 5.9: Distribution of loans (i.e., the number of loans) across world regions, sectors, borrower genders, and repayment intervals

The graphs in *Figure 5.9* and *Figure 5.10* use Sankey diagrams. The code to generate these Sankey diagrams in Plotly is included in the utility script `plotly_utils` (see *Reference 7* for a link to the book code repository). The code is too large to include here completely, so we only include the prototype and parameters definition in the following code snippet:

```
def plotly_sankey(df,cat_cols=[],value_cols='',title='Sankey Diagram',
    color_palette=None, height=None):
    """

    Plot a Sankey diagram
```

```
Args:
    df: dataframe with data
    cat_cals: grouped by features
    valie_cols: feature grouped on
    title: graph title
    color_palette: list of colors
    height: graph height
Returns:
    figure with the Sankey diagram
"""
```

Next, look at *Figure 5.10* for loan amounts in USD only:

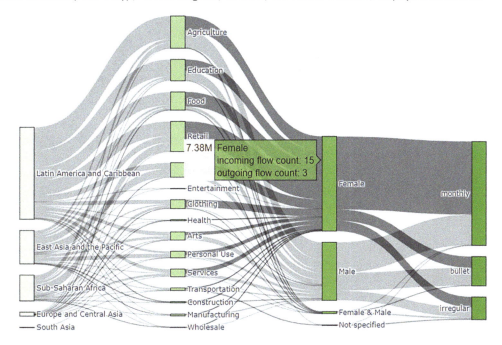

Figure 5.10: Distribution of the loan amount (USD) across world regions, sectors, borrower genders, and repayment intervals

We would like to also correlate several numerical features with MPI. We start with the information available in the Kiva dataset. In *Figure 5.11*, we can see the correlation matrix between the number of male borrowers, the number of female borrowers, the loan amount, the funded amount, the term in months, and the MPI value. Note that we not only selected columns that appear as poverty factors in the calculation of MPI but also other features.

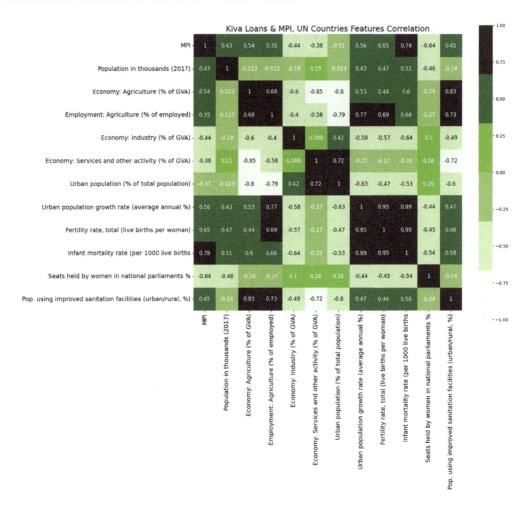

Figure 5.11: Correlation matrix between MPI, the loan data features, and the UNData selected columns

The number of males and females is inversely correlated (which is normal, since a loan would have either male or female borrowers, and when the number in one category increases, the other will decrease).

There is always a very high correlation between the funded amount and the borrowed amount. There is a very small inverse correlation (that is, no correlation, since this value is, as an absolute value, smaller than 0.1) between MPI and any of the Kiva numerical indicators included. We will need to look at the correlation between MPI and features from UNData, where we do have many poverty-related indicators.

To prepare the preceding correlation matrix (shown in *Figure 5.11*), we merged loan data with MPI data and UNData:

```
kiva_mpi_un_df = loan_mpi_df.merge(kiva_country_profiles_variables_df)
kiva_loans_corr = kiva_mpi_un_df.loc[loan_mpi_df.currency=="USD"][sel_
columns].corr()
fig, ax = plt.subplots(1, 1, figsize = (16, 16))
sns.heatmap(kiva_loans_corr,
            xticklabels=kiva_loans_corr.columns.values,
            yticklabels=kiva_loans_corr.columns.values,
            cmap=cmap_custom, vmin=-1, vmax=1, annot=True, square=True,
            annot_kws={"size":8})
plt.suptitle('Kiva Loans & MPI, UN Countries Features Correlation')
plt.show()
```

From the inspection of *Figure 5.11*, we can observe that MPI has a very strong positive correlation with infant mortality rate and is correlated with a fertility rate (0.78). It is also positively correlated with the population, using improved sanitation facilities (0.45), urban population growth rate (0.56), the percentage of agriculture in the economy (0.54), or the percentage of the population involved in agriculture (0.35). These are examples of factors that will increase when there is more poverty. It is interesting that the urban population growth rate is correlated with MPI. This is because population displacement is not always caused by more people moving to cities for employment but because many people are displaced, due to a lack of resources in rural areas. It is also inversely correlated with total expenditure for health (-0.2), the seats held by women in parliaments (-0.64), and the percentage of industry (-0.21) and services in the economy (-0.36).

Industry development and more services are attributes of a developed economy, with more opportunities for the poor; therefore, MPI decreases with an increase in these factors (industry development and services). A very interesting factor (strong inverse correlation) is the presence of women in the national parliaments. This signals a more developed, inclusive, and affluent society that is ready to empower women and give them more opportunities.

Radar visualization of poverty dimensions

We started this section by exploring the information about the borrowers. We learned that they are mostly female, from impoverished regions in the Sub-Saharan area or South Asia. However, there is a large diversity of needs, and the sector information does not reveal all of it. Only by looking at the detailed activity associated with each sector can we start to unveil the specific needs of each borrower and, therefore, reveal the special conditions that cause poverty.

From both the Kiva data and the UN's definition of MPI, we understand that poverty is a combination of factors. This specific combination of factors leading to poverty depends on each region, and even on each specific case. We adopt visualization tools to highlight this multidimensional essence of poverty. We will use radar (a.k.a. spider) graphs for several countries with selected dimensions relevant to poverty. In a radar (or spider – so-named because it resembles a spider web) graph, the axes (radial) represent individual features under consideration. The area of the graph reflects the magnitude of the cumulative effect of the individual features. For small features, we obtain a small area. For large features, the area is large. In our case, we want to illustrate poverty (or the MPI cumulative factor) by the number of features or the factors that contribute to poverty.

The following code snippets prepare data for visualization with custom-built radar graphs, using Plotly. We group the data by country and calculate average values per country:

```
region_df = kiva_mpi_region_locations_df.loc[~kiva_mpi_region_locations_
df.MPI.isna()]
df = region_df.groupby(["country"])["MPI"].agg(["mean", "median"]).reset_
index()
df.columns = ["country", "MPI_mean", "MPI_median"]
kiva_mpi_country_df = kiva_country_profiles_variables_df.merge(df)
df = kiva_mpi_country_df.sort_values(by="MPI_median", ascending = False)
[0:10]
df['MPI_median'] = df['MPI_median'] * 100
df['MPI_mean'] = df['MPI_mean'] * 100
```

We selected only features that range between 1 and 100 (and we scaled some, like MPI, to be in the same interval). We also calculated *100 – value*, when the value is inversely correlated with the MPI values. We do this so that the features we represent on the axes of the radar graph are all positively correlated with the MPI:

```
df['Infant mortality rate /1000 births'] = df['Infant mortality rate (per
1000 live births']
```

```
df["Employment: Agriculture %"] = df['Employment: Agriculture (% of
employed)'].apply(lambda x: abs(x))
df["No improved sanitation facilit. %"] = df['Pop. using improved
sanitation facilities (urban/rural, %)'].apply(lambda x: 100 - float(x))
df ['No improved drinking water % (U)'] = df['Pop. using improved drinking
water (urban/rural, %)'].apply(lambda x: 100 - float(x.split("/")[0]))
df ['No improved drinking water % (R)'] = df['Pop. using improved drinking
water (urban/rural, %)'].apply(lambda x: 100 - float(x.split("/")[1]))
```

Then, we define the radar graph features:

```
radar_columns = ["No improved sanitation facilit. %",
                 "MPI_median", "MPI_mean",
                 'No improved drinking water % (U)',
                 'No improved drinking water % (R)',
                 'Infant mortality rate /1000 births',
                 "Employment: Agriculture %"]
```

The radar plot is created with the following code:

```
fig = make_subplots(rows=1, shared_xaxes=True)
for _, row in df.iterrows():
    r = []
    for f in radar_columns:
        r.append(row[f])
    radar = go.Scatterpolar(r=r,
      theta=radar_columns,
       fill = 'toself',
       opacity=0.7,
       name = row['country'])
    fig.add_trace(radar)
fig.update_layout(height=900, width=900,
        title="Selcted poverty dimmensions in the 10 countries with
highest median MPI rate",
        polar=dict(
            radialaxis=dict(visible=True, range=[0,100],
gridcolor='black'),
            bgcolor='white',
            angularaxis=dict(visible=True, linecolor='black',
gridcolor='black')
```

```
        ),
        margin=go.layout.Margin(l=200,r=200,b=50, t=100)
    )
fig.show()
```

The resulting graph is shown in *Figure 5.12*. What we get is a radar chart, with selected poverty dimensions in the 10 countries with the highest median (calculated per country) MPI rate. The dimensions are selected to be positively correlated with the MPI. A larger total area results in higher actual poverty.

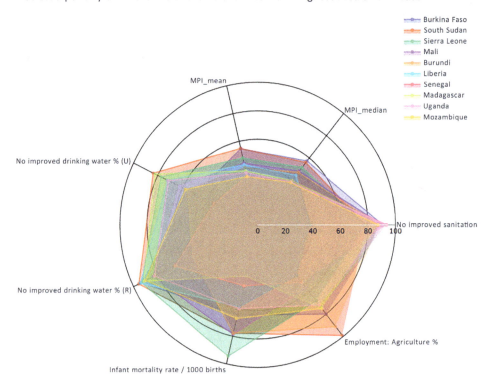

Figure 5.12: Radar chart with selected poverty dimensions in the 10 countries with the highest median MPI rate

We identified the factors that are correlated with poverty, using a radar graph to show both these factors and their cumulative effect on maintaining poverty.

Final remarks

We analyzed a part of the Kiva data competition, focusing less on actual loans and the field partners of Kiva and more on borrowers and what defines their poverty. Our intention was to create an analysis targeting the factors of poverty, understanding these factors and how they each contribute to maintaining poverty. We started by explaining that when we start working on an analytics competition, we need to start with a hypothesis or a subject and restrict our analysis to a part of the data – one that is relevant to our direction of research.

Rather than building a story around a full, comprehensive data analysis, we need to navigate through data to tell the story we want. We didn't describe here the preliminary steps, where we conduct an exhaustive analysis of data (like we did in the previous chapter, where a final analysis using both the Starbucks and pubs data was prepared and supported by our preliminary EDAs for the two datasets separately). Our focus was on understanding what defines poverty best, and for this, we combined Kiva data with additional data from the UN.

In conclusion, we can state that Kiva can be improved by targeting with priority the countries, regions, and categories that are most exposed to the different aspects that characterize poverty. A radar chart can be a useful tool. In designing it, we selected those metrics or modified some of them, giving us a higher total area with higher poverty.

GDP per capita is not the only metric that characterizes poverty; it can take different forms and be defined by multiple and, sometimes, interdependent factors. Targeting the factors that have the potential to also influence others, like increased school attendance, improved sanitation conditions, alimentation, and healthcare, also through Kiva anti-poverty programmes, might increase the positive social impact.

Telling a different story from a different dataset

We started this chapter by analyzing the data from one of the first analytics competitions held by Kaggle, more than 5 years ago. We will continue looking at data from more recent competitions, particularly those using Kaggle's own data. We will look at the data in the Meta Kaggle dataset (see *Reference 2*) and attempt to answer a question related to the perception of a recent trend in creating large teams for competitions. The ultimate intention is to show that we can get important insights by carefully inspecting the available data.

The plot

A few years ago, in 2019, there was a discussion toward the end of a competition about the recent trend of having a higher number of competitors teaming up, especially for high-profile, featured competitions. I was intrigued by this claim trending on the discussion boards, and I decided to use Kaggle's own data from the Meta Kaggle dataset (which is constantly updated by Kaggle) to verify this information. To maintain the results of that analysis, I will restrict the data from Meta Kaggle to values before the end of 2019. Since 2019, some of the metadata keywords have changed. Competitions that used to be named "In Class" are now renamed "Community." Although in current versions of the dataset, the category now has the name "Community," we will use both terms, and sometimes only "In Class," as it was used at the time this analysis was first performed.

The actual history

If we look at the number of teams grouped by year and team size, we can observe that large teams were not restricted only to 2017 or 2018. Let's look at these statistics, as shown in *Figure 5.13*.

The largest teams were in:

- 2012 (with 40 and 23 team members)
- 2013 (the largest team had 24 team members)
- 2014 (having teams with as many as 25 team members)
- 2017 (with the largest team having 34 team members)

What happened in 2017 and 2018 was that there was a sudden increase in the number of teams (2017) and medium-sized teams (4–8 team members).

When checking the number of competitions per year, we also notice that what happened in 2018 was that the number of competitions without a limit on the team size increased, as a percentage of the total number of competitions. This will explain in part the pattern we observed – that there were more teams that were larger in size in 2018.

Number of teams grouped by year and by team size

Team size	2010	2011	2012	2013	2014	2015	2016	2017	2018	2019
1	9953	61010	90146	165621	442937	474822	382000	743655	955532	951251
2	24	153	592	1045	1292	2590	2704	3717	6719	11068
3	7	41	190	353	399	940	956	1313	2403	4373
4	3	8	78	145	126	416	431	653	857	1776
5		2	40	54	48	133	149	233	408	927
6		1	24	22	14	52	54	94	161	122
7			6	19	6	14	24	33	60	42
8			2	9	7	6	15	20	33	26
9			3	1	3	4	6	5	21	
10			5	2	1	3	2	6	11	
11			4	1	3	3	2	6	7	
12		1	1		2	1		4	5	
13					2		1	2	3	
14					1			1	2	
15			1		1			1	2	
16					1				2	
17								1		
18				1		1		1		
19					1			2		
20								1	1	
22					2					
23			2						1	
24				2	1					
25					1					
34								1		
40		1								

Figure 5.13: Number of teams grouped by year and team size

If we eliminate the Community competitions, we obtain the stats shown in *Figure 5.14*. The statistics have not changed very much with respect to larger teams, since the majority of teams with multiple participants were formed for competitions other than the Community type.

Number of teams grouped by year and by team size (no InClass comp.)

Team size	2010	2011	2012	2013	2014	2015	2016	2017	2018	2019
1	9953	61010	90146	165621	442937	474822	382000	743655	955532	951251
2	24	153	592	1045	1292	2590	2704	3717	6719	11068
3	7	41	190	353	399	940	956	1313	2403	4373
4	3	8	78	145	126	416	431	653	857	1776
5		2	40	54	48	133	149	233	408	927
6		1	24	22	14	52	54	94	161	122
7			6	19	6	14	24	33	60	42
8			2	9	7	6	15	20	33	26
9			3	1	3	4	6	5	21	
10			5	2	1	3	2	6	11	
11			4	1	3	3	2	6	7	
12		1	1		2	1		4	5	
13					2		1	2	3	
14					1			1	2	
15			1		1			1	2	
16					1				2	
17								1		
18				1		1		1		
19					1			2		
20								1	1	
22					2					
23			2						1	
24				2	1					
25					1					
34								1		
40			1							

Figure 5.14: Number of teams grouped by year and by team size, except the Community competition

Let's look at the distribution over time of the gold, silver, and bronze medals, using a Plotly Express scatter plot with the medals grouped as separate traces per team size.

On the y axis, we used a log scale for the number of teams; on the x axis, we showed the team size, and the size of the markers is proportional to the medal importance (gold being the largest, and bronze being the smallest). As can be seen in *Figure 5.15*, we show these results for one selected year. We can observe that the largest teams that won medals in each year were as follows:

- 2010: 1 team winning gold, with 4 members.
- 2011: 1 team winning gold, with 12 members.
- 2012: 1 team winning bronze, with 40 members.
- 2013: 2 teams winning gold, with 24 members.
- 2014: 1 team winning bronze, with 6 members.
- 2015: 1 team winning bronze, with 18 members.
- 2016: 1 team winning gold, with 13 members.
- 2017: 1 team winning bronze, with 34 members.
- 2018: 1 team winning silver, with 23 members.
- 2019: 2 teams winning gold, with 8 members, and 4 teams winning silver, with 8 members; please note that for 2019, the results are still partial.

Let's also look at a heatmap with the number of winning teams grouped by year and team size, where we select only the featured competitions. These are the highest profile competitions and, therefore, attract the highest interest, and also, the largest teams. In *Figure 5.16*, we show this heatmap. We can observe several things:

- In 2018, the number of gold-winning teams increased only for teams with 2, 5, and 7 members.
- The largest teams winning gold were in 2013 (24 and 10 members), 2012 (23, 15, and 12 members), 2011 (12 members), 2016 (13 and 11 members), and 2017 (10 members).

Therefore, the perception that the number of large teams in featured competition only recently increased is false. Actually, the largest team winning a medal was in 2012 (40 team members), and in 2013, there were two teams with 24 members that won gold!

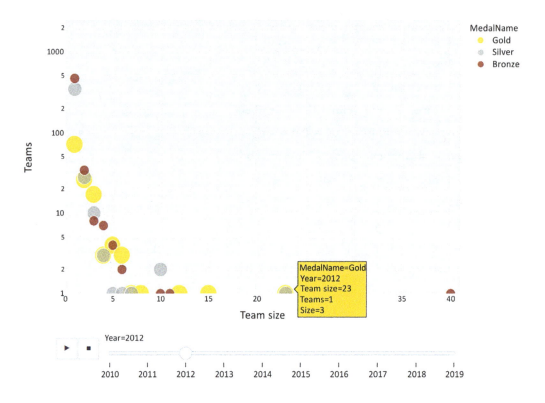

Figure 5.15: Number of teams vs. team size, grouped by medals (gold, silver, and bronze) and filtered by year

Similar observations can be made for research competitions. The largest teams winning a medal in research competitions were, in each year:

- 2012: 1 team winning gold and 1 silver, with 11 members
- 2013: 1 team winning bronze, with 9 members
- 2014: 1 team winning bronze, with 24 members
- 2015: 1 team winning silver, with 8 members
- 2016: 1 team winning silver, with 8 members
- 2017: 4 teams winning bronze, with 8 members
- 2018: 1 team winning gold, with 9 members

The conclusion is that large teams winning bronze, silver, or gold medals in research competitions is not a recent trend. As far back as 2012, teams with 11 members won gold and silver. In 2017, there were four teams that won bronze.

Number of Gold winning teams grouped by year and by team size (Featured competitions)

Team size	2010	2011	2012	2013	2014	2015	2016	2017	2018	2019
1	33	106	90	100	68	129	132	125	135	158
2	5	16	29	20	19	51	44	35	78	50
3		3	17	11	9	26	26	25	31	40
4	1		6	6	1	7	20	19	25	26
5			4	3	4	5	7	8	18	28
6		1	3	1		4	4	5	14	3
7			1	3		1	3	2	8	1
8			1	1			3	2	6	2
9									1	
10				1				1	1	
11							2	1		
12		1		1					1	
13							1			
15			1							
23			1							
24				2						

Figure 5.16: Number of winning teams grouped by year and team size (featured competitions only)

We select the teams for featured competitions and check if the team's size is correlated in any way with the team rankings. To do this, we count the number of team members for each team and year. We then merge the results with the Teams dataset to have, in one dataset, the number of team members per team and the public and private leaderboard rank. *Figure 5.17* shows the heatmap with the team size and team ranking (the public and private leaderboard) for the years between 2010 and 2019. Although there is a very small negative correlation value, we observe the following for the value of correlation between the private leaderboard and public leaderboard ranks and the team size. There exists a very small inverse correlation factor, signifying that team size tends to increase as the rank value decreases. In other words, the closer a team is to the top, the larger its size becomes. Values are between -0.02 and -0.12 (very small inverse correlation values) and increase (in absolute values) over time.

In general, inverse correlations for **Public** are larger, meaning teams tend to be larger for higher positions on the public leaderboard; this would maybe allow us to speculate on the opportunistic quality of the large teams, especially very large teams. In reality, there is too low a correlation to extract any meaningful insights from it.

On analyzing the competitions and teams data, we understand that large teams winning medals were equally frequent in past years, with very large-sized teams winning competitions as early as 2012. A team of 40 members won a bronze medal in 2012, and a team with 13 members won gold in 2016, both in featured competitions. Comparatively, one team won silver in 2018 with 23 members.

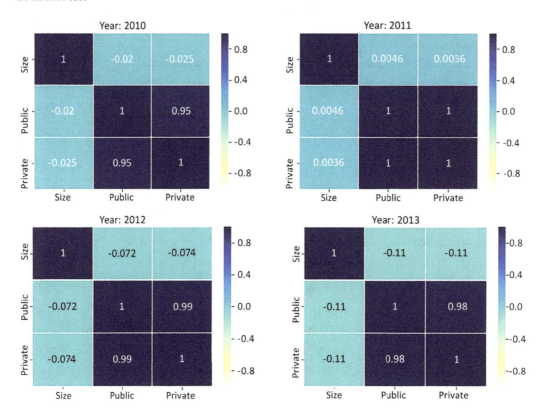

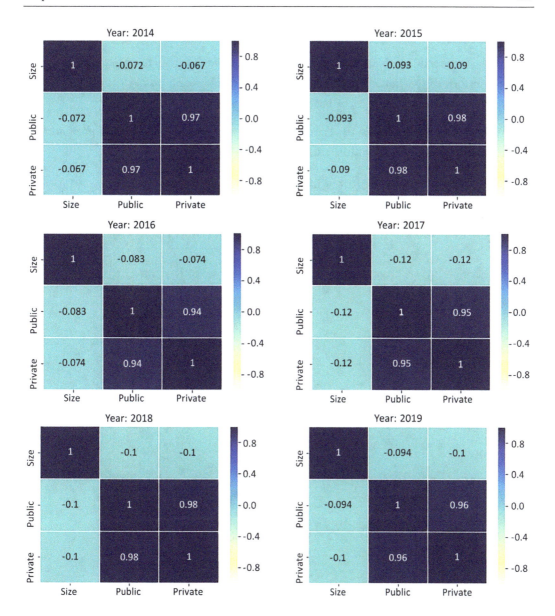

Figure 5.17: Correlation matrices for public and private leaderboard rankings and team size

We can observe that while there is an obviously strong correlation between the public and private leaderboard ranks, there is no correlation (for values under 0.1 and negative) between the team size and the public or private leaderboard rank.

Conclusion

The conclusion is that, although there was a recent perception of an increase in the frequency of large teams formed to win medals, this is not a recent phenomenon (as per 2018–2019 observations); there were larger teams in the past that won medals.

What changed dramatically recently is the number of Kagglers. Let's check this information as well. *Figure 5.18* shows the Kaggle user distribution until 2019.

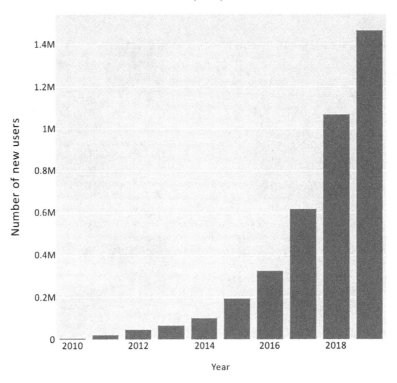

Figure 5.18: User dynamics from 2010 to 2019

This dynamic shows that 70% of the current users of Kaggle were not actually around a few years ago – this includes me, actually. The increase in the number of new users is really exponential. Therefore, what is perceived as community memory might be a biased image, since the majority of Kagglers were not around to experience large teams just a few years ago.

Summary

In this chapter, we explored analytics competitions, analyzing the data from the Kiva analytics competition and then from the *Meta Kaggle* dataset, which is frequently updated by Kaggle and is also the subject of numerous analytics notebooks.

With Kiva data, we chose to investigate one topic – understanding what poverty is – rather than perform an exhaustive exploratory data analysis. With the Meta Kaggle dataset, we chose to answer a question related to the perception of what appeared to be a recent trend in creating large teams for competitions, especially for participants aiming to win medals in high-profile competitions. Building an articulate narrative, supported by well-documented data and clear visualization, is a more effective approach in an analytics competition than exhaustive exploratory data analytics.

We also started to use Plotly as a visualization library in this chapter. In the next chapters, we will reuse some of the visualization scripts that we developed for Kiva and Meta Kaggle analyses.

References

1. Data Science for Good: Kiva Crowdfunding, Kaggle dataset: `https://www.kaggle.com/kiva/data-science-for-good-kiva-crowdfunding`

2. Meta Kaggle, Kaggle dataset: `https://www.kaggle.com/datasets/kaggle/meta-kaggle`

3. Country Statistics – UNData, Kaggle dataset: `https://www.kaggle.com/sudalairajkumar/undata-country-profiles`

4. Kiva Microloans – A Data Exploration, Kaggle notebook: `https://github.com/PacktPublishing/Developing-Kaggle-Notebooks/blob/develop/Chapter-05/kiva-microloans-a-data-exploration.ipynb`

5. Multidimensional poverty index (MPI): `http://hdr.undp.org/en/content/multidimensional-poverty-index-mpi`

6. Multidimensional poverty index on Wikipedia: `https://en.wikipedia.org/wiki/Multidimensional_Poverty_Index`

7. `plotly-utils`, Kaggle utility script: `https://github.com/PacktPublishing/Developing-Kaggle-Notebooks/blob/develop/Chapter-05/plotly-utils.ipynb`

8. Kiva: Loans that change lives: `https://theglobalheroes.wordpress.com/2012/11/01/kiva-loans-that-change-lives/`

9. Understanding Poverty to Optimize Microloans, Kaggle notebook: `https://github.com/PacktPublishing/Developing-Kaggle-Notebooks/blob/develop/Chapter-05/understand-poverty-to-optimize-microloans.ipynb`

Join our book's Discord space

Join our Discord community to meet like-minded people and learn alongside more than 5000 members at:

`https://packt.link/kaggle`

6

Can You Predict Bee Subspecies?

In this chapter, we will learn how to work with image data and start building models to classify images. Computer vision's part in data science and data analysis has grown in an exponential way over the years. Some of the most high-profile (with a large number of upvotes and forks, e.g., copying and editing) notebooks on Kaggle are not **Exploratory Data Analysis (EDA)** notebooks or just EDAs but, instead, notebooks to build models.

In this chapter, we will demonstrate how to use your in-depth data analysis to prepare to build a model, and we will also give you some insights into the process of iteratively refining a model. It will be not for a competition but, instead, for an image dataset. The dataset is the *BeeImage Dataset: Annotated Honey Bee Images* (see *Reference 1*). In the previous chapter, we also started to use Plotly as a visualization library. In this chapter, we will continue to use Plotly for visualization of the dataset features. We grouped a few useful functions for visualization with Plotly in a utility script, `plotly-utils` (see *Reference 2*). The notebook associated with this chapter is *Honeybee Subspecies Classification* (see *Reference 3*).

This chapter will cover the following topics:

- A comprehensive data exploration of the *BeeImage Dataset: Annotated Honey Bee Images*.
- Preparation of a model baseline followed by step-by-step model refinement, analyzing the effect of the changes performed on the evolution of train and validation metrics, and taking new actions to further improve the model.

Data exploration

The *BeeImage Dataset: Annotated Honey Bee Images* contains one **comma-delimited format (.csv)** file, bee_data.csv, with 5172 rows and 9 columns, along with a folder with 5172 images:

	file	date	time	location	zip code	subspecies	health	pollen_carrying	caste
1931	040_330.png	8/21/18	15:56	Athens, GA, USA	30607	Italian honey bee	few varrao, hive beetles	False	worker
1258	005_249.png	7/7/18	12:56	Saratoga, CA, USA	95070	Italian honey bee	healthy	False	worker
236	003_218.png	7/2/18	13:57	Saratoga, CA, USA	95070	Italian honey bee	healthy	False	worker
3921	032_885.png	8/21/18	9:00	Des Moines, IA, USA	50315	Russian honey bee	healthy	False	worker
4312	038_128.png	8/18/18	12:30	Athens, Georgia, USA	30607	1 Mixed local stock 2	Varroa, Small Hive Beetles	False	worker

Figure 6.1: Sample of the bee_data.csv data file

As you can see, the preceding dataframe contains the following columns:

- **file**: the image filename
- **date**: the date when the picture was taken
- **time**: the time when the picture was taken
- **location**: the US location, with city, state, and country names
- **zip code**: the ZIP code associated with the location
- **subspecies**: the subspecies to whom the bee in the current image belongs
- **health**: the health state of the bee in the current image
- **pollen_carrying**: indicates whether the picture shows the bee with pollen attached to its legs or not
- **caste**: the bee's caste

We will start the data exploration journey with a few quality checks, focusing on the bee_data.csv file, followed by the images. For the data quality checks, we will use one of the utility scripts previously introduced in *Chapter 4*, data_quality_stats.

Data quality checks

The dataset does not have any missing values, as you can see in the following figure. All the features are of the string type.

	file	date	time	location	zip code	subspecies	health	pollen_carrying	caste
Total	0	0	0	0	0	0	0	0	0
Percent	0.0	0.0	0.0	0.0	0.0	0.0	0.0	0.0	0.0
Types	object	object	object	object	int64	object	object	bool	object

Figure 6.2: Missing values in the bee_data.csv file. The result was obtained using the data_quality_stats functions

In *Figure 6.3*, we show the unique values of the dataset features. The data was collected:

- at 6 different dates and 35 different times
- in 8 locations with 7 different ZIP codes

In the data, there are seven subspecies represented with six different health problems.

	file	date	time	location	zip code	subspecies	health	pollen_carrying	caste
Total	5172	5172	5172	5172	5172	5172	5172	5172	5172
Uniques	5172	16	35	8	7	7	6	2	1

Figure 6.3: Unique values in the bee_data.csv file. The result was obtained using the data_quality_stats functions

From the data shown in *Figure 6.4*, 21% of the images are from one single date (out of 16 different dates). There was a time when 11% of images were collected. There is one single location (Saratoga, California, with the ZIP code 95070) where 2000 (or 39% of the) images were collected. Italian honeybee is the most frequent species. 65% of the images represent healthy bees. Almost all the images show bees that do not carry pollen, and all are from the worker caste.

	file	date	time	location	zip code	subspecies	health	pollen_carrying	caste
Total	5172	5172	5172	5172	5172	5172	5172	5172	5172
Most frequent item	041_066.png	8/21/18	15:56	Saratoga, CA, USA	95070	Italian honey bee	healthy	False	worker
Frequence	1	1080	579	2000	2000	3008	3384	5154	5172
Percent from total	0.019	20.882	11.195	38.67	38.67	58.159	65.429	99.652	100.0

Figure 6.4: The most frequent values in the bee_data.csv file. The result was obtained using data_quality_stats functions

Next, we will review the image data in parallel with the features in bee_data.csv. We will also introduce functions to read and visualize the images.

Exploring image data

First, we check that all the image names present in the dataset are also present in the folder with images:

```
file_names = list(honey_bee_df['file'])
print("Matching image names: {}".format(len(set(file_names).
intersection(image_files))))
```

The result is that all the images indexed in the .csv file are present in the images folder. Next, we check the image sizes. For this, we can use the following code to read images:

```
def read_image_sizes(file_name):
    """

    Read images size using skimage.io
    Args:
        file_name: the name of the image file
    Returns:
        A list with images shape
    """

    image = skimage.io.imread(config['image_path'] + file_name)
    return list(image.shape)
```

Alternatively, we can use the following code to read images based on the OpenCSV (cv2) library:

```
def read_image_sizes_cv(file_name):
    """

    Read images size using OpenCV
    Args:
        file_name: the name of the image file
    Returns:
        A list with images shape
    """

    image = cv2.imread(config['image_path'] + file_name)
    return list(image.shape)
```

We now compare the speed of the preceding two methods using a subsample of all the images. The following code snippet measures the execution time to read the images, using the method based on skimage.io:

```
%timeit m = np.stack(subset.apply(read_image_sizes))
```

The code below is used to measure the execution time to read the images, using the method based on opencv:

```
%timeit m = np.stack(subset.apply(read_image_sizes_cv))
```

The comparison shows that the execution was faster using the opencv-based method:

- With skimage.io:

  ```
  129 ms ± 4.12 ms per loop (mean ± std. dev. of 7 runs, 1 loop each)
  ```

- With opencv:

  ```
  127 ms ± 6.79 ms per loop (mean ± std. dev. of 7 runs, 10 loops each)
  ```

Then, we apply the fastest approach to extract the shape of each image (the width, height, and depth, or the number of color dimensions) and add it to the dataset for each image:

```
t_start = time.time()
m = np.stack(honey_bee_df['file'].apply(read_image_sizes_cv))
df = pd.DataFrame(m,columns=['w','h','c'])
honey_bee_df = pd.concat([honey_bee_df,df],axis=1, sort=False)
t_end = time.time()
print(f"Total processing time (using OpenCV): {round(t_end-t_start, 2)}
sec.")
```

The output of executing the preceding code is:

```
Total processing time (using OpenCV): 34.38 sec.
```

We can check the image size distribution using the following code snippet. Notice that we use Plotly to create this visualization. We create two traces of the type boxplot. In the first, we show the image width distribution, and in the second, the image height distribution. The boxplot shows the minimum, first quartile, median, third quartile, and maximum values in the distribution of the value we plot. We also show the outliers' values as points on each of the traces:

```
traceW = go.Box(
    x = honey_bee_df['w'],
    name="Width",
    marker=dict(
                color='rgba(238,23,11,0.5)',
                line=dict(
                    color='red',
                    width=1.2),
```

```
                    ),
        orientation='h')
traceH = go.Box(
        x = honey_bee_df['h'],
        name="Height",
        marker=dict(
                        color='rgba(11,23,245,0.5)',
                        line=dict(
                            color='blue',
                            width=1.2),
                    ),
        orientation='h')
data = [traceW, traceH]
layout = dict(title = 'Width & Heights of images',
            xaxis = dict(title = 'Size', showticklabels=True),
            yaxis = dict(title = 'Image dimmension'),
            hovermode = 'closest',
            )
fig = dict(data=data, layout=layout)
iplot(fig, filename='width-height')
```

The result is plotted in *Figure 6.5*. Median values for width and height are 61 and 62, respectively. There are many outliers for both width (the maximum value being 520) and height (the maximum value is 392).

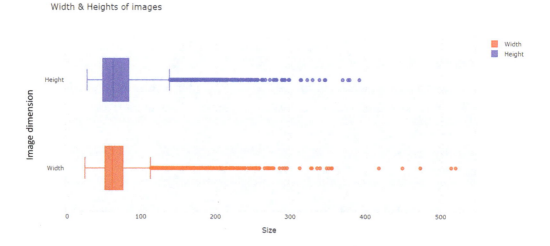

Figure 6.5: Width and height distribution of images

In our analysis, we include all the features in the dataset, not only the ones related to images. We want to understand, before we start building a baseline for the prediction model, all aspects related to *The BeeImage Dataset: Annotated Honey Bee Images*.

Locations

By grouping the data in our dataset by locations where the pictures were shot and ZIP code, we can observe that there is one location with the same ZIP code and similar name:

	zip code	location	Images
0	3431	Keena, NH, USA	92
1	30607	Athens, GA, USA	579
2	30607	Athens, Georgia, USA	472
3	50315	Des Moines, IA, USA	973
4	70115	New Orleans, LA, USA	170
5	77511	Alvin, TX, USA	737
6	95070	Saratoga, CA, USA	2000
7	95124	San Jose, CA, USA	149

Figure 6.6: Locations and ZIP codes where the pictures with bees were taken

We can observe that Athens, Georgia, USA appears with two slightly different names. We just merge them using the following lines of code:

```
honey_bee_df = honey_bee_df.replace({'location':'Athens, Georgia, USA'},
'Athens, GA, USA')
```

Now, let's visualize, using one of the functions in the Plotly utility script module, the distribution of the resulting location data:

```
tmp = honey_bee_df.groupby(['zip code'])['location'].value_counts()
df = pd.DataFrame(data={'Images': tmp.values}, index=tmp.index).reset_
index()
df['code'] = df['location'].map(lambda x: x.split(',', 2)[1])

plotly_barplot(df, 'location', 'Images', 'Tomato', 'Locations', 'Number of
images', 'Number of bees images per location')
```

The code for the function `plotly_barplot` is given here:

```python
def plotly_barplot(df, x_feature, y_feature, col, x_label, y_label,
title):
    """
    Plot a barplot with number of y for category x
    Args:
        df: dataframe
        x_feature: x feature
        y_feature: y feature
        col: color for markers
        x_label: x label
        y_label: y label
        title: title

    Returns:
        None
    """
    trace = go.Bar(
            x = df[x_feature],
            y = df[y_feature],
            marker=dict(color=col),
            #text=df['Location']
        )
    data = [trace]

    layout = dict(title = title,
            xaxis = dict(title = x_label, showticklabels=True,
tickangle=15),
            yaxis = dict(title = y_label),
            hovermode = 'closest'
            )
    fig = dict(data = data, layout = layout)
    iplot(fig, filename=f'images-{x_feature}-{y_feature}')
```

In *Figure 6.7*, we show the distribution of the locations where the bee images were taken. Most of the images are from Saratoga, CA (2000 images), followed by Athens, GA, and Des Moines, IA.

Number of bees images per location

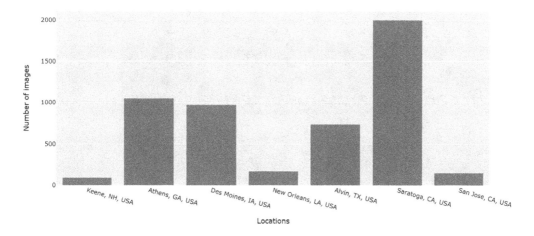

Figure 6.7: Location distribution

We also build a function for the visualization of subsets of images, based on a selected criterion. The following code is to select images based on location and display a subset of them (five images in a row, from the same location):

```
#List of locations

locations = (honey_bee_df.groupby(['location'])['location'].nunique()).
index
def draw_category_images(var,cols=5):
    categories = (honey_bee_df.groupby([var])[var].nunique()).index
    f, ax = plt.subplots(nrows=len(categories),ncols=cols,
figsize=(2*cols,2*len(categories)))
    # draw a number of images for each location
    for i, cat in enumerate(categories):
        sample = honey_bee_df[honey_bee_df[var]==cat].sample(cols)
        for j in range(0,cols):
            file=config['image_path'] + sample.iloc[j]['file']
            im=imageio.imread(file)
            ax[i, j].imshow(im, resample=True)
            ax[i, j].set_title(cat, fontsize=9)
    plt.tight_layout()
    plt.show()
```

In *Figure 6.8*, a fraction of this selection is shown (just for the first two locations). The full image can be seen in the associated notebook:

Figure 6.8: Bee images from two locations (a selection from the full picture, obtained with the preceding code)

Date and time

Let's continue with the detailed analysis of the features in our dataset. We start now to analyze the date and time data. We will convert the date to datetime and extract the year, month, and day. We also convert time and extract the hour and minute:

```
honey_bee_df['date_time'] = pd.to_datetime(honey_bee_df['date'] + ' ' +
honey_bee_df['time'])
honey_bee_df["year"] = honey_bee_df['date_time'].dt.year
honey_bee_df["month"] = honey_bee_df['date_time'].dt.month
honey_bee_df["day"] = honey_bee_df['date_time'].dt.day
honey_bee_df["hour"] = honey_bee_df['date_time'].dt.hour
honey_bee_df["minute"] = honey_bee_df['date_time'].dt.minute
```

A visualization of the number of bee images per date and approximative hour and location is shown in *Figure 6.9*. The code for this visualization starts by grouping the data by date_time and hour and calculating the number of images collected on each date and the time of day:

```
tmp = honey_bee_df.groupby(['date_time', 'hour'])['location'].value_
counts()
df = pd.DataFrame(data={'Images': tmp.values}, index=tmp.index).reset_
index()
```

Then, we build the text displayed when we hover over one point displayed in the graph. This text will include the hour, location, and the number of images. We then add the hover texts as a new column in the new dataset:

```
hover_text = []
for index, row in df.iterrows():
    hover_text.append(('Date/time: {}<br>'+
                       'Hour: {}<br>'+
                       'Location: {}<br>'+
                       'Images: {}').format(row['date_time'],
                                            row['hour'],
                                            row['location'],
                                            row['Images']))
df['hover_text'] = hover_text
```

Then, we represent, for each location, a scatter plot with the time and hour when pictures were collected. Each point's size is proportional to the number of images taken in that location, at a certain time of day, and on a certain date:

```
locations = (honey_bee_df.groupby(['location'])['location'].nunique()).
index
data = []
for location in locations:
    dfL = df[df['location']==location]
    trace = go.Scatter(
        x = dfL['date_time'],y = dfL['hour'],
        name=location,
        marker=dict(
            symbol='circle',
            sizemode='area',
            sizeref=0.2,
            size=dfL['Images'],
            line=dict(
                width=2
            ),),
        mode = "markers",
        text=dfL['hover_text'],
    )
```

```
    data.append(trace)

layout = dict(title = 'Number of bees images per date, approx. hour and
    location',
            xaxis = dict(title = 'Date', showticklabels=True),
            yaxis = dict(title = 'Hour'),
            hovermode = 'closest'
            )
fig = dict(data = data, layout = layout)


iplot(fig, filename='images-date_time')
```

In the next image, *Figure 6.9*, we see the result of running the aforementioned code. Most pictures were taken around August. Most of the pictures were also taken in the afternoon hours.

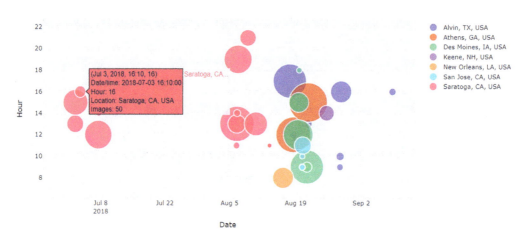

Figure 6.9: Number of bee images per date and the approximate hour and location

Subspecies

We use the same `plotly_barplot` function to visualize the distribution of subspecies. Most of the bees are Italian honey bees, followed by Russian honey bees and Carniolan honey bees (see *Figure 6.10*). Some of the 428 images are not classified (with a label value of **-1**). We will keep the images not classified as one subspecies category.

Number of bees images per subspecies

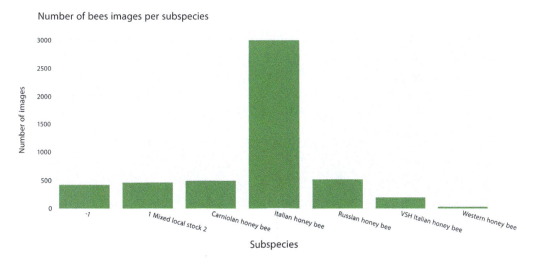

Figure 6.10: Number of bee images per date and the approximate hour and location

In *Figure 6.11*, we show a selection of images, with samples for just a few of the subspecies:

Figure 6.11: Samples of bee images from a few subspecies

Now, let's represent the number of images per subspecies and location, as well as the number of images per subspecies and hour (see *Figure 6.12*). The largest number of images were collected from Saratoga, CA, and all were Italian honey bees (1972 images). The largest number of images were collected at hour 13, and all were of Italian honey bees (909 images).

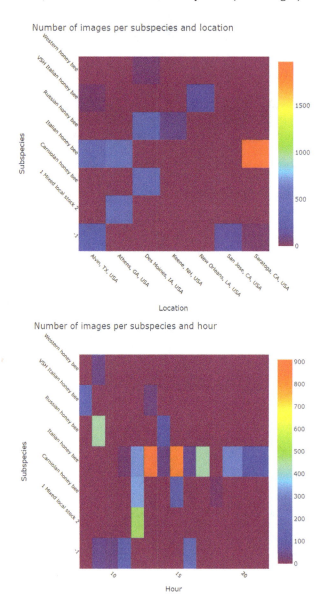

Figure 6.12: Number of images per subspecies and location (upper) and the number of images per subspecies and hour (lower)

The Subspecies images have a large variety of weights and heights. *Figure 6.13* shows this distribution, using a boxplot, for the weight and the height.

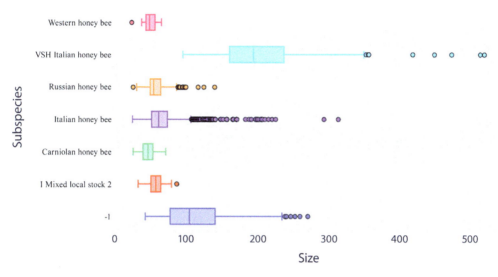

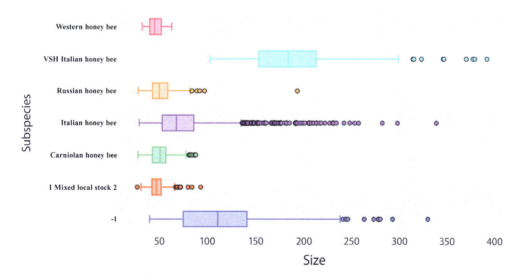

Figure 6.13: Image size distribution per each subspecies – width (upper) and height (lower)

VSH Italian honey bee has the largest average and also the largest variance for both width and height. **Western honey bee, Carniolan honey bee**, and **Mixed local stock 2** have the most compact distribution of weight and height (and lower variance). The *Italian honey bee*, the most numerous subspecies, shows both a small median and a large variance, with a lot of outliers. In the next figure, we show the weight and the height distribution combined on the same scatter plot:

Width and height of images per subspecies

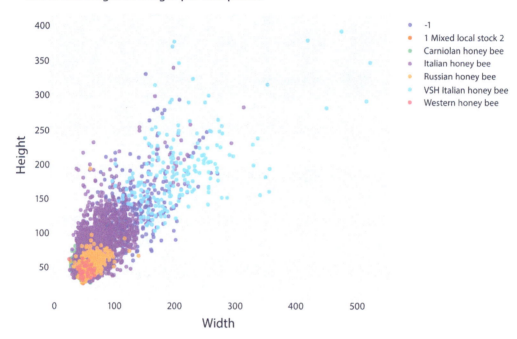

Figure 6.14: Image size distribution per each subspecies – scatter plot

The preceding figure shows this distribution, using a scatter plot, for the weight and the height. The code for this visualization is shown in the following. First, we start by defining a function to draw a scatter plot, with the image width on the x scale and the image height on the y scale:

```python
def draw_trace_scatter(dataset, subspecies):
    dfS = dataset[dataset['subspecies']==subspecies];
    trace = go.Scatter(
        x = dfS['w'],y = dfS['h'],
        name=subspecies,
```

```
        mode = "markers",
        marker = dict(opacity=0.8),
        text=dfS['subspecies'],
    )
    return trace
```

We now use the function defined above to draw the scatter plot for each subspecies. Each function call will create a trace, and we add the traces to the Plotly plot:

```
subspecies = (honey_bee_df.groupby(['subspecies'])['subspecies'].
nunique()).index
def draw_group(dataset, title,height=600):
    data = list()
    for subs in subspecies:
        data.append(draw_trace_scatter(dataset, subs))

    layout = dict(title = title,
                xaxis = dict(title = 'Width',showticklabels=True),
                yaxis = dict(title = 'Height', showticklabels=True,
tickfont=dict(
                    family='Old Standard TT, serif',
                    size=8,
                    color='black'),),
                hovermode = 'closest',
                showlegend=True,
                    width=800,
                    height=height,
                )
    fig = dict(data=data, layout=layout)
    iplot(fig, filename='subspecies-image')

draw_group(honey_bee_df,  "Width and height of images per subspecies")
```

Health

Figure 6.15 shows the distribution of images with various health problems. The majority of images are for **healthy** bees (3384), followed by **few varrao, hive beetles** (579), **Varroa, Small Hive Beetles** (472), and **ant problems** (457):

Number of bees images per health

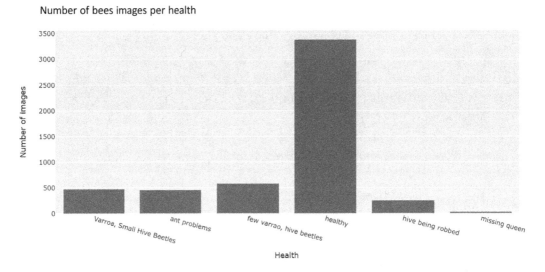

Figure 6.15: Number of images with different health problems

If we analyze the number of images per subspecies and health (see *Figure 6.16*), we can observe that only a reduced number of combinations of health and subspecies values are present. Most images are **healthy Italian honey bee** (1972), followed by **few varroa, hive beetles**, then **Italian honey bee** (579), and lastly, **healthy Russian honey bee** (527). The unknown subspecies are either **healthy** (177) or **hive being robbed** (251).

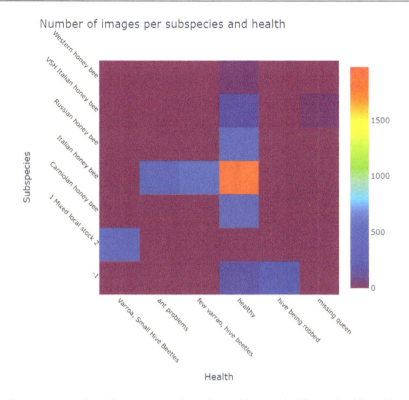

Figure 6.16: Number of images per subspecies and bees with different health problems

In *Figure 6.17*, we plot the number of images per location, subspecies, and health problems:

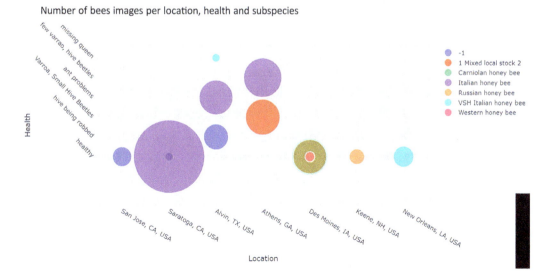

Figure 6.17: Number of images per location, subspecies, and health problems

Others

There is a small number of images with bees carrying pollen. *Figure 6.18* shows a few images of bees carrying pollen and some not carrying pollen. All the bees are from only one caste: the worker caste.

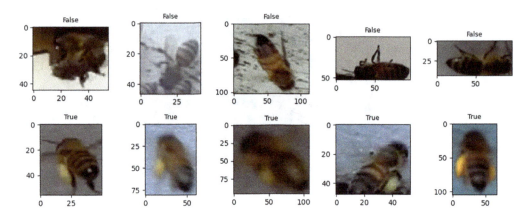

Figure 6.18: Selection of images with bees carrying pollen and not carrying pollen

Conclusion

We use a Sankey diagram, drawn with the `plotly_sankey` script from the `plotly_utils` utility script module, to draw the summary graph in *Figure 6.19*. A Sankey diagram is used mainly to visualize processes or flows, for example, the production of energy, with its sources and consumers, in an economy. I use it here with another purpose, to summarize the distribution of data with multiple features. It shows on the same plot the distribution of images per date, time, location, ZIP code, subspecies, and health. The adaptation code for the Sankey diagram is not given here for limited space reasons (refer *Reference 2* for the code samples associated with the chapter); we just include the code to adapt the honey bee data for the use of this function:

```
tmp = honey_bee_df.groupby(['location', 'zip code', 'date', 'time',
'health'])['subspecies'].value_counts()
df = pd.DataFrame(data={'Images': tmp.values}, index=tmp.index).reset_
index()

fig = plotly_sankey(df,cat_cols=['date', 'time', 'location', 'zip code',
'subspecies', 'health'],value_cols='Images',
                    title='Honeybee Images: date | time | location | zip
code | subspecies | health',
```

```
                color_palette=[ "darkgreen", "lightgreen", "green",
 "gold", "black", "yellow"],
          height=800)
iplot(fig, filename='Honeybee Images')
```

The visualization in *Figure 6.19*, a funnel-like graph, allows us to capture in one single graph the relationship between multiple features:

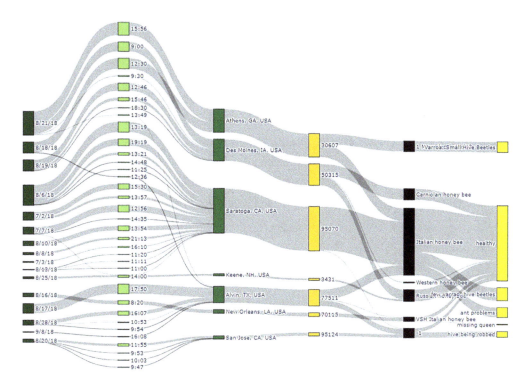

Figure 6.19: Summary of images

Until now, we analyzed the distribution of features in the dataset. Now, we have a better understanding of the data in the dataset. In the following section of this chapter, we will start preparation to build a machine learning model to classify images on subspecies, which is the second and more important objective of this chapter.

Subspecies classification

The objective of this section will be to use the images investigated until now to build a machine learning model that will correctly predict the subspecies. Since we have one dataset only, we will start by splitting the data into three subsets: for train, validation, and test data. We will use train and validation during the training process: the train data to feed the model and the validation data to verify how well the model predicts the class (i.e., the subspecies) with the new data. Then, the model trained and validated will be used to predict the class in the test set, which was not used either in train or validation.

Splitting the data

First, we split the data into `train` and `test`, using an 80%–20% split. Then, the `train` data is split again, in to train and validation, using the same 80%–20% split. The splits are performed using `stratify` with `subspecies` as a parameter, ensuring balanced subsets that respect the overall distribution of classes in the subsampled sets of train, validation, and test. The percent values for train/validation/test splits are chosen arbitrarily here and are not the result of a study or optimization. In your experiments, you can work with different values for train/validation/ test subsets, and you can also choose to not use `stratify`:

```
train_df, test_df = train_test_split(honey_bee_df, test_size=config['test_
size'], random_state=config['random_state'],
            stratify=honey_bee_df['subspecies'])
train_df, val_df = train_test_split(train_df, test_size=config['val_
size'], random_state=config['random_state'],
            stratify=train_df['subspecies'])
```

Ultimately, we will have three subsets, as follows:

- Train set rows: 3309
- Validation set rows: 828
- Test set rows: 1035

We will split the images into subsets, corresponding to the image names' subsets. We create functions to read images and rescale them all to the same dimension, as specified in the configuration structure we defined, using `skimage.io` and `opencv`. We decided to rescale all images to 100 x 100 pixels. Our decision was based on the analysis of the images' size distribution. You can choose to modify the code in the notebook given at *Reference 3* and experiment with different image sizes.

The following code reads an image (using `skimage.io`) and resizes it according to the size set in the configuration. You can change the configuration and resize the image, using different values for the image height and width:

```
def read_image(file_name):
    """

    Read and resize the image to image_width x image_height
    Args:
        file_name: file name for current image
    Returns:
        resized image
    """

    image = skimage.io.imread(config['image_path'] + file_name)
    image = skimage.transform.resize(image, (config['image_width'],
config['image_height']), mode='reflect')
    return image[:,:,:config['image_channels']]
```

The code below reads and resizes an image using opencv. The function differs from the previous one shown above just by the method to read the image file:

```
def read_image_cv(file_name):
    """

    Read and resize the image to image_width x image_height
    Args:
        file_name: file name for current image
    Returns:
        resized image
    """

    image = cv2.imread(config['image_path'] + file_name)
    image = cv2.resize(image, (config['image_width'], config['image_
height']))
    return image[:,:,:config['image_channels']]
```

We then apply one of these functions to all dataset files to read and rescale the images in the dataset.

We also create dummy variables corresponding to the categorical target variables. We prefer to use this approach because we will prepare a model for multiclass classification that outputs probabilities per class:

```python
def categories_encoder(dataset, var='subspecies'):
    X = np.stack(dataset['file'].apply(read_image))
    y = pd.get_dummies(dataset[var], drop_first=False)
    return X, y


s_time = time.time()
X_train, y_train = categories_encoder(train_df)
X_val, y_val = categories_encoder(val_df)
X_test, y_test = categories_encoder(test_df)
e_time = time.time()
print(f"Total time: {round(e_time-s_time, 2)} sec.")
```

With that, we've shown how to read and rescale our images. Next, we will see how we can multiply our images to have more data in the train set so that we present to the model a larger variety of data.

Data augmentation

We will use a deep learning model to classify the subspecies in our images. Typically, deep learning models perform better when trained with a larger amount of data. Using data augmentation, we also create a larger variety in the data, which is also beneficial for the model quality. Our model will improve its generalization if we expose it to more diverse data during training.

We define a component for data augmentation, based on `ImageDataGenerator` from `keras.preprocessing.image`. In this notebook, we will use Keras to build various components of the model. The `ImageDataGenerator` component is initialized with various parameters to create random variations of the training dataset, by applying:

- a rotation (in a range of 0 to 180 degrees) of the original images
- a zoom (10%)
- a shift in horizontal and vertical directions (10%)
- a horizontal and vertical shift (10%)

These variations can be controlled separately. Not all use cases will allow, or benefit from applying, all the transformations listed above (think about, for example, images with buildings or other landmarks, for which rotations do not make too much sense). The following code can be used in our case to initialize and fit the image generator:

```
image_generator = ImageDataGenerator(
        featurewise_center=False,
        samplewise_center=False,
        featurewise_std_normalization=False,
        samplewise_std_normalization=False,
        zca_whitening=False,
        rotation_range=180,
        zoom_range = 0.1,
        width_shift_range=0.1,
        height_shift_range=0.1,
        horizontal_flip=True,
        vertical_flip=True)


image_generator.fit(X_train)
```

We then move on to building and training a baseline model.

Building a baseline model

It is almost always recommended to start your work with a simple model and then conduct an error analysis. Based on the error analysis, you will have to further refine your model. If, for example, you observe that you obtained, with your baseline model, a large error for training, you need to start by improving the training. You can do this by perhaps adding more data, improving your data labeling, or creating better features. If your training error is small but you have instead a high validation error, it means that your model probably overfits on the training data. In such a case, you need to try to improve your model generalization. You can try various techniques to improve your model generalization. See more about this kind of analysis in *Reference 4* at the end of this chapter.

We will use the Keras library to define our models. Keras (see *Reference 5*) is a wrapper over the TensorFlow machine learning platform (see *Reference 6*). It allows you to create powerful deep learning models by defining a sequential structure with specialized layers. We will add the following layers to our model:

- One Conv2D layer, with 16 filters of dimension 3
- One MaxPooling2D layer, with reduction factor 2
- One convolutional layer, with 16 filters of dimension 3
- A Flatten layer
- A Dense layer, with the dimension the number of classes of the subspecies target feature

The preceding architecture is a very simple example of a **convolutional neural network**. The role of the convolutional2d layer is to apply sliding convolutional filters to a 2D input. The maxpool2d layer will down-sample the input along its spatial dimension (width and height) by taking the maximum value over an input window (see *Reference 5* for more details).

The code to build the described architecture will be:

```
model1=Sequential()
model1.add(Conv2D(config['conv_2d_dim_1'],
                  kernel_size=config['kernel_size'],
                  input_shape=(config['image_width'], config['image_
height'],config['image_channels']),
                  activation='relu', padding='same'))
model1.add(MaxPool2D(config['max_pool_dim']))
model1.add(Conv2D(config['conv_2d_dim_2'], kernel_size=config['kernel_
size'],
                  activation='relu', padding='same'))
model1.add(Flatten())
model1.add(Dense(y_train.columns.size, activation='softmax'))
model1.compile(optimizer='adam', loss='categorical_crossentropy',
metrics=['accuracy'])
```

In *Figure 6.20*, we show the summary information of the model. As you can see, the total number of trainable parameters is 282,775:

```
Model: "sequential"

_____
 Layer (type)                Output Shape              Param #
=================================================================
 conv2d (Conv2D)             (None, 100, 100, 16)      448


 max_pooling2d (MaxPooling2D  (None, 50, 50, 16)       0
 )


 conv2d_1 (Conv2D)           (None, 50, 50, 16)        2320


 flatten (Flatten)           (None, 40000)             0


 dense (Dense)               (None, 7)                 280007


=================================================================
Total params: 282,775
Trainable params: 282,775
Non-trainable params: 0
_____
```

Figure 6.20: Summary of the baseline model

For the baseline, we start with a small model and train for a reduced number of epochs. The size of the input images is 100 x 100 x 3 (as we explained previously). We will train this model for five epochs. The batch size is set to 32. The code to run the training is shown here:

```
train_model1  = model1.fit_generator(image_generator.flow(X_train, y_
train, batch_size=config['batch_size']),
                        epochs=config['no_epochs_1'],
                        validation_data=[X_val, y_val],
                        steps_per_epoch=len(X_train)/config['batch_size'])
```

Figure 6.21 shows the training log for the baseline model. We are not saving the best model version during training; the model weights at the last step will be used for the test.

```
Epoch 1/5
103/103 [==============================] - 20s 187ms/step - loss: 1.0271 - accuracy: 0.6860 - val_loss: 0.6962 - val_ac
curacy: 0.7548
Epoch 2/5
103/103 [==============================] - 20s 189ms/step - loss: 0.6707 - accuracy: 0.7510 - val_loss: 0.6134 - val_ac
curacy: 0.7295
Epoch 3/5
103/103 [==============================] - 20s 191ms/step - loss: 0.5676 - accuracy: 0.7752 - val_loss: 0.5358 - val_ac
curacy: 0.7742
Epoch 4/5
103/103 [==============================] - 20s 192ms/step - loss: 0.5216 - accuracy: 0.7894 - val_loss: 0.4610 - val_ac
curacy: 0.8080
Epoch 5/5
103/103 [==============================] - 20s 189ms/step - loss: 0.4735 - accuracy: 0.8108 - val_loss: 0.4146 - val_ac
curacy: 0.8321
```

Figure 6.21: The training log for the baseline model. The training loss and accuracy and validation loss and accuracy for each step are shown

The training loss and accuracy are updated after each batch, and the validation loss and accuracy are calculated at the end of each epoch. Next, with the model trained and validated, we will evaluate the test set loss and accuracy:

```
score = model1.evaluate(X_test, y_test, verbose=0)
print('Test loss:', score[0])
print('Test accuracy:', score[1])
```

In *Figure 6.22*, we show the training and validation loss and the training and validation accuracy:

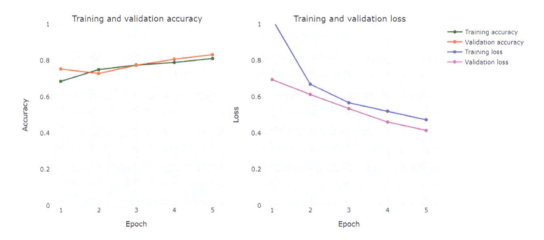

Figure 6.22: Baseline model – the training and validation accuracy (left) and the training and validation loss (right)

The results obtained are as follows:

- Test loss: **0.42**
- Test accuracy: **0.82**

The test loss refers to the loss function, a mathematical function that measures the difference between the predicted values and the true values. By measuring this value during training, for both
the train and validation sets, we can monitor how the model learns and improves its predictions.

Using a metrics classification report (`metrics.classification_report`) from sklearn, we calculate the precision, recall, f1-score, and accuracy per each class in train data. The code for that
is given here:

```
def test_accuracy_report(model):
    predicted = model.predict(X_test)
    test_predicted = np.argmax(predicted, axis=1)
    test_truth = np.argmax(y_test.values, axis=1)
    print(metrics.classification_report(test_truth, test_predicted,
target_names=y_test.columns))
    test_res = model.evaluate(X_test, y_test.values, verbose=0)
    print('Loss function: %s, accuracy:' % test_res[0], test_res[1])
```

In *Figure 6.23*, we show this classification report for the test set, where we applied the baseline
model fit with train data. The macro average of the precision, recall, and f1-score are **0.78**, **0.72**,
and **0.74**, respectively (the support data is **1035**). The weighted average precision, recall, and f1-
score are **0.82**, **0.83**, and **0.82**, respectively.

```
33/33 [==============================] - 2s 44ms/step
                        precision   recall  f1-score   support

                   -1       0.71     0.57      0.63        86
   1 Mixed local stock 2    0.52     0.50      0.51        94
    Carniolan honey bee     0.95     0.99      0.97       100
       Italian honey bee    0.85     0.90      0.88       602
       Russian honey bee    0.88     0.93      0.91       106
   VSH Italian honey bee    0.68     0.33      0.44        40
       Western honey bee    0.86     0.86      0.86         7

             accuracy                          0.83      1035
            macro avg       0.78     0.72      0.74      1035
         weighted avg       0.82     0.83      0.82      1035

Loss function: 0.4225456118583679, accuracy: 0.825120747089386
```

Figure 6.23: Classification report for test data using the baseline model

These weighted average scores are higher because unlike the simple averages of all class scores, these are weighted averages, so the higher scores associated with better-represented classes will have a higher contribution to the overall average. The worst scores for precision/class are for **1 Mixed local stock 2** (0.52) and **VSH Italian honey bee** (0.68). The worst overall score is for **VSH Italian honey bee,** where the recall is 0.33.

Iteratively refining the model

If we go back now to the training and validation errors, we can see that validation and training accuracies are around 0.81 and 0.82.

We will continue to train the model, and to avoid overfitting, we will also introduce two Dropout layers, each with a coefficient of 0.4. A Dropout layer is used as a regularization method in neural networks. Its purpose is to prevent overfitting and improve generalization of the model. The coefficient given as a parameter is the percentage of inputs randomly selected during training to be set to zero at each training epoch. The structure of the model is described in *Figure 6.24*. The number of trainable parameters will remain the same.

```
Model: "sequential_1"

_____
 Layer (type)                Output Shape              Param #
=================================================================
 conv2d_2 (Conv2D)           (None, 100, 100, 16)      448

 max_pooling2d_1 (MaxPooling  (None, 50, 50, 16)       0
 2D)

 dropout (Dropout)           (None, 50, 50, 16)        0

 conv2d_3 (Conv2D)           (None, 50, 50, 16)        2320

 dropout_1 (Dropout)         (None, 50, 50, 16)        0

 flatten_1 (Flatten)         (None, 40000)             0

 dense_1 (Dense)             (None, 7)                 280007

=================================================================
Total params: 282,775
Trainable params: 282,775
Non-trainable params: 0
_____
```

Figure 6.24: Refined model summary. Two Dropout layers were added

We also extend the number of epochs to 10. Let's see the results in *Figure 6.25*, where we show the training and validation accuracy and the training and validation loss.

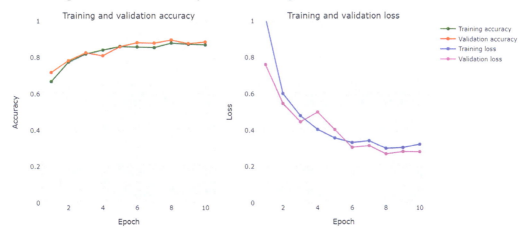

Figure 6.25: Refined model (version 2) – the training and validation accuracy (left) and the training and validation loss (right)

The final training loss is 0.32, and the final training accuracy is 0.87. The final validation loss is 0.28, and the final validation accuracy is 0.88. These are improved results. Of course, training accuracy is mainly improved due to the fact that we trained for more epochs.

```
33/33 [==============================] - 1s 38ms/step
                        precision    recall  f1-score   support

                   -1       0.98      0.70      0.82        86
  1 Mixed local stock 2     0.63      0.56      0.60        94
    Carniolan honey bee     0.88      1.00      0.93       100
       Italian honey bee    0.90      0.94      0.92       602
       Russian honey bee    0.94      0.94      0.94       106
   VSH Italian honey bee    0.97      0.72      0.83        40
       Western honey bee    0.54      1.00      0.70         7

             accuracy                           0.89      1035
            macro avg       0.83      0.84      0.82      1035
         weighted avg       0.89      0.89      0.88      1035


Loss function: 0.3087160289287567, accuracy: 0.8850241303443909
```

Figure 6.26: Classification report for test data using the second refined model (the training epochs increased to 10 and Dropout layers added)

As per validation accuracy, the result is due to both more training epochs as well as adding Dropout layers, which kept overfitting under control. Let's now check the test loss and accuracy as well as look at the entire classification report for test data.

Both macro averaged and weighted averaged metrics improved for precision, recall, and f1-score. Also, we can see much-improved precision, recall, and f1-scores for the classes with small scores obtained with the baseline. **1 Mixed local stock 2** had 0.52 precision, and now, precision is 0.63. As for **VSH Italian honey bee**, precision was 0.68 and is now 0.97. We see a degradation of the precision of **Western honey bee**, but the support for this minority class is only 7, so this result is expected.

We continue to refine our model to improve the validation and test metrics – in other words, to improve the model performance. In the next iteration, we will increase the number of training epochs to 50. Also, we will add three callback functions, as follows:

- A learning rate scheduler, to implement a nonlinear function for variation of the learning rate. By changing the learning rate at each epoch, we can improve the training process. The function we introduce to control the learning rate will gradually decrease the learning function value.

- An early stopper to stop training epochs, based on the loss function evolution (if loss does not improve for a certain number of epochs) and a patience factor (the number of epochs, after which, if we don't see any improvement of the monitored function, we stop training).

- A check pointer to save the best-performing models every time we obtain the best accuracy. This will allow us to use not the model parameters at the last training epoch but, instead, the best-performing model of all the epochs.

The code for the three callback functions is given below:

```
annealer3 = LearningRateScheduler(lambda x: 1e-3 * 0.995 ** (x+config['no_
epochs_3']))
earlystopper3 = EarlyStopping(monitor='loss', patience=config['patience'],
verbose=config['verbose'])
checkpointer3 = ModelCheckpoint('best_model_3.h5',
                                monitor='val_accuracy',
                                verbose=config['verbose'],
                                save_best_only=True,
                                save_weights_only=True)
```

The code to fit the model is also given below:

```
train_model3  = model3.fit_generator(image_generator.flow(X_train, y_
train, batch_size=config['batch_size']),
                        epochs=config['no_epochs_3'],
                        validation_data=[X_val, y_val],
                        steps_per_epoch=len(X_train)/config['batch_size'],
                        callbacks=[earlystopper3, checkpointer3,
   annealer3])
```

The training can take as many as the maximum number of epochs assigned or, if the early stopping criteria are met (i.e., no loss function improvement after a number of epochs equal to the patience factor), it might end earlier. Either way, the model for which the best validation accuracy was achieved is saved and will be used for testing.

In *Figure 6.27*, we show the evolution of the training and validation accuracy and the training and validation loss for this further refined model. The final training loss obtained is 0.18, and the final training accuracy is 0.93. For validation, the last validation loss is 0.21, and the last validation accuracy is 0.91. The learning rate at the final epoch is 6.08e-4. The best validation accuracy obtained was for epoch 46, 0.92.

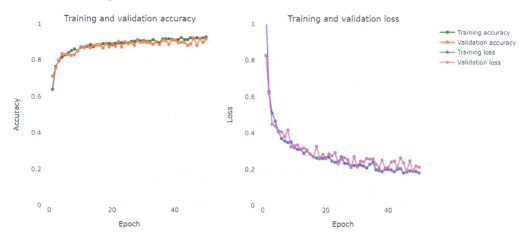

Figure 6.27: Refined model (version 3, with a learning rate scheduler, early stop, and checkpoint) – the training and validation accuracy (left) and the training and validation loss (right)

We use the model checkpoint saved (for epoch 46) to predict for the test data. In *Figure 6.28*, we show the classification report for the third model.

Macro average metrics are further improved to the precision, recall, and f1-score values of 0.88, 0.90, and 0.89, respectively. The weighted average values for precision, recall, and f1-score are also improved to 0.91, 0.90, and 0.90, respectively.

```
33/33 [==============================] - 2s 43ms/step
                        precision    recall  f1-score   support

                    -1       0.93      0.80      0.86        86
   1 Mixed local stock 2     0.59      0.72      0.65        94
    Carniolan honey bee      0.98      1.00      0.99       100
       Italian honey bee     0.94      0.91      0.93       602
       Russian honey bee     0.91      0.99      0.95       106
   VSH Italian honey bee     0.92      0.88      0.90        40
       Western honey bee     0.88      1.00      0.93         7

              accuracy                           0.90      1035
             macro avg       0.88      0.90      0.89      1035
          weighted avg       0.91      0.90      0.90      1035

Loss function: 0.23610743880271912, accuracy: 0.9004830718040466
```

Figure 6.28: Classification report for test data using the third refined model (the training epochs increased to 50 and a learning rate scheduler, early stopper, and model checkpoint added)

Here, we will stop the process of iteratively improving the model. You can continue to refine it. You can try to add more convolutional and maxpool layers, using a different number of kernels and values of stride to work with different hyperparameters, including a different batch size or learning rate scheduler. Also, you can change the optimization scheme. Another way to change the model is to control, through data augmentation, the balance of the class images (currently, the bee images are unbalanced with respect to the subspecies class).

You can also experiment with various data augmentation parameters and try to use a different data augmentation solution. See *Reference 5* for one example of an image data augmentation library that is very much used currently, **Albumentations**, created by a group of data scientists, researchers, and computer vision engineers, including the famous Kaggle Grandmaster Vladimir Iglovikov.

Summary

In this chapter, we started by introducing a new dataset, with metadata about images collected at different dates and in different locations, including various bee subspecies that have various diseases. We also introduced a few functions to read, rescale, and extract features from images, based on skimage.io and opencv (cv2).

We used a newly created utility script to visualize tabular data, based on Plotly, and created insightful visualizations by leveraging the flexibility of Plotly to create customized graphics. We also created visualization functions for images.

After the detailed EDA, we moved on to building a predictive model for bee subspecies. Here, we introduced a method for data augmentation to multiply the initial available training data, by creating variations (rotations, zoom, shift, and mirroring) from the original image sets. We split the data into train, validation, and test subsets, using `stratify` to account for the class imbalance when randomly sampling the three subsets. We started by training and validating a baseline model, and then, after performing error analysis, we gradually improved the initial model, by adding more steps, introducing `Dropout` layers, and then using several callbacks: the learning rate scheduler, early stopper, and model checkpoints. We analyzed the iterative improvement for the training, validation, and test errors, looking not only at the training and validation loss and accuracy but also at the classification report for test data.

In the following chapter, we will introduce techniques and tools for text data analysis, showing you how to prepare your data to create baseline models using text data.

References

1. The BeeImage Dataset: Annotated Honey Bee Images: `https://www.kaggle.com/datasets/jenny18/honey-bee-annotated-images`

2. `plotly-script` and Kaggle Utility Script: `https://github.com/PacktPublishing/Developing-Kaggle-Notebooks/blob/develop/Chapter-06/plotly-utils.ipynb`

3. Honeybee Subspecies Classification, Kaggle Notebook: `https://github.com/PacktPublishing/Developing-Kaggle-Notebooks/blob/develop/Chapter-06/honeybee-subspecies-classification.ipynb`

4. Andrew Ng, Machine Learning Yearning: `https://info.deeplearning.ai/machine-learning-yearning-book`

5. Keras: `https://keras.io/`

6. TensorFlow: `https://www.tensorflow.org/`

7. Using Albumentations with Tensorflow: `https://github.com/albumentations-team/albumentations_examples/blob/master/notebooks/tensorflow-example.ipynb`

Join our book's Discord space

Join our Discord community to meet like-minded people and learn alongside more than 5000 members at:

```
https://packt.link/kaggle
```

7

Text Analysis Is All You Need

In this chapter, we will learn how to analyze text data and create machine learning models to help us. We will use the *Jigsaw Unintended Bias in Toxicity Classification* dataset (see *Reference 1*). This competition had the objective of building models that detect toxicity and reduce unwanted bias toward minorities that might be wrongly associated with toxic comments. With this competition, we introduce the field of **Natural Language Processing (NLP)**.

The data used in the competition originates from the Civil Comments platform, which was founded by Aja Bogdanoff and Christa Mrgan in 2015 (see *Reference 2*) with the aim of solving the problem of civility in online discussions. When the platform was closed in 2017, they chose to keep around 2 million comments for researchers who want to understand and improve civility in online conversations. Jigsaw was the organization that sponsored this effort and then started a competition for language toxicity classification. In this chapter, we're going to transform pure text into meaningful, model-ready numbers to be able to classify them into groups according to the toxicity of the comments.

In a nutshell, this chapter will cover the following topics:

- Data exploration of the *Jigsaw Unintended Bias in Toxicity Classification* competition dataset
- Introduction to NLP-specific processing and analysis techniques, including word frequency, tokenization, part-of-speech tagging, named entity recognition, and word embeddings
- The iterative refinement of the preprocessing of text data to prepare a model baseline
- A model baseline for this text classification competition

What is in the data?

The data from the *Jigsaw Unintended Bias in Toxicity Classification* competition dataset contains 1.8 million rows in the training set and 97,300 rows in the test set. The test data contains only a **comment** column and does not contain a target (the value to predict) column. Training data contains, besides the **comment** column, another 43 columns, including the target feature. The target is a number between 0 and 1, which represents the annotation that is the objective of the prediction for this competition. This target value represents the degree of toxicity of a comment (0 means zero/no toxicity and 1 means maximum toxicity), and the other 42 columns are flags related to the presence of certain sensitive topics in the comments. The topic is related to five categories: race and ethnicity, gender, sexual orientation, religion, and disability. In more detail, these are the flags per each of the five categories:

- **Race and ethnicity**: asian, black, jewish, latino, other_race_or_ethnicity, and white
- **Gender**: female, male, transgender, and other_gender
- **Sexual orientation**: bisexual, heterosexual, homosexual_gay_or_lesbian, and other_sexual_orientation
- **Religion**: atheist, buddhist, christian, hindu, muslim, and other_religion
- **Disability**: intellectual_or_learning_disability, other_disability, physical_disability, and psychiatric_or_mental_illness

There are also a few features (a.k.a. columns in the dataset) that serve for identifying the comment: created_data, publication_id, parent_id, and article_id. Also provided are several user feedback information features associated with the comments: rating, funny, wow, sad, likes, disagree, and sexual_explicit. Finally, there are also two fields relative to annotations: identity_annotator_count and toxicity_annotator_count.

Let's start with a quick analysis of the target feature and the sensitive features.

Target feature

We would like to look first at the distribution of the target feature. Let's look at the histogram for these values' distribution in *Figure 7.1*:

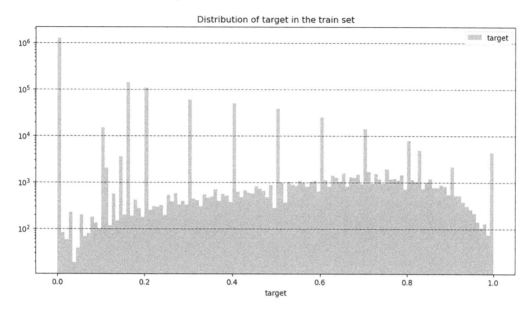

Figure 7.1: Distribution of target values (training data, 1.9 million columns)

For this histogram, we've used a logarithmic scale on the y axis; the reason behind this is that we want to see the skewed distribution of values toward 0. As we do this, we observe that we have a bimodal distribution: peak values at around 0.1 intervals, decreasing in amplitude, and less frequent values with a slowly rising trend, superposed. Most of the target values (above 1 million) are 0.

Sensitive features

We will look at the distribution of sensitive features as listed earlier (race and ethnicity, gender, sexual orientation, religion, and disability). We will again use a logarithmic scale on the y axis due to the skewness of the distribution (similar to the target, we have a concentration at 0).

Figure 7.2 shows the distribution of race and ethnicity feature values. These look discontinuous and very discrete, with the histogram showing a few separate peaks:

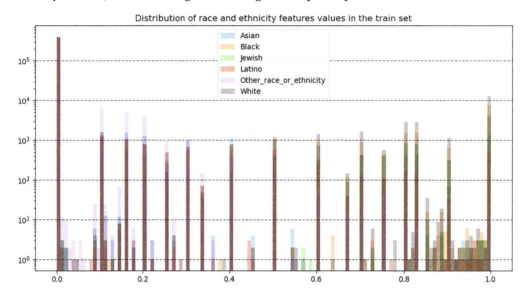

Figure 7.2: Distribution of race and ethnicity feature values

We can observe a similar distribution for the gender feature values in *Figure 7.3*:

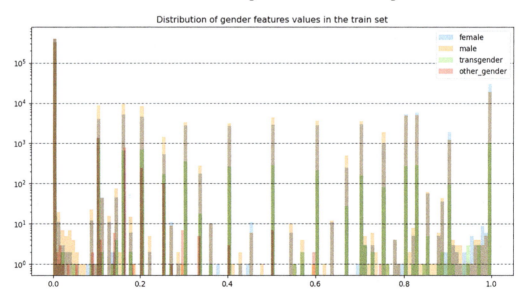

Figure 7.3: Distribution of gender feature values

In *Figure 7.4*, we show the distribution of the additional toxicity features (severe_toxicity, obscene, identity_attack, insult, or threat) values. As you can see, the distribution is more even, and with an increasing trend for insult:

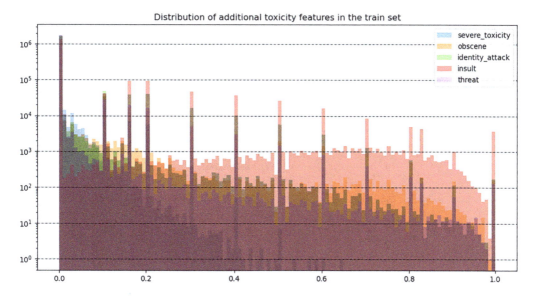

Figure 7.4: Distribution of additional toxicity feature values

Let us also look at the correlation between the target values and the race or ethnicity, gender, sexual orientation, religion, and disability feature values. We are not showing here the correlation matrix for all the features, but you can inspect it in the notebook associated with this chapter. Here, we only show the first 16 features correlated with the target, ordered by correlation factor:

```
train_corr['target'].sort_values(ascending=False)[1:16]
```

Let's look at the top 15 features ordered by correlation factor with the target in *Figure 7.5*:

```
                        Insult      0.93
                       Obscene      0.49
               Identity_attack      0.45
               Severe_toxicity      0.39
                        Threat      0.29
                         White      0.19
                         Black      0.17
                        Muslim      0.13
      Homosexual_gay_or_lesbian      0.13
                          Male      0.07
                        Female      0.06
    Psychiatric_or_mental_illness  0.06
                        Jewish      0.05
                   Transgender      0.04
                  Heterosexual      0.04
```

Figure 7.5: Top 15 correlation factors of other features with the target feature

Next, in *Figure 7.6*, we represent the correlation matrix for these selected features and the target feature:

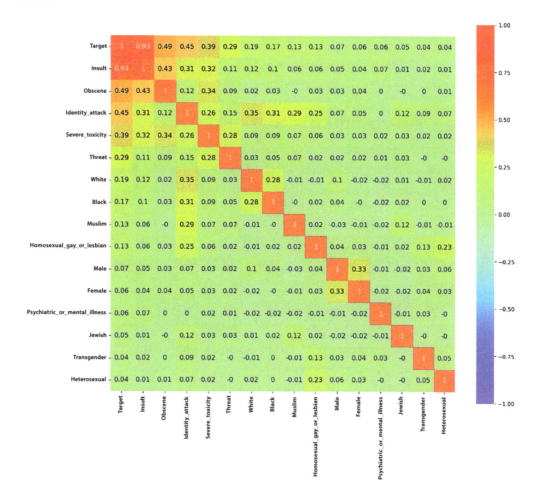

Figure 7.6: Correlation matrix between the target and 15 features with the highest correlation with it

We can observe that target is highly correlated with insult (0.93), obscene (0.49), and identity_ attack (0.45). Also, severe_toxicity is correlated positively with insult and obscene. identity_ attack has a small correlation with being white, black, muslim, and homosexual_gay_or_lesbian.

We investigated the distribution of the target feature (feature to predict) and of the sensitive features. Now we will move to the main topic of analysis for this chapter: the comments text. We will apply several NLP-specific analysis techniques.

Analyzing the comments text

NLP is a field of AI that involves the use of computational techniques to enable computers to understand, interpret, transform, and even generate human language. NLP uses several techniques, algorithms, and models to process and analyze large datasets of text. Among these techniques, we can mention:

- **Tokenization:** Breaks down text into smaller units, like words, parts of words, or characters
- **Lemmatization or stemming:** Reduces the words to dictionary form or removes the last few characters to get to a common form (stem)
- **Part-of-Speech (POS) tagging:** Assigns a grammatical category (for example, nouns, verbs, proper nouns, and adjectives) to each word in a sequence
- **Named Entity Recognition (NER):** Identifies and classifies entities (for example, names of people, organizations, and places)
- **Word embeddings:** Use a high-dimensional space to represent the words, a space in which the position of each word is determined by its relationship with other words
- **Machine learning models:** Train models on annotated datasets to learn patterns and relationships in language data

NLP applications can include sentiment analysis, machine translation, question answering, text summarization, and text classification.

With that quick introduction to NLP, let us inspect the actual comment text. We will build a few word cloud graphs (using a 20,000-comment subset of the entire dataset). We will look first at the overall word distribution (see the notebook associated with this chapter), then at the distribution of words with target values above 0.75 and below 0.25:

Figure 7.7: Prevalent words (1-gram) in comments with low target score < 0.25 (left) and high
target score > 0.75 (right)

target is very highly correlated with insult, and we expect to see a rather close distribution of words in the word clouds for the two features. This hypothesis is confirmed, and *Figure 7.8* illustrates this very well (both for low score and high score):

Figure 7.8: Prevalent words (1-gram) in comments with low insult score < 0.25 (left) and high
insult score > 0.75 (right)

As you can see, distributions show similar words with high frequency for both low scores and high scores for **target** and **insult**.

More word clouds are available in the associated notebook for threat, obscene, and other features. These word clouds give us a good initial intuition for the most frequent words. We will perform a more detailed analysis of word frequency in the entire corpus vocabulary in the *Building the vocabulary* and *Checking vocabulary coverage* sections. For now, we can observe that the analysis we performed is limited to individual word frequency, without capturing how these words are grouped over the entire corpus – in other words, how various words are used together and, based on this, identifying the main themes in the corpus. Such processing, aimed to reveal the underlying semantic structure of the entire corpus, is called **topic modeling**. The analysis of co-occurrence patterns of words in this approach allows us to reveal the latent topics existent in the text.

The inspiration for the implementation of the topic modeling approach in the associated notebook is from a set of articles and tutorials on topic modeling using latent Dirichlet allocation (see *References 5–10*).

Topic modeling

We start by preprocessing the comments text, using the gensim library to eliminate special charac-ters, frequently used words, connection words (or stopwords), and words with lengths less than 2:

```
def preprocess(text):
    result = []
    for token in gensim.utils.simple_preprocess(text):
        if token not in gensim.parsing.preprocessing.STOPWORDS and
len(token) > 2:
            result.append(token)
    return result
```

The following code applies the defined preprocess function to all the comments:

```
%%time
preprocessed_comments = train_subsample['comment_text'].map(preprocess)
```

Then, we create a dictionary of words using dictionary from gensim/corpora. We also filter extremes, to eliminate less frequent words and limit the size of the vocabulary:

```
%%time
dictionary = gensim.corpora.Dictionary(preprocessed_comments)
dictionary.filter_extremes(no_below=10, no_above=0.5, keep_n=75000)
```

With these restrictions, we go then to the next step and generate a *bag of words* (bow) corpus from the dictionary. Then we apply **TF-IDF** (**Term Frequency-Inverse Document Frequency**) to this corpus, which provides a numerical representation of the importance of a word within a document in a collection or corpus of documents.

The tf component measures how frequently a word appears in a document. The idf component shows the significance of a word across the entire corpus of documents (in our case, over the full set of comments). This factor decreases with a higher occurrence of a term in the documents. Therefore, after the tfidf transform, the coefficient for one word and one document is larger for words that are infrequent at the corpus level and appear with higher frequency inside the current document:

```
%%time
bow_corpus = [dictionary.doc2bow(doc) for doc in preprocessed_comments]
tfidf = models.TfidfModel(bow_corpus)
corpus_tfidf = tfidf[bow_corpus]
```

We then apply *Latent Dirichlet Allocation* (lda), a topic model that generates topics based on word frequency on this corpus, using the gensim implementation for parallel processing (LdaMulticore):

```
%%time
lda_model = gensim.models.LdaMulticore(corpus_tfidf, num_topics=20,
                                       id2word=dictionary, passes=2,
workers=2)
```

Let's represent the first 10 topics, with 5 words for each of them:

```
topics = lda_model.print_topics(num_words=5)
for i, topic in enumerate(topics[:10]):
    print("Train topic {}: {}".format(i, topic))
```

The topic words are shown with the associated relative weight in the topic, as shown here:

```
Train topic 0: (0, '0.006*"tax" + 0.005*"yes" + 0.005*"income" + 0.005*"lol" + 0.003*"think"')
Train topic 1: (1, '0.008*"good" + 0.005*"mean" + 0.004*"yep" + 0.003*"like" + 0.003*"years"')
Train topic 2: (2, '0.005*"think" + 0.005*"money" + 0.004*"job" + 0.004*"trump" + 0.004*"fraud"')
Train topic 3: (3, '0.004*"obama" + 0.004*"vote" + 0.003*"surprise" + 0.003*"quebec" + 0.003*"book"')
Train topic 4: (4, '0.004*"people" + 0.004*"trump" + 0.004*"like" + 0.003*"obama" + 0.003*"know"')
Train topic 5: (5, '0.004*"water" + 0.003*"taxes" + 0.003*"people" + 0.003*"like" + 0.003*"pay"')
Train topic 6: (6, '0.005*"like" + 0.004*"people" + 0.004*"pay" + 0.003*"trump" + 0.003*"point"')
Train topic 7: (7, '0.005*"trump" + 0.004*"wrong" + 0.004*"people" + 0.003*"agree" + 0.003*"work"')
Train topic 8: (8, '0.005*"thanks" + 0.004*"know" + 0.003*"guns" + 0.003*"immigrants" + 0.003*"won"')
Train topic 9: (9, '0.005*"trump" + 0.005*"people" + 0.004*"like" + 0.003*"good" + 0.003*"white"')
```

Figure 7.9: Top 10 topics, with 5 words (most relevant) selected per topic

Once we extract the topics, we can go through the documents and identify which topics are present in the current document (in our case, comment). In *Figure 7.10*, we show the dominant topics (with the relative weights) for one document (the following is the code used to generate the list of topics for a selected comment):

```
for index, score in sorted(lda_model[bd5], key=lambda tup: -1*tup[1]):
    print("\nScore: {}\t \nTopic: {}".format(score, lda_model.print_
topic(index, 5)))
```

```
Score: 0.82851642370224
Topic: 0.004*"muslim" + 0.004*"trump" + 0.004*"people" + 0.003*"read" + 0.003*"like"

Score: 0.10221932083368301
Topic: 0.004*"obama" + 0.004*"vote" + 0.003*"surprise" + 0.003*"quebec" + 0.003*"book"
```

Figure 7.10: Topics associated (each with relative importance) with one comment

We prefer the **pyLDAvis** visualization tool to represent the topics. In *Figure 7.11*, we show a screenshot of this tool (in the notebook, we generated 20 topics for train data and, separately, for test data). The dashboard in *Figure 7.11* displays the **Intertopic Distance Map**. Here, the topic's relative dimension (or influence) is represented by the size of the disks and the topic's relative distance by their mutual distance. On the right side, for the currently selected topic (in the left-side panel), we can see the top 30 most relevant terms per topic.

The disks with a light color (blue in the notebook) represent the overall word frequency. The darker colored disks (red in the notebook) represent the estimated word frequency within the selected topic. We can use a slide as well to adjust the relevance metric (in the picture, this is set to 1). We can further refine this analysis by improving the preprocessing step (for example, we can add more stopwords, specific to this corpus), adjusting the parameters for the dictionary formation, and controlling the parameters for `tfidf` and `lda`. Due to the complexity of the LDA procedure, we also reduced the size of the corpus, by subsampling the train data.

As shown in the following screenshot, on the left panel of the topic modeling dashboard generated using the pyLDAvis tool, we see the **Intertopic Distance Map** – with relative dimension of topic influence in the corpus and the relative topic's distance:

Figure 7.11: Topic modeling dashboard generated using the pyLDAvis tool (left panel)

On the right-side panel of the topic modeling dashboard generated using the pyLDAvis tool, for the selected topic, we see the top 30 most relevant terms per topic, with blue for the overall term frequency in the corpus and red for the estimated term frequency within the selected topic:

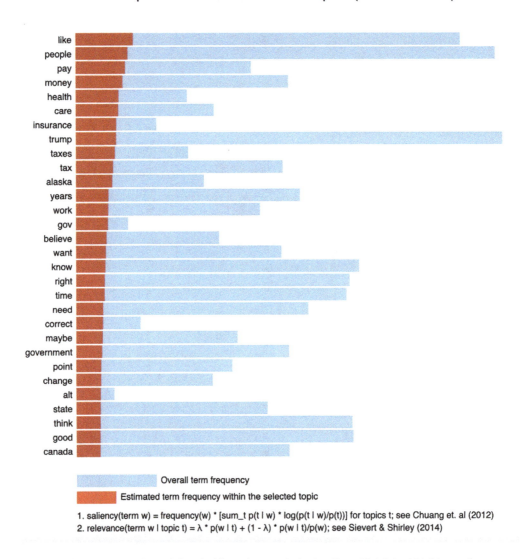

Figure 7.12: Topic modeling dashboard generated using the pyLDAvis tool (right panel)

We can repeat the analysis over the entire corpus, but this will require more computational resources than are available on Kaggle.

And with that, we have explored the topics in the comments text corpus, using the lda method. With this procedure, we revealed one of the hidden (or latent) structures in the corpus of the text. Now we can better understand not only the frequency of the words but also how words are associated in comments, to form topics discussed by the commentators. Let's continue to explore the corpus, from a different perspective. We will take every comment and analyze, using NER, what types of concepts are present in the text. Then, we will start to look at the syntactic elements and use POS tagging to extract the nouns, verbs, adjectives, and other parts of speech.

The reason we review these NLP techniques is twofold. First, we want to give you a glimpse of the richness of the tools and techniques available in NLP. Second, for more complex machine learning models, you can include features derived using these methods. For example, you can add, besides other features extracted from the text, features obtained by the use of NER or POS tagging.

Named entity recognition

Let's perform NER on a selection of comments. NER is an information extraction task that aims to identify and extract named entities in unstructured data (text). Named entities are people, organizations, geographical places, dates and times, amounts, and currencies. There are several available methods to identify and extract named entities, with the most frequently used being spacy and transformers. In our case, we will use spacy to perform NER. We prefer spacy because it requires fewer resources compared with transformers and yet gives good results. Something to note here is that spacy is also available in 23 languages, including English, Portuguese, Spanish, Russian, and Chinese.

First, we initialize an nlp object using the spacy.load function:

```
import spacy
nlp = spacy.load('en_core_web_sm')
```

This will load the 'en_core_web_sm' (sm stands for small) spacy pipeline, which includes the tok2vec, tagger, parser, senter, ner, attribute_ruler, and lemmatizer components. We will not use all the functionality provided by this pipeline; we are interested in the nlp component.

Then, we create a selection of comments. We filter documents that contain either the name Obama or the name Trump and have less than 100 characters. For the purpose of this demonstration, we do not want to manipulate large sentences; it will be easier to follow the demonstrations if we operate with smaller sentences. The next code fragment will perform the selection:

```
selected_text = train.loc[train['comment_text'].str.contains("Trump") |
train['comment_text'].str.contains("Obama")]

selected_text["len"] = selected_text['comment_text'].apply(lambda x:
len(x))

selected_text = selected_text.loc[selected_text.len < 100]
selected_text.shape
```

We can visualize the result of applying NER in two ways. One way is to print out the text's start and end characters and the entity label for each entity identified in the current comment. An alternative way is to use displacy rendering from spacy, which will decorate each entity with a selected color and add the entity name beside the entity text (see *Figure 7.13*).

The following code is for the extraction of entities using nlp and the preparation of visualization using displacy. Before showing the annotated text using displacy, we are printing each entity text, followed by its position (start and end character positions) and the entity label:

```
for sentence in selected_text["comment_text"].head(5):
    print("\n")
    doc = nlp(sentence)
    for ent in doc.ents:
        print(ent.text, ent.start_char, ent.end_char, ent.label_)
    displacy.render(doc, style="ent",jupyter=True)
```

There are multiple labels predefined in spacy nlp. We can extract the meaning of each one with a simple piece of code:

```
import spacy
nlp = spacy.load("en_core_web_sm")
labels = nlp.get_pipe("ner").labels

for label in labels:
    print(f"{label} - {spacy.explain(label)}")
```

Here is the resulting list of labels and the meaning of each one:

- **CARDINAL**: Numerals that do not fall under another type
- **DATE**: Absolute or relative dates or periods
- **EVENT**: Named hurricanes, battles, wars, sports events, and so on
- **FAC**: Buildings, airports, highways, bridges, and so on
- **GPE**: Countries, cities, or states
- **LANGUAGE**: Any named language
- **LAW**: Named documents made into laws
- **LOC**: Non-GPE locations, mountain ranges, or bodies of water
- **MONEY**: Monetary values, including units
- **NORP**: Nationalities or religious or political groups
- **ORDINAL**: first, second, and so on
- **ORG**: Companies, agencies, institutions, and so on
- **PERCENT**: Percentage, including %
- **PERSON**: People, including fictional
- **PRODUCT**: Objects, vehicles, foods, and so on (not services)
- **QUANTITY**: Measurements, such as weight or distance
- **TIME**: Times less than a day
- **WORK_OF_ART**: Titles of books, songs, and so on

```
Bernie 32 38 PERSON
Trump 71 76 ORG
```

Is there evidence that it was a Bernie **PERSON** supporter? Last time I checked, Trump **ORG** supporters poop too.

```
Obama 38 43 PERSON
```

The discourse may have been civil but Obama **PERSON** 's presidency has been obscene.

Figure 7.13: NER using spacy and displacy for visualization of NER results

In the top example of the preceding screenshot, Bernie (Sanders) is recognized correctly as a person (**PERSON**), while (Donald) Trump is identified as an organization (**ORG**). This might be because former president Trump frequently used his name as part of the name of several of the organizations he founded while being a businessperson.

In the bottom example, Obama (also a former president and a frequent topic in disputed political debates) is recognized correctly as **PERSON**. In both cases, we are also showing the list of
extracted entities, complemented with the starting and ending positions of each identified entity.

POS tagging

With NER analysis, we identified names specific to various entities like people, organizations,
places, and so on. These help us to associate various terms with a certain semantic group. We can
go further and explore the comments text so that we understand what POS (like noun or verb)
each word is, and understand the syntax of each phrase.

Let's start with using nltk (an alternative nlp library) to extract parts of speech from the same
small selection of phrases we used for NER experiments. We chose nltk here because, as well as
being even less resource-hungry than spacy, it provides good-quality results. We also want to be
able to compare the results of both (spacy and nltk):

```
for sentence in selected_text["comment_text"].head(5):
    print("\n")
    tokens = twt().tokenize(sentence)
    tags = nltk.pos_tag(tokens, tagset = "universal")
    for tag in tags:
        print(tag, end=" ")
```

The results will be as follows:

```
('Is', 'VERB') ('there', 'DET') ('evidence', 'NOUN') ('that', 'ADP') ('it', 'PRON') ('was', 'VER
B') ('a', 'DET') ('Bernie', 'NOUN') ('supporter', 'NOUN') ('?', '.') ('Last', 'ADJ') ('time', 'N
OUN') ('I', 'PRON') ('checked', 'VERB') (',', '.') ('Trump', 'NOUN') ('supporters', 'NOUN') ('po
op', 'VERB') ('too', 'ADV') ('.', '.')

('Go', 'NOUN') ('Trump', 'NOUN') (',', '.') ('Go', 'NOUN') ('!', '.') ('!', '.')

('I', 'PRON') ('agree.', 'VERB') ('Go', 'NOUN') ('Trump', 'NOUN') (',', '.') ('and', 'CONJ') ('t
ake', 'VERB') ('Ted', 'NOUN') ('with', 'ADP') ('you', 'PRON') ('.', '.')

('The', 'DET') ('discourse', 'NOUN') ('may', 'VERB') ('have', 'VERB') ('been', 'VERB') ('civil',
'ADJ') ('but', 'CONJ') ('Obama', 'NOUN') ("'s", 'PRT') ('presidency', 'NOUN') ('has', 'VERB')
('been', 'VERB') ('obscene', 'VERB') ('.', '.')

('Exactly.', 'NOUN') ('And', 'CONJ') ('already', 'ADV') ('the', 'DET') ('republicans', 'NOUN')
('are', 'VERB') ("'digging", 'VERB') ('in', 'ADP') ("'", '.') ('and', 'CONJ') ('threatening', 'V
ERB') ('Obama', 'NOUN') ('.', '.')
```

Figure 7.14: POS tagging using nltk

We can perform the same analysis using spacy as well:

```
for sentence in selected_text["comment_text"].head(5):
    print("\n")
    doc = nlp(sentence)
    for token in doc:
        print(token.text, token.pos_, token.ent_type_, end=" | ")
```

The results will be as follows:

```
Is AUX  | there PRON  | evidence NOUN  | that SCONJ  | it PRON  | was AUX  | a DET  | Bernie PRO
PN PERSON | supporter NOUN  | ? PUNCT  | Last ADJ  | time NOUN  | I PRON  | checked VERB  | , PU
NCT  | Trump NOUN ORG | supporters NOUN  | poop VERB  | too ADV  | . PUNCT  |

Go VERB  | Trump PROPN  | , PUNCT  | Go PROPN  | ! PUNCT  | ! PUNCT  |

I PRON  | agree VERB  | . PUNCT  | Go VERB  | Trump PROPN PERSON  | , PUNCT  | and CCONJ  | take
VERB  | Ted PROPN PERSON | with ADP  | you PRON  | . PUNCT  |

The DET  | discourse NOUN  | may AUX  | have AUX  | been AUX  | civil ADJ  | but CCONJ  | Obama
PROPN PERSON | 's PART  | presidency NOUN  | has AUX  | been AUX  | obscene ADJ  | . PUNCT  |

Exactly ADV  | . PUNCT  | And CCONJ  | already ADV  | the DET  | republicans PROPN NORP | are AU
X  | ' PUNCT  | digging VERB  | in ADP  | ' PUNCT  | and CCONJ  | threatening VERB  | Obama PROP
N LOC | . PUNCT  |
```

Figure 7.15: POS tagging using spacy

Let's compare the two outputs in *Figures 7.14* and *7.15*. The two libraries generate slightly different POS results. Some of the differences are due to the different mapping of actual parts of speech on categories. For nltk, the word "is" represents an AUX (auxiliary), while the same "is" for spacy is a verb. spacy distinguishes between proper nouns (names of persons, places, and so on) and regular nouns (NOUN), whereas nltk does not differentiate.

With some phrases having a non-standard structure, both outputs wrongly identify the verb "Go" as a noun (nltk) and a proper noun (spacy). In the case of spacy, it is somewhat expected, since "Go" is written in uppercase after a comma. spacy differentiates between a coordinating conjunction (**CCONJ**) and a subordinating conjunction (**SCONJ**), while nltk will only recognize that there are conjunctions (**CONJ**).

With the same library extension for spacy that we used to highlight NER in the previous subsection, we can also represent the syntactic structure of phrases and paragraphs. In *Figure 7.16*, we show one example of such a representation. In the notebook, we show all the comment (set of phrases) visualizations using `displacy` with the "dep" (dependency) flag.

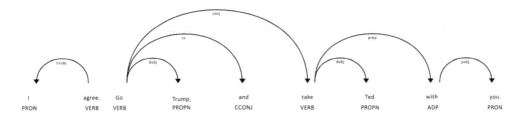

Figure 7.16: POS tagging using spacy and dependency to show phrase structure with the dependency between the parts of speech

We saw how we can use dependency to show entities and the category for each of them using dependency, and also how we can use the same function to show both the parts of speech and the phrase structure. With inspiration from *Reference 11*, we extended the code sample given there (and transitioned from using `nltk` to `spacy` for POS extraction, given that nltk is not fully aligned with spacy) so that we can show the parts of speech highlighted in the same way as we represented the named entities.

The modified code (including some minor bug fixing, besides the changes mentioned already) from *Reference 11* is given here (code explanation follows after the code block):

```
import re
def visualize_pos(sentence):
    colors = {"PRON": "blueviolet",
              "VERB": "lightpink",
              "NOUN": "turquoise",
              "PROPN": "lightgreen",
              "ADJ" : "lime",
              "ADP" : "khaki",
              "ADV" : "orange",
              "AUX" : "gold",
              "CONJ" : "cornflowerblue",
              "CCONJ" : "magenta",
              "SCONJ" : "lightmagenta",
              "DET" : "forestgreen",
```

```
                "NUM" : "salmon",
                "PRT" : "yellow",
                "PUNCT": "lightgrey"}

    pos_tags = ["PRON", "VERB", "NOUN", "PROPN", "ADJ", "ADP",
                "ADV", "AUX", "CONJ", "CCONJ", "SCONJ",  "DET", "NUM",
"PRT", "PUNCT"]

    # Fix for issues in the original code
    sentence = sentence.replace(".", " .")
    sentence = sentence.replace("'", "")
    # Replace nltk tokenizer with spacy tokenizer and POS tagging
    doc = nlp(sentence)
    tags = []
    for token in doc:
        tags.append((token.text, token.pos_))

    # Get start and end index (span) for each token
    span_generator = twt().span_tokenize(sentence)
    spans = [span for span in span_generator]

    # Create dictionary with start index, end index,
    # pos_tag for each token
    ents = []
    for tag, span in zip(tags, spans):
        if tag[1] in pos_tags:
            ents.append({"start" : span[0],
                         "end" : span[1],
                         "label" : tag[1] })

    doc = {"text" : sentence, "ents" : ents}

    options = {"ents" : pos_tags, "colors" : colors}

    displacy.render(doc,
                    style = "ent",
                    options = options,
                    manual = True,
                    )
```

Let's understand the preceding code better. In the function `visualise_pos`, we first define a mapping between parts of speech and colors (how a part of speech will be highlighted). Then, we define the parts of speech that we will consider. Then, we correct a bug existing in the original code (from *Reference 11*) using some replacements for special characters. We also use a spacy tokenizer and add, in the `tags` list, the text and part of speech for each pos extracted using `nlp` from spacy. Then, we calculate the position of each pos identified and create a dictionary with the pos tokens and their position in the text, to be able to highlight them with different colors. At the end, we render the document with all pos highlighted using `displacy`.

In *Figure 7.17*, we show the result of applying this procedure to our sample of comments. We can now see some of the errors of spacy easier. In the second comment, it misinterprets the second "Go" as a proper noun (**PROPN**). This is somewhat explainable, since normally, after a comma, only proper nouns will be written in uppercase in English.

Figure 7.17: POS tagging using spacy and dependency with the procedure modified from Reference 8 to show POSs highlighted inline in text

We can observe other errors as well. In the first comment, "Trump" appears as **NOUN** – that is, a simple noun. The term "republicans" is categorized as **PROPN**, which is likely accurate in the context of U.S. politics where "Republicans" is treated as a proper noun. However, in our context, this is inaccurate, as it represents a simple noun in plural form, identifying a group of individuals advocating for a republican government.

We reviewed several NLP techniques that helped us to get a better understanding of the word distribution, topics, POS, and concepts present in the text. Optionally, we can also use these techniques to generate features to include in a machine learning model.

In the next section, we will start the analysis targeted at preparing a supervised NLP model for the classification of comments.

Preparing the model

The model preparation, depending on the method we will implement, might be more or less complex. In our case, we opt to start the first baseline model with a simple deep learning architecture (which was the standard approach at the time of the competition), including a word embeddings layer (using pretrained word embeddings) and one or more bidirectional LSTM layers. This architecture was a common choice at the time when this competition took place, and it is still a good option for a baseline for a text classification problem. **LSTM** stands for **Long Short-Term Memory**. It is a type of recurrent neural network architecture designed to capture and remember long-term dependencies in sequential data. It is particularly effective for text classification problems due to its ability to handle and model intricate relationships and dependencies in sequences of text.

For this, we will need to perform some comment data preprocessing (we also performed preprocessing when preparing to build the topic modeling model). This time, we will perform the preprocessing steps gradually, and monitor how these steps are affecting the result not of the model, but of one prerequisite of a well-performing language model, which is the vocabulary coverage of the word embeddings.

We will then use word embeddings in the first baseline model to extend the generalization power of our model so that the words that are not present in the train set but are in the test set would benefit from the vicinity of words that exist in the word embeddings. Finally, to ensure that our approach will be effective, we will need the pretrained word embeddings to have as large a vocabulary coverage as possible. Thus, we will also measure the vocabulary coverage and suggest methods for improving it.

For now, we start by building the initial vocabulary.

Building the vocabulary

We performed the earlier experiments with word frequency, word distribution associated with various values of the target and other features, topic modeling, NER, and POS tagging with a subset of the entire comments corpus. For the following experiment, we will start using the entire dataset. We will use word embeddings with an embedding size of 300.

Word embeddings are numerical representations of a word. They map words to vectors. The embedding size refers to the number of components (or dimensions) of these vectors. This procedure enables computers to understand and compare relationships between words. Because all the words are first transformed using word embeddings (and in the word embeddings space, the relationship between words is represented by relationships between vectors), words with similar meanings will be represented by vectors aligned in the word embeddings space.

At testing time, new words, not present in the training data, will be represented in the word embeddings space as well, and their relationship with other words, present in the training data, will be exploited by the algorithm. The effect will be to enhance the algorithm we are using for text classification.

Additionally, we will set the number of characters (or length of comments) to a fixed number; we chose this dimension to be 220. For shorter comments, we will pad the comment sequence (that is, add spaces), and for larger comment sequences, we will truncate them (to 220 characters). This procedure will ensure we will have inputs for the machine learning model with the same dimension. Let's first define a function for building the vocabulary. For building these functions, we used sources from *References 12* and *13*.

The following code is used to build the vocabulary (that is, the corpus of words present in the comments). We apply a split on each comment and gather all data in a list of sentences. We then parse all these sentences to create a dictionary with the vocabulary. Each time a word parsed is found as a key in the dictionary, we increment the value associated with the key. What we obtain is a vocabulary dictionary with the count (or overall frequency) of each word in the vocabulary:

```
def build_vocabulary(texts):
    """
    Build the vocabulary from the corpus
    Credits to: [9] [10]
    Args:
        texts: list of list of words
    Returns:
        dictionary of words and their count
    """
    sentences = texts.apply(lambda x: x.split()).values
    vocab = {}
    for sentence in tqdm(sentences):
        for word in sentence:
            try:
                vocab[word] += 1
            except KeyError:
                vocab[word] = 1
    return vocab
```

We create the overall vocabulary by concatenating `train` and `test`:

```
# populate the vocabulary
df = pd.concat([train ,test], sort=False)
vocabulary = build_vocabulary(df['comment_text'])
```

We can check the first 10 elements in the vocabulary to have an intuition of what this vocabulary looks like:

```
# display the first 10 elements and their count


print({k: vocabulary[k] for k in list(vocabulary)[:10]})
```

The following image shows the result of running the preceding code. It shows the most frequent words in the text. As expected, the most used words are some of the most frequently used words in the English language.

```
{'This': 127947, 'is': 1534062, 'so': 222745, 'cool.': 503, "It's": 86489, 'like,': 2430, "'w
ould": 13, 'you': 773969, 'want': 101084, 'your': 309288}
```

Figure 7.18: Vocabulary without any preprocessing – uppercase and lowercase words, and possibly wrongly spelled expressions

We will use the earlier introduced function, `build_vocabulary`, repeatedly every time we perform an additional (sometimes repeated) text transformation. We perform successive text transformations to ensure that, while using pretrained word embeddings, we have good coverage with the words in the pretrained word embeddings of the vocabulary in the comments. With a larger coverage, we ensure a better accuracy of the model that we are building. Let's continue by loading some pretrained word embeddings.

Embedding index and embedding matrix

We will now build a dictionary with the words in word embeddings as keys and the arrays of their embedding representations as values. We call this dictionary the embedding index. We will then also build the embedding matrix, which is a matrix representation of embeddings. We will use GloVe's pretrained embeddings (with 300 dimensions) for our experiments. **GloVe** stands for **Global Vectors for Word Representation** and is an unsupervised algorithm that produces word embeddings. It works by analyzing global text statistics over a very large text corpus to create vector representations and capture semantic relationships between words.

The following code loads the pretrained word embeddings:

```
def load_embeddings(file):
    """
    Load the embeddings
    Credits to: [9] [10]
    Args:
        file: embeddings file
    Returns:
        embedding index
    """
    def get_coefs(word,*arr):
        return word, np.asarray(arr, dtype='float32')
    embeddings_index = dict(get_coefs(*o.split(" ")) for o in open(file,
encoding='latin'))
    return embeddings_index


%%time
GLOVE_PATH = '../input/glove840b300dtxt/'
print("Extracting GloVe embedding started")
embed_glove = load_embeddings(os.path.join(GLOVE_PATH,'glove.840B.300d.
txt'))
print("Embedding completed")
```

The size of the embedding structure obtained is 2.19 million items. Next, we create the embedding matrix using the word index and the embedding index we just created:

```
def embedding_matrix(word_index, embeddings_index):
    '''
    Create the embedding matrix
    credits to: [9] [10]
    Args:
        word_index: word index (from vocabulary)
        embedding_index: embedding index (from embeddings file)
    Returns:
        embedding matrix
    '''
    all_embs = np.stack(embeddings_index.values())
    emb_mean, emb_std = all_embs.mean(), all_embs.std()
```

```
    EMBED_SIZE = all_embs.shape[1]
    nb_words = min(MAX_FEATURES, len(word_index))
    embedding_matrix = np.random.normal(emb_mean, emb_std, (nb_words,
EMBED_SIZE))
    for word, i in tqdm(word_index.items()):
        if i >= MAX_FEATURES:
            continue
        embedding_vector = embeddings_index.get(word)
        if embedding_vector is not None:
            embedding_matrix[i] = embedding_vector
    return embedding_matrix
```

We use the parameter MAX_FEATURES to limit the dimension of the embedding matrix.

Checking vocabulary coverage

We introduced the functions to read the word embeddings and compute the embedding matrix. Now we will continue with introducing the functions to evaluate the vocabulary coverage with words from the word embeddings. The larger the vocabulary coverage, the better the accuracy of the model we are building.

To check the coverage of the vocabulary by the embeddings, we are going to use the following function:

```
def check_coverage(vocab, embeddings_index):
    '''
    Check the vocabulary coverage by the embedding terms
    credits to: [9] [10]
    Args:
        vocab: vocabulary
        embedding_index: embedding index (from embeddings file)
    Returns:
        list of unknown words; also prints the vocabulary coverage of
embeddings and
        the % of comments text covered by the embeddings
    '''
    known_words = {}
    unknown_words = {}
    nb_known_words = 0
    nb_unknown_words = 0
    for word in tqdm(vocab.keys()):
```

```
        try:
            known_words[word] = embeddings_index[word]
            nb_known_words += vocab[word]
        except:
            unknown_words[word] = vocab[word]
            nb_unknown_words += vocab[word]
            pass
    print('Found embeddings for {:.3%} of vocabulary'.format(len(known_
words)/len(vocab)))
    print('Found embeddings for {:.3%} of all text'.format(nb_known_words/
(nb_known_words + nb_unknown_words)))
    unknown_words = sorted(unknown_words.items(), key=operator.
itemgetter(1))[::-1]
    return unknown_words
```

The preceding code browses through all the vocabulary items (that is, the words present in the comments text) and counts the unknown words (that is, words in the text but not in the list of embeddings words). Then, it calculates the percentage of words in the vocabulary that exist in the word embeddings index. This percentage is calculated in two ways: with each word in the vocabulary unweighted and with words weighted by their frequency in the text.

We will apply this function repeatedly to check the vocabulary coverage after each step of pre-processing. Let's start with checking the vocabulary coverage for the initial vocabulary, where we haven't applied any preprocessing to the comments text yet.

Iteratively improving vocabulary coverage

We apply the function check_coverage to check the vocabulary coverage, passing the two parameters: vocabulary and embedding matrix. In the following notation, **oov** stands for **out of vocabulary**:

```
print("Verify the initial vocabulary coverage")
oov_glove = check_coverage(vocabulary, embed_glove)
```

The result of the first iteration is not great. Although we have almost 90% of the text covered, only 15.5% of the words in the vocabulary are covered by the word embeddings:

```
            Found embeddings for 15.520% of vocabulary
            Found embeddings for 89.609% of all text
```

Figure 7.19: Vocabulary coverage – first iteration

We can also look at the list of not covered terms. Because, in oov_glove, we stored the not covered terms in descending order by the number of appearances in the corpus, we can see, by selecting the first terms in this list, the most important words not included in the word embeddings. In *Figure 7.20*, we show the first 10 terms in this list – the top 10 words not covered. Here, *not covered* refers to words that appear in the vocabulary (are present in the comments texts) but not in the word embeddings index (are not present in the pretrained word embeddings):

```
[("isn't", 42161),
 ("That's", 39552),
 ("won't", 30975),
 ("he's", 25704),
 ("Trump's", 24736),
 ("aren't", 21626),
 ("wouldn't", 20569),
 ('Yes,', 20092),
 ('that,', 19237),
 ("wasn't", 19107)]
```

Figure 7.20: Most frequent 10 words from the vocabulary not covered by the word embeddings in the first iteration

By quickly inspecting the list in *Figure 7.20*, we see that some of the frequent words are either contracted, or colloquial, non-standard forms of spoken English. It is normal to see such forms in online comments. We will perform several steps of preprocessing to try to improve the vocabulary coverage by correcting the issues we find. After each step, we will also measure the vocabulary coverage again.

Transforming to lowercase

We will start by converting all text to lowercase and adding it to the vocabulary. In word embeddings, the words will be all lowercase:

```
def add_lower(embedding, vocab):
    '''
    Add lower case words
    credits to: [9] [10]
    Args:
        embedding: embedding matrix
        vocab: vocabulary
    Returns:
```

```
      None
      modify the embeddings to include the lower case from vocabulary
  '''

  count = 0
  for word in tqdm(vocab):
      if word in embedding and word.lower() not in embedding:
          embedding[word.lower()] = embedding[word]
          count += 1
  print(f"Added {count} words to embedding")
```

We apply this lowercase transformation to both the train and test sets and then we rebuild the vocabulary and calculate the vocabulary coverage:

```
train['comment_text'] = train['comment_text'].apply(lambda x: x.lower())
test['comment_text'] = test['comment_text'].apply(lambda x: x.lower())
print("Check coverage for vocabulary with lower case")
oov_glove = check_coverage(vocabulary, embed_glove)
add_lower(embed_glove, vocabulary) # operates on the same vocabulary
oov_glove = check_coverage(vocabulary, embed_glove)
```

Figure 7.21 shows the new vocabulary coverage after we applied the lowercase transformation:

```
Found embeddings for 15.639% of vocabulary
Found embeddings for 89.638% of all text
```

Figure 7.21: Vocabulary coverage – second iteration with lowercase of all words

We can observe a few small improvements in the word percentage and text percentage coverage. Let's continue by removing contractions in the comments text.

Removing contractions

Next, we will remove contractions. These are modified forms of words and expressions. We will use a predefined dictionary of usually encountered contractions. These will be mapped on words that exist in embeddings. Because of limited space, we are just including here a few examples of items in the contractions dictionary, but the entire resource is available in the notebook associated with this chapter:

```
contraction_mapping = {"ain't": "is not", "aren't": "are not","can't":
"cannot", "'cause": "because", "could've": "could have", "couldn't":
"could not", "didn't": "did not",  "doesn't": "does not", "don't": "do
not", "hadn't": "had not", "hasn't": "has not",
```

```
...
}
```

With the following function, we can get the list of known contractions in GloVe embeddings:

```
def known_contractions(embed):
    '''

    Add know contractions
    credits to: [9] [10]
    Args:
        embed: embedding matrix
    Returns:
        known contractions (from embeddings)
    '''

    known = []
    for contract in tqdm(contraction_mapping):
        if contract in embed:
            known.append(contract)
    return known
```

We can use the next function to clean the known contractions from the vocabulary – that is, replace them by using the contractions dictionary:

```
def clean_contractions(text, mapping):
    '''

    Clean the contractions

    credits to: [9] [10]
    Args:
        text: current text
        mapping: contraction mappings
    Returns: modify the comments to use the base form from contraction
mapping
    '''

    specials = ["'", "'", "'", "`"]
    for s in specials:
        text = text.replace(s, "'")
    text = ' '.join([mapping[t] if t in mapping else t for t in text.
split(" ")])
    return text
```

After we apply `clean_contractions` to both the train and test sets and again apply the function to build the vocabulary and measure vocabulary coverage, we get the new stats about the vocabulary coverage:

```
Found embeddings for 13.503% of vocabulary
Found embeddings for 90.395% of all text
```

Figure 7.22: Vocabulary coverage – third iteration, after replacing contractions using the contractions dictionary

Further refinement of the contractions dictionary is possible by inspecting expressions without coverage and enhancing it to equate not covered expressions in the corpus with words or groups of words where each word is represented in the embedding vector.

Removing punctuation and special characters

Next, we will remove punctuation and special characters. The following lists and functions are useful for this step. First, we list the unknown punctuation:

```
punct_mapping = "/-'?!.,#$%\'()*+-/:;<=>@[\\]^_`{|}~" + '""""''' + '∞θ÷α•à–
β∅³π'₹´°£€\×™√²—–&'
punct_mapping += '©^®` <→°€™' ♥←×§″′Â▇½à…"*"–•â►–¢²┐▇¶↑±¿▾=¦‖–¥▉–'–▇:
¼⊕▼■↑■'▉'▇♫☆é¯◆¤▲è¸¾Ã('∞·) ↓、 │ ◇、 ♪╨╚3 · ╥╖ ╾♥ï∅¹≤‡√'

def unknown_punct(embed, punct):
    '''
    Find the unknown punctuation
    credits to: [9] [10]
    Args:
        embed: embedding matrix
        punct: punctuation
    Returns:
        unknown punctuation
    '''
    unknown = ''
    for p in punct:
        if p not in embed:
            unknown += p
            unknown += ' '
    return unknown
```

Then we clean the special characters and punctuation:

```
puncts = {"'": "'", "'": "'", "°": "", "€": "euro", "–": "-", "—": "-",
"'": "'", "_": "-", "`": "'", "‛": "'", "„": "'", "‟": "'", "£": "pound",
          '∞': 'infinity', 'θ': 'theta', '÷': '/', 'α': 'alpha', '•': '.',
'à': 'a', '−': '-', 'β': 'beta', 'Ø': '', '³': '3', 'π': 'pi', '…': ' '}


def clean_special_chars(text, punct, mapping):
    '''
    Clean special characters
    credits to: [9] [10]
    Args:
        text: current text
        punct: punctuation
        mapping: punctuation mapping
    Returns:
        cleaned text
    '''
    for p in mapping:
        text = text.replace(p, mapping[p])
    for p in punct:
        text = text.replace(p, f' {p} ')
    return text
```

Let's check the vocabulary coverage again in *Figure 7.23*. This time, we increased the word vocabulary coverage by word embeddings from around 15% to 54%. Additionally, text coverage increased from 90% to 99.7%.

```
Found embeddings for 54.389% of vocabulary
Found embeddings for 99.718% of all text
CPU times: user 1min 5s, sys: 1.14 s, total: 1min 6s
Wall time: 1min 6s
```

Figure 7.23: Vocabulary coverage – fourth iteration, after cleaning punctuation and special characters

Looking at the top 20 words not covered, we see that we have small words with accents, special characters, and idiomatic expressions. We extend the punctuation dictionary to include the most frequent special characters, and after we run `build_vocabulary` and `check_coverage` again, we get a new status of the vocabulary coverage:

```
more_puncts = {'█': '.', '▪': '.', 'é': 'e', 'è': 'e', 'ï': 'i','☆':
'star', 'A': 'A', 'AND': 'and', '»': ' '}

train['comment_text'] = train['comment_text'].apply(lambda x: clean_
special_chars(x, punct_mapping, more_puncts))
test['comment_text'] = test['comment_text'].apply(lambda x: clean_special_
chars(x, punct_mapping, more_puncts))

%%time
df = pd.concat([train ,test], sort=False)
vocab = build_vocabulary(df['comment_text'])
print("Check coverage after additional punctuation replacement")
oov_glove = check_coverage(vocab, embed_glove)
```

There is a trivial improvement this time, but we can continue with addressing either frequent expressions or frequent special character replacements until we get a significant improvement.

An alternative way to further improve the comments corpus vocabulary coverage by the embeddings is to add an additional embedding source to current pretrained embeddings. Let's try this. We used pretrained embeddings from GloVe. We can also use FastText from Facebook. FastText is a very practical industry-standard library that is commonly used in search and recommendation engines in several companies daily. Let us load the embeddings and recreate the embeddings index with the combined embeddings vectors.

After we merge both word embedding dictionaries, with dimensions of 2.19 million and 2.0 million entries (both with a vector dimension of 300), we obtain a dictionary with a dimension of 2.8 million entries (due to many common words in the two dictionaries). We then recalculate the vocabulary coverage. In *Figure 7.24*, we show the result of this operation.

```
Found embeddings for 54.390% of vocabulary
Found embeddings for 99.727% of all text
CPU times: user 1min 15s, sys: 1.85 s, total: 1min 16s
Wall time: 1min 16s
```

Figure 7.24: Vocabulary coverage – fifth iteration, after adding the FastText pretrained word embeddings to the initial GloVe embedding dictionary

To summarize our process here, our intention was to build a baseline solution based on the use of pretrained word embeddings. We introduced two pretrained word embedding algorithms, GloVe and FastText. Pretrained means that we used the already trained algorithms; we didn't calculate the word embeddings from the corpus of comments in our dataset. To be effective, we need to ensure that we have good coverage with these word embeddings of the comments text vocabulary. Initially, the coverage was rather poor (15% of the vocabulary and 86% of the entire text). We improved these statistics gradually by transforming to lowercase, removing contractions, removing punctuation, and replacing special characters. In the last step, we extended the embeddings dictionary by adding pretrained embeddings from an alternative source. In the end, we were able to ensure a 56% coverage of the vocabulary and 99.75% of the entire text.

The next step is to go ahead and create a baseline model in a separate notebook. We will only reuse a part of the functions we created for the experiments in the current notebook.

Building a baseline model

These days, everybody will build a baseline model by at least fine-tuning a Transformer architecture. Since the 2017 paper *Attention Is All You Need* (*Reference 14*), the performance of these solutions has continuously improved, and for competitions like *Jigsaw Unintended Bias in Toxicity Classification*, a recent Transformer-based solution will probably take you easily into the gold zone.

In this exercise, we will start with a more classical baseline. The core of this solution is based on contributions from Christof Henkel (Kaggle nickname: Dieter), Ane Berasategi (Kaggle nickname: Ane), Andrew Lukyanenko (Kaggle nickname: Artgor), Thousandvoices (Kaggle nickname), and Tanrei (Kaggle nickname); see *References 12, 13, 15, 16, 17,* and *18*.

The solution includes four steps. In the first step, we load the train and test data as pandas datasets and then we perform preprocessing on the two datasets. The preprocessing is largely based on the preprocessing steps we performed before, and hence, we won't repeat those steps here.

In the second step, we perform tokenization and prepare the data to present it to the model. The tokenization is performed as shown in the following code excerpt (we are not showing the entire procedure here):

```
logger.info('Fitting tokenizer')
tokenizer = Tokenizer()
tokenizer.fit_on_texts(list(train[COMMENT_TEXT_COL]) +
list(test[COMMENT_TEXT_COL]))
word_index = tokenizer.word_index
X_train = tokenizer.texts_to_sequences(list(train[COMMENT_TEXT_COL]))
```

```
    X_test = tokenizer.texts_to_sequences(list(test[COMMENT_TEXT_COL]))
    X_train = pad_sequences(X_train, maxlen=MAX_LEN)
    X_test = pad_sequences(X_test, maxlen=MAX_LEN)
```

We used a basic tokenizer here from keras.preprocessing.text. After tokenization, each input sequence is padded with a predefined MAX_LEN, which was selected as an optimum considering the average/median length of sequences for the entire comments corpus and also considering the available memory and runtime constraints.

In the third step, we build the embedding matrix and the model structure. The code for building the embedding matrix is largely based on the procedures we already presented in the previous sections. Here, we just systematize it:

```
def build_embedding_matrix(word_index, path):
    '''
    Build embeddings
    '''

    logger.info('Build embedding matrix')
    embedding_index = load_embeddings(path)
    embedding_matrix = np.zeros((len(word_index) + 1, EMB_MAX_FEAT))
    for word, i in word_index.items():
        try:
            embedding_matrix[i] = embedding_index[word]
        except KeyError:
            pass
        except:
            embedding_matrix[i] = embeddings_index["unknown"]

    del embedding_index
    gc.collect()
    return embedding_matrix

def build_embeddings(word_index):
    '''
    Build embeddings
    '''

    logger.info('Load and build embeddings')
    embedding_matrix = np.concatenate(
        [build_embedding_matrix(word_index, f) for f in EMB_PATHS], axis=-
```

```
1)
    return embedding_matrix
```

The model is a deep learning architecture with a word embeddings layer, a `SpatialDropout1D` layer, two bidirectional LSTM layers, a concatenation of `GlobalMaxPooling1D` with a `GlobalAveragePooling1D`, two dense layers with `'relu'` activation, and one dense layer with `'sigmoid'` activation for the target output.

In the word embedding layer, the input is transformed so that each word is represented by its corresponding vector. After this transformation, the information about the semantic distance between words in the input is captured by the model. The `SpatialDropout1D` layer helps prevent overfitting by randomly deactivating neurons during training (the coefficient gives the percentage of neurons deactivated each epoch). The bidirectional LSTM layer's role is to process the input sequences in both forward and backward directions, enhancing contextual understanding for better predictions. The role of the `GlobalAveragePooling1D` layer is to compute the average of each feature across the entire sequence, reducing the dimensionality while retaining essential information in the 1D (sequential) data. This amounts to revealing a latent representation of the sequences. The dense layers' output is the prediction of the model. See *References 17* and *18* for more details regarding the implementation:

```python
def build_model(embedding_matrix, num_aux_targets, loss_weight):
    '''

        Build model
    '''

    logger.info('Build model')
    words = Input(shape=(MAX_LEN,))
    x = Embedding(*embedding_matrix.shape, weights=[embedding_matrix],
trainable=False)(words)
    x = SpatialDropout1D(0.3)(x)
    x = Bidirectional(CuDNNLSTM(LSTM_UNITS, return_sequences=True))(x)
    x = Bidirectional(CuDNNLSTM(LSTM_UNITS, return_sequences=True))(x)

    hidden = concatenate([GlobalMaxPooling1D()(x),GlobalAveragePooling1D()
(x),])
    hidden = add([hidden, Dense(DENSE_HIDDEN_UNITS, activation='relu')
(hidden)])
    hidden = add([hidden, Dense(DENSE_HIDDEN_UNITS, activation='relu')
(hidden)])
    result = Dense(1, activation='sigmoid')(hidden)
```

```
    aux_result = Dense(num_aux_targets, activation='sigmoid')(hidden)


    model = Model(inputs=words, outputs=[result, aux_result])
    model.compile(loss=[custom_loss,'binary_crossentropy'], loss_
weights=[loss_weight, 1.0], optimizer='adam')


    return model
```

In the fourth step, we run the training, prepare the submission, and submit. To reduce the memory used during runtime, we are using temporary storage and performing garbage collection after deleting non-used allocated data. We run the model twice for a specified number of NUM_EPOCHS (representing one complete pass of training data through the algorithm) and then average the test predictions using variable weights. Then we submit the predictions:

```
def run_model(X_train, y_train, y_aux_train, embedding_matrix, word_index,
loss_weight):
    '''
        Run model
    '''
    logger.info('Run model')

    checkpoint_predictions = []
    weights = []
    for model_idx in range(NUM_MODELS):
        model = build_model(embedding_matrix, y_aux_train.shape[-1], loss_
weight)
        for global_epoch in range(NUM_EPOCHS):
            model.fit(
                X_train, [y_train, y_aux_train],
                batch_size=BATCH_SIZE, epochs=1, verbose=1,
                callbacks=[LearningRateScheduler(lambda epoch: 1.1e-3 *
(0.55 ** global_epoch))]
            )
            with open('temporary.pickle', mode='rb') as f:
                X_test = pickle.load(f) # use temporary file to reduce
memory
            checkpoint_predictions.append(model.predict(X_test, batch_
size=1024)[0].flatten())
            del X_test
```

```
            gc.collect()
            weights.append(2 ** global_epoch)
        del model
        gc.collect()

    preds = np.average(checkpoint_predictions, weights=weights, axis=0)
    return preds

def submit(sub_preds):
    logger.info('Prepare submission')
    submission = pd.read_csv(os.path.join(JIGSAW_PATH,'sample_submission.
csv'), index_col='id')
    submission['prediction'] = sub_preds
    submission.reset_index(drop=False, inplace=True)
    submission.to_csv('submission.csv', index=False)
```

With this solution (for the full code, see *Reference 16*), we can obtain, via a late submission, a core of 0.9328 and, consequently, a ranking in the upper half of the private leaderboard. Next, we will show how, by using a Transformer-based solution, we can obtain a higher score, in the upper silver medal or even gold medal zone for this competition.

Transformer-based solution

At the time of the competition, BERT and some other Transformer models were already available and a few solutions with high scores were provided. Here, we will not attempt to replicate them but we will just point out the most accessible implementations.

In *Reference 20*, Qishen Ha combines a few solutions, including BERT-Small V2, BERT-Large V2, XLNet, and GPT-2 (fine-tuned models using competition data included as datasets) to obtain a 0.94656 private leaderboard score (late submission), which would put you in the top 10 (both gold medal and prize area for this competition).

A solution with only the BERT-Small model (see *Reference 21*) will yield a private leaderboard score of 0.94295. Using the BERT-Large model (see *Reference 22*) will result in a private leaderboard score of 0.94388. Both these solutions will be in the silver medal zone (around places 130 and 80, respectively, in the private leaderboard, as late submissions).

Summary

In this chapter, we learned how to work with text data, using various approaches to explore this type of data. We started by analyzing our target and text data, preprocessing text data to include it in a machine learning model. We also explored various NLP tools and techniques, including topic modeling, NER, and POS tagging, and then prepared the text to build a baseline model, passing through an iterative process to gradually improve the data quality for the objective set (in this case, the objective being to improve the coverage of word embeddings for the vocabulary in the corpus of text from the competition dataset).

We introduced and discussed a baseline model (based on the work of several Kaggle contributors). This baseline model architecture includes a word embedding layer and bidirectional LSTM layers. Finally, we looked at some of the most advanced solutions available, based on Transformer architectures, either as single models or combined, to get a late submission with a score in the upper part of the leaderboard (silver and gold zones).

In the next chapter, we will start working with signal data. We will introduce data formats specific to various signal modalities (sound, image, video, experimental, or sensor data). We will analyze the data from the *LANL Earthquake Prediction* Kaggle competition.

References

1. Jigsaw Unintended Bias in Toxicity Classification, Kaggle competition dataset: `https://www.kaggle.com/c/jigsaw-unintended-bias-in-toxicity-classification/`

2. Aja Bogdanoff, Saying goodbye to Civil Comments, Medium: `https://medium.com/@aja_15265/saying-goodbye-to-civil-comments-41859d3a2b1d`

3. Gabriel Preda, Jigsaw Comments Text Exploration: `https://github.com/PacktPublishing/Developing-Kaggle-Notebooks/blob/develop/Chapter-07/jigsaw-comments-text-exploration.ipynb`

4. Gabriel Preda, Jigsaw Simple Baseline: `https://github.com/PacktPublishing/Developing-Kaggle-Notebooks/blob/develop/Chapter-07/jigsaw-simple-baseline.ipynb`

5. Susan Li, Topic Modeling and Latent Dirichlet Allocation (LDA) in Python: `https://towardsdatascience.com/topic-modeling-and-latent-dirichlet-allocation-in-python-9bf156893c24`

6. Aneesha Bakharia, Improving the Interpretation of Topic Models: `https://towardsdatascience.com/improving-the-interpretation-of-topic-models-87fd2ee3847d`

7. Carson Sievert, Kenneth Shirley, LDAvis: A method for visualizing and interpreting topics: `https://www.aclweb.org/anthology/W14-3110`

8. Lucia Dosin, Experiments on Topic Modeling – PyLDAvis: `https://www.objectorientedsubject.net/2018/08/experiments-on-topic-modeling-pyldavis/`

9. Renato Aranha, Topic Modelling (LDA) on Elon Tweets: `https://www.kaggle.com/errearanhas/topic-modelling-lda-on-elon-tweets`

10. Latent Dirichlet Allocation, Wikipedia: `https://en.wikipedia.org/wiki/Latent_Dirichlet_allocation`

11. Leonie Monigatti, Visualizing Part-of-Speech Tags with NLTK and SpaCy: `https://towardsdatascience.com/visualizing-part-of-speech-tags-with-nltk-and-spacy-42056fcd777e`

12. Ane, Quora preprocessing + model: `https://www.kaggle.com/anebzt/quora-preprocessing-model`

13. Christof Henkel (Dieter), How to: Preprocessing when using embeddings: `https://www.kaggle.com/christofhenkel/how-to-preprocessing-when-using-embeddings`

14. Ashish Vaswani, Noam Shazeer, Niki Parmar, Jakob Uszkoreit, Llion Jones, Aidan N. Gomez, Lukasz Kaiser, Illia Polosukhin, Attention Is All You Need: `https://arxiv.org/abs/1706.03762`

15. Christof Henkel (Dieter), keras baseline lstm + attention 5-fold: `https://www.kaggle.com/christofhenkel/keras-baseline-lstm-attention-5-fold`

16. Andrew Lukyanenko, CNN in keras on folds: `https://www.kaggle.com/code/artgor/cnn-in-keras-on-folds`

17. Thousandvoices, Simple LSTM: `https://www.kaggle.com/code/thousandvoices/simple-lstm/s`

18. Tanrei, Simple LSTM using Identity Parameters Solution: `https://www.kaggle.com/code/tanreinama/simple-lstm-using-identity-parameters-solution`

19. Gabriel Preda, Jigsaw Simple Baseline: `https://www.kaggle.com/code/gpreda/jigsaw-simple-baseline`

20. Qishen Ha, Jigsaw_predict: `https://www.kaggle.com/code/haqishen/jigsaw-predict/`

21. Gabriel Preda, Jigsaw_predict_BERT_small: `https://www.kaggle.com/code/gpreda/jigsaw-predict-bert-small`

22. Gabriel Preda, Jigsaw_predict_BERT_large: `https://www.kaggle.com/code/gpreda/jigsaw-predict-bert-large`

Join our book's Discord space

Join our Discord community to meet like-minded people and learn alongside more than 5000 members at:

https://packt.link/kaggle

8

Analyzing Acoustic Signals to Predict the Next Simulated Earthquake

In the previous chapters, we explored basic table-formatted data, covering categories like categorical, ordinal, and numerical data, as well as text, geographical coordinates, and imagery. The current chapter shifts our focus to a different data category, specifically, simulated or experimental signal data. This data type often appears in a range of formats beyond the standard CSV file format.

Our primary case study will be data from the *LANL Earthquake Prediction* Kaggle competition (see *Reference 1*). I contributed to this competition with a widely recognized and frequently forked notebook titled *LANL Earthquake EDA and Prediction* (see *Reference 2*), which will serve as the foundational resource for this chapter's principal notebook. We'll then delve into feature engineering, employing a variety of signal analysis techniques vital for developing a predictive model for the competition. Our goal will be to construct an initial model that predicts the competition's target variable: the time until failure, which is the remaining time before the next simulated lab earthquake.

The research in the domain of earthquake prediction has shown that before earthquakes, the movement of the tectonic plates generates signals in a low-frequency acoustic spectrum. By studying these signals, researchers try to understand the relationship between the signal's profile and the moment when the failure (that is, the earthquake) occurs. In a laboratory, the sliding and shearing of tectonic plates are simulated. This competition uses the laboratory measurement data, including the acoustic signals, as well as the time when failures occur.

To sum up, this chapter will cover the following topics:

- Data formats used for various signal data
- Exploration of the *LANL Earthquake Prediction* Kaggle competition data
- Feature engineering
- Training the model for the competition *LANL Earthquake Prediction*

Introducing the LANL Earthquake Prediction competition

The *LANL Earthquake Prediction* competition centers on utilizing seismic signals to determine the precise timing of a laboratory-induced earthquake. Currently, predicting natural earthquakes remains beyond the reach of our scientific knowledge and technological capabilities. The ideal scenario for scientists is to predict the timing, location, and magnitude of such an event.

Simulated earthquakes, however, created in highly controlled artificial environments, mimic real-world seismic activities. These simulations enable attempts to forecast lab-generated quakes using the same types of signals observed in natural settings. In this competition, participants use an acoustic data input signal to estimate the time until the next artificial earthquake occurs, as detailed in *Reference 3*. The challenge is to predict the timing of the earthquake, addressing one of the three critical unknowns in earthquake forecasting: when it will happen, where it will occur, and how powerful it will be.

The training data is a single file with two columns: acoustic signal amplitude and time to failure. The test data consists of multiple files (2,526 in total) with acoustic signal amplitude segments for which we will have to predict the time to failure. A sample submission file has one column with the segment ID, seg_id, and the value to predict: time_to_failure.

The competitors are tasked with training their models with the acoustic signal and time-to-failure data in the training file and predicting the time-to-failure for each segment from each file in the test folder. This competition data is in a very convenient format, that is, **comma-separated values (CSV)** format, but this is not a requirement. Other competitions or datasets on Kaggle with signal data use different, less common formats. Because this chapter is about analyzing signal data, this is the right place to review this format. Let's first look into some of these formats.

Formats for signal data

Several competitions on Kaggle used sound data as an addition to regular tabular features. There were three competitions organized by Cornell Lab of Ornithology's BirdCLEF (LifeCLEF Bird Recognition Challenge) in 2021, 2022, and 2023 for predicting a bird species from samples of bird songs (see *Reference 4* for an example of one of these competitions). The format used in these competitions was .ogg. The .ogg format is used to store audio data with less bandwidth. It is considered technically superior to the .mp3 format.

We can read these types of file formats using the librosa library (see *Reference 5*). The following code can be used to load an .ogg file and display the sound wave:

```python
import matplotlib.pyplot as plt
import librosa


def display_sound_wave(sound_path=None,
                text="Test",
                color="green"):
    """
    Display a sound wave
    Args
        sound_path: path to the sound file
        text: text to display
        color: color for text to display
    Returns
        None
    """

    if not sound_path:
        return
    y_sound, sr_sound = librosa.load(sound_path)
    audio_sound, _ = librosa.effects.trim(y_sound)
    fig, ax = plt.subplots(1, figsize = (16, 3))
    fig.suptitle(f'Sound Wave: {text}', fontsize=12)
    librosa.display.waveshow(y = audio_sound, sr = sr_sound, color =
color)
```

The library librosa, when loading the audio sound, will return values as a time series with floating-point values (see *Reference 6*). It isn't just the .ogg format that is supported; it will work with any code supported by soundfile or Audioread. The default sampling rate is 22050 but this can be also set upon load, using the parameter *sr*. Other parameters that can be used when loading an audio wave are the offset and the duration (both given in seconds – together, they allow you to select the time interval of the sound wave you will load).

In an earlier version of the BirdCLEF competition, *Cornell Birdcall Identification* (see *Reference 7*), audio sounds in the dataset were given in .mp3 format. For this format, we can use librosa to load, transform, or visualize the sound waves. **Waveform Audio File** format (or **WAV**), another frequently used format, can also be loaded using librosa.

For .wav format, we can alternatively use the scipy.io module wavfile to load data. The following code will load and display a file in .wav format. In this case, the amplitude is not scaled down to a -1:1 interval (the maximum value is 32K):

```python
import matplotlib.pyplot as plt
from scipy.io import wavfile


def display_wavefile(sound_path=None,
                text="Test",
                color="green"):
    """
    Display a sound wave - load using wavefile
    sr: sample rate
    y_sound: sound samples
    Args
        sound_path: path to the sound file
        text: text to display
        color: color for text to display
    Returns
        None
    """
    if not sound_path:
        return
    sr_sound, y_sound = wavfile.load(sound_path)
    fig, ax = plt.subplots(1, figsize = (16, 3))
    fig.suptitle(f'Sound Wave: {text}', fontsize=12)
    ax.plot(np.linspace(0, sr_sound/len(y_sound), sr_sound), y_sound)
```

Signal, not specifically audio signal, data can also be stored in .npy or .npz format, which are both numpy formats to store array data. These formats can be loaded using numpy functions, as you can see in the following code snippets. For npy format, this will load a multi-column array:

```python
import numpy as np
f = np.load('data_path/file.npy', allow_pickle=True)
columns_, data_  = f
data_df = pd.DataFrame(data_, columns = columns_)
```

For .npz format, the following code will load a similar structure, previously compressed (one file only):

```python
import numpy as np
f = np.load('data_path/file.npz', allow_pickle=True)
columns_, data_ = f['arr_0']
data_df = pd.DataFrame(data_, columns = columns_)
```

For data stored in .rds format, an R-specific format for saving data, we can load the data using the following code:

```python
!pip install pyreadr
import pyreadr
f = pyreadr.read_r('data_path/file.rds')
data_df = f[None]
```

To store multi-dimensional array data, **NetCDF-4** format (**Network Common Data Form, version 4**) is used. In *Reference 8*, we have an example of such multi-dimensional signal data, from Earthdata NASA satellite measurements, from the dataset EarthData MERRA2 CO. The following code snippet reads a subset of measurements for CO, focusing on the COCL dimension (Column Burden kg m-2), and includes values for latitude, longitude, and time:

```python
from netCDF4 import Dataset

data = Dataset(file_path, more="r")
lons = data.variables['lon'][:]
lats = data.variables['lat'][:]
time = data.variables['time'][:]
COCL = data.variables['COCL'][:,:,:]; COCL = COCL[0,:,:]
```

For more details, you can consult *Reference 9*. For now, let's get back to our competition data, which is in CSV format, although it represents an audio signal (sound waves), as we already clarified.

Exploring our competition data

The `LANL Earthquake Prediction` dataset consists of the following data:

- A `train.csv` file, with two columns only:

    - `acoustic_data`: This is the amplitude of the acoustic signal.

    - `time_to_failure`: This is the time to failure corresponding to the current data segment.

- A test folder with 2,624 files with small segments of acoustic data.

- A `sample_submission.csv` file; for each test file, those competing will need to give an estimate for time to failure.

The training data (9.56 GB) contains 692 million rows. The actual time constant for the samples in the training data results from the continuous variation of `time_to_failure` values. The acoustic data is integer values, from -5,515 to 5,444, with an average of 4.52 and a standard deviation of 10.7 (values oscillating around 0). The `time_to_failure` values are real numbers, ranging from 0 to 16, with a mean of 5.68 and a standard deviation of 3.67. To reduce the memory footprint for the training data, we read the data with a reduced dimension for both acoustic data and time_to_failure:

```
%%time
train_df = pd.read_csv(os.path.join(PATH,'train.csv'), dtype={'acoustic_
data': np.int16, 'time_to_failure': np.float32})
```

Let's check the first values in the `training data`. We will not use all the `time_to_failure` data (only values associated with the end-of-time interval for which we will aggregate interval acoustic data); therefore, rounding in order to reduce the size of the time to failure from double to float is not important here:

	acoustic_data	time_to_failure
0	12	1.469099998474121
1	6	1.469099998474121
2	8	1.469099998474121
3	5	1.469099998474121
4	8	1.469099998474121
5	8	1.469099998474121
6	9	1.469099998474121
7	7	1.469099998474121
8	-5	1.469099998474121
9	3	1.469099998474121

Figure 8.1. First rows of data in the training data

Let's visualize, on the same graph, the acoustic signal values and the time to failure. We will use a subsampling rate of 1/100 (sample each 100th row) to represent the full training data (see *Figure 8.2*). We will use the following code to represent these graphs:

```
def plot_acc_ttf_data(idx, train_ad_sample_df, train_ttf_sample_df,
title="Acoustic data and time to failure: 1% sampled data"):
    """
    Plot acoustic data and time to failure
    Args:
        train_ad_sample_df: train acoustic data sample
        train_ttf_sample_df: train time to failure data sample
        title: title of the plot
    Returns:
        None
    """

    fig, ax1 = plt.subplots(figsize=(12, 8))
    plt.title(title)
    plt.plot(idx, train_ad_sample_df, color='r')
    ax1.set_ylabel('acoustic data', color='r')
    plt.legend(['acoustic data'], loc=(0.01, 0.95))
    ax2 = ax1.twinx()
    plt.plot(idx, train_ttf_sample_df, color='b')
    ax2.set_ylabel('time to failure', color='b')
    plt.legend(['time to failure'], loc=(0.01, 0.9))
    plt.grid(True)
```

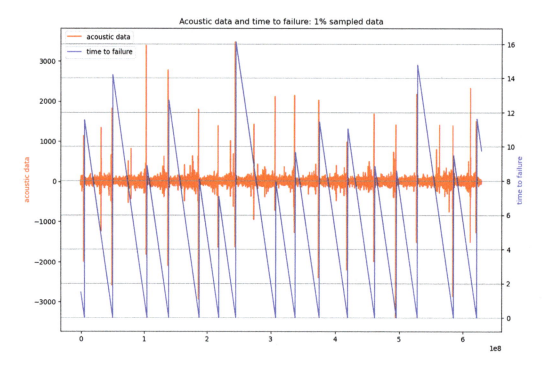

Figure 8.2. Acoustic signal data and time to failure data over an entire training set, subsampled at 1/100

Let's zoom into the first part of the time interval. We will show the first 1% of the data (no subsampling). In *Figure 8.3*, we are showing, on the same graph, the acoustic signal and time to failure for the first 6.29 million rows of data. We can observe that before the failure (but not very close in time), there is a large oscillation, with both negative and positive peaks. This oscillation is also preceded by a few smaller ones, at irregular time intervals.

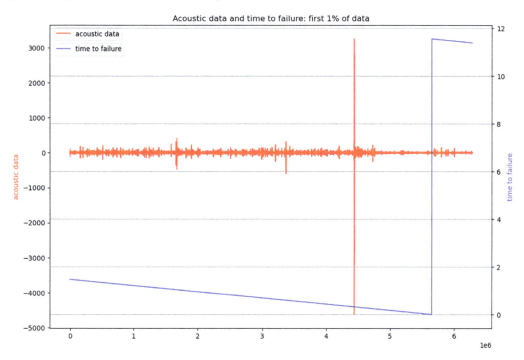

Figure 8.3: Acoustic signal data and time to failure data for the first 1% of the data

Let's also look at the next 1% of the training data (without subsampling). In *Figure 8.4*, we show this time series for acoustic signal values and time to failure. There is no failure during this time interval. We observe many irregular small oscillations, with both negative and positive peaks.

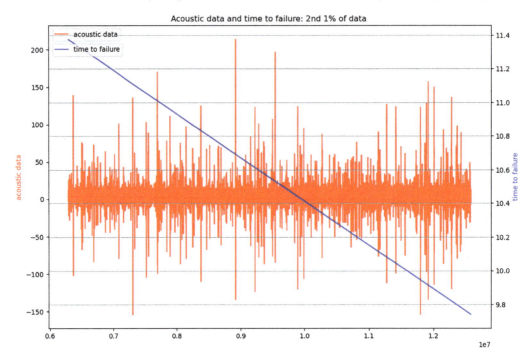

Figure 8.4: Acoustic signal data and time to failure for the second 1% of the data in the training set

Let's also look at the last few percentages of the data (last 5% of time) in the training set. In *Figure 8.5*, we observe the same pattern of several larger oscillations superposed on smaller irregular oscillations, and with a major oscillation just before the failure:

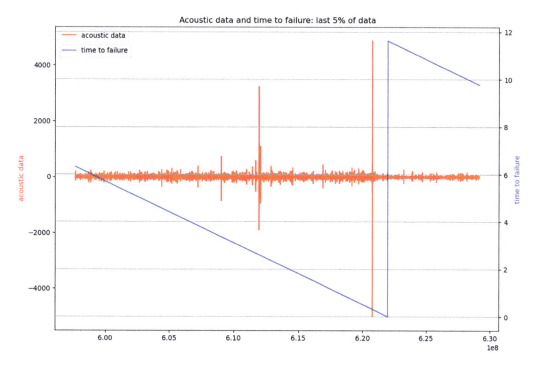

Figure 8.5: Acoustic signal data and time to failure for the last 5% of the data in the training set

Let's now also look at a few examples of variations of the acoustic signal in the test data samples. There are 2,624 data segment files in the test data. We will select a few of them to visualize. We will use a modified visualization function since in the test data, we only have the acoustic signals:

```python
def plot_acc_data(test_sample_df, segment_name):
    """
    Plot acoustic data for a train segment
    Args:
        test_sample_df: test acoustic data sample
        segment_name: title of the plot
    Returns:
        None
    """
    fig, ax1 = plt.subplots(figsize=(12, 8))
    plt.title(f"Test segment: {segment_name}")
    plt.plot(test_sample_df, color='r')
    ax1.set_ylabel('acoustic data', color='r')
    plt.legend([f"acoustic data: {segment_name}"], loc=(0.01, 0.95))
    plt.grid(True)
```

In *Figure 8.6*, we are showing the acoustic signal graph for the segment **seg_00030f**:

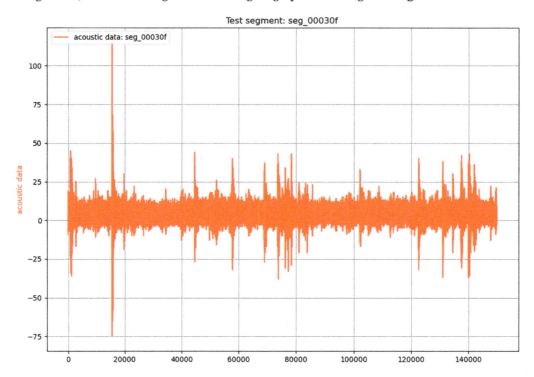

Figure 8.6: Acoustic signal data for test segment seg_00030f

In the next figure, we are showing the acoustic signal graph for segment **seg_0012b5**:

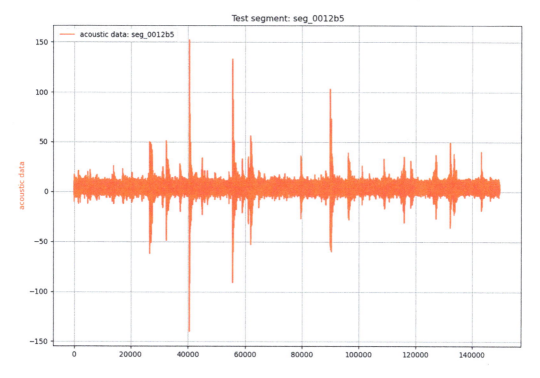

Figure 8.7: Acoustic signal data for test segment seg_0012b5

In the notebooks associated with this chapter, you can see more examples of such test acoustic signals. The test segments show quite a large variety of signal profiles, depicting the same sequence of small oscillations with intercalated peaks with variable amplitude, similar to what we can see in the `training` data subsampled earlier.

Solution approach

The task in the competition is to accurately forecast a singular `time_to_failure` value for each segment in the test dataset. Each segment of the test set comprises 150,000 data rows. In contrast, the `training` dataset is vast, encompassing 692 million rows, with one column dedicated to our target variable: the time until failure. We plan to divide the training data into uniform segments, each containing 150,000 rows, and use the final time-to-failure value from each segment as the target variable for that segment. This approach is designed to align the training data with the format of the test data, facilitating more effective model training.

Additionally, we will engineer new features by aggregating values across both the training and test datasets, resulting in a single row that encapsulates multiple features for each data segment. The subsequent section will delve into the signal processing techniques employed for feature generation.

Feature engineering

We will use several libraries specific to signal processing to generate most of the features. From SciPy (Python scientific library), we are using a few functions from the `signal` module. The Hann function returns a Hann window, which modifies the signal to smooth the values at the end of the sampled signal to 0 (uses a cosine "bell" function). The Hilbert function computes the analytic signal, using the `Hilbert` transform. The Hilbert transform is a mathematical technique used in signal processing, with a property that shifts the phase of the original signal by 90 degrees.

Other library functions used are from `numpy`: Fast Fourier Transform (FFT), `mean`, `min`, `max`, `std` (standard deviation), `abs` (absolute value), `diff` (the difference between two successive values in the signal), and `quantile` (where a sample is divided into equal-sized, adjacent groups). We are also using a few statistical functions that are available from `pandas`: `mad` (median absolute deviation), `kurtosis`, `skew`, and `median`. We are implementing functions to calculate trend features and classic STA/LTA. Classic STA/LTA represents the ratio between the amplitude of the signal of a short time window of length STA and a long time window, LTA. Let's dive in!

Trend feature and classic STA/LTA

We start by defining two functions, for the calculation of a trend feature and classic **Short-Term Average/Long-Term Average (STA/LTA)**. STA/LTA is a seismic signal analysis technique used in seismology. It measures the ratio of short-term to long-term signal averages. It is useful in earthquake detection as it identifies distinct patterns in seismic data. Therefore, it will also be a useful feature to include in our model.

We show here the code to calculate the trend feature. This is calculated using a linear regression model (for 1D data) and retrieves the slope of the resulting regression line. We use the option to transform all the sampled data into positive values before performing regression (that is, calculating the slope/trend for the absolute values of the data). The trend data contains important information about the overall signal:

```
def add_trend_feature(arr, abs_values=False):
    """

    Calculate trend features
```

```
    Uses a linear regression algorithm to extract the trend
    from the list of values in the array (arr)
    Args:
        arr: array of values
        abs_values: flag if to use abs values, default is False

    Returns:
        trend feature
    """
    idx = np.array(range(len(arr)))
    if abs_values:
        arr = np.abs(arr)
    lr = LinearRegression()
    lr.fit(idx.reshape(-1, 1), arr)
    return lr.coef_[0]
```

Next, we calculate the classic STA/LTA, which represents the ratio between the amplitude of the signal of a short time window of length STA and a long time window, LTA. The function receives as parameters the signal and the length for the short-time average and long-time average windows:

```
def classic_sta_lta(x, length_sta, length_lta):
    """
    Calculate classic STA/LTA
    STA/LTA represents the ratio between amplitude of the
    signal on a short time window of length LTA and on a
    long time window LTA
    Args:
        length_sta: length of short time average window
        length_lta: length of long time average window
    Returns:
        STA/LTA
    """
    sta = np.cumsum(x ** 2)
    # Convert to float
    sta = np.require(sta, dtype=np.float)
    # Copy for LTA
    lta = sta.copy()
    # Compute the STA and the LTA
```

```
sta[length_sta:] = sta[length_sta:] - sta[:-length_sta]
sta /= length_sta
lta[length_lta:] = lta[length_lta:] - lta[:-length_lta]
lta /= length_lta
# Pad zeros
sta[:length_lta - 1] = 0
# Avoid division by zero by setting zero values to tiny float
dtiny = np.finfo(0.0).tiny
idx = lta < dtiny
lta[idx] = dtiny
return sta / lta
```

Next, we implement the function to calculate features, which receives as parameters the sample index, the data subsample, and a handle to the transformed training data. This function will use various signal processing algorithms to build aggregated features from the time variation acoustic signal per segment. In the case of the training data, we use windows of 150K rows from the training set (without stride). In the case of the test set, each test file represents a segment of 150K. In the following subsections, we will review the engineered features that will be included in the model.

FFT-derived features

One of the features of the model is the **Fast Fourier Transform** (**FFT**) applied to the entire segment; this is not directly used as a feature but as a basis for the calculation of multiple aggregation functions (see next subsection). The FFT is calculated using a fast implementation of the discrete Fourier transform.

We are using numpy implementations for **FFT** for one-dimensional arrays (`fft.fft`), which is extremely fast, numpy being based on **BLAS** (**Basic Linear Algebra Subprograms**) and **Lapack** (**Linear Algebra PACkage**), two libraries that provide routines for performing basic vector and matrix operations and solving linear algebra equations. The output of the function used here is a one-dimensional array of complex values. Then, we extract the vectors of real and imaginary parts from the array of complex values, and we calculate the following features:

- Extract real and imaginary parts of the FFT; this is the first part of further processing the Fourier fast transform of the acoustic signal.
- Calculate the mean, standard deviation, min, and max for both the real and imaginary parts of the FFT. From the previous transformation, which separates the real and imaginary parts of the FFT, we then calculate these aggregate functions.

- Calculate the mean, standard deviation, min and max for both the real and imaginary parts of the FFT for 5K and 15K data points from the end of the FFT vector.

The code to create the file segment as well as the FFT and FFT-derived features is given here. First, we calculate the FFT for the subset of the acoustic data. Then, we calculate the real and imaginary parts of the FFT. From the real FFT component, we calculate, using pandas' aggregated functions, the mean, standard deviation, max, and min values. We then calculate similar values from the imaginary part of the FFT signal:

```python
def create_features(seg_id, seg, X):
    """
    Create features
    Args:
        seg_id: the id of current data segment to process
        seg: the current selected segment data
        X: transformed train data
    Returns:
        None
    """
    xc = pd.Series(seg['acoustic_data'].values)
    zc = np.fft.fft(xc)


    #FFT transform values
    realFFT = np.real(zc)
    imagFFT = np.imag(zc)
    X.loc[seg_id, 'Rmean'] = realFFT.mean()
    X.loc[seg_id, 'Rstd']  = realFFT.std()
    X.loc[seg_id, 'Rmax']  = realFFT.max()
    X.loc[seg_id, 'Rmin']  = realFFT.min()
    X.loc[seg_id, 'Imean'] = imagFFT.mean()
    X.loc[seg_id, 'Istd']  = imagFFT.std()
    X.loc[seg_id, 'Imax']  = imagFFT.max()
    X.loc[seg_id, 'Imin']  = imagFFT.min()

    X.loc[seg_id, 'Rmean_last_5000']  = realFFT[-5000:].mean()
    X.loc[seg_id, 'Rstd__last_5000']  = realFFT[-5000:].std()
    X.loc[seg_id, 'Rmax_last_5000']   = realFFT[-5000:].max()
```

```
    X.loc[seg_id, 'Rmin_last_5000']   = realFFT[-5000:].min()
    X.loc[seg_id, 'Rmean_last_15000'] = realFFT[-15000:].mean()
    X.loc[seg_id, 'Rstd_last_15000']  = realFFT[-15000:].std()
    X.loc[seg_id, 'Rmax_last_15000']  = realFFT[-15000:].max()
    X.loc[seg_id, 'Rmin_last_15000']  = realFFT[-15000:].min()
```

We then follow with calculating features derived from various aggregated functions.

Features derived from aggregate functions

The mean, standard deviation, max, and min applied to the entire segment are calculated with the following code, using pandas' aggregate functions mean, std, max, and min:

```
    xc = pd.Series(seg['acoustic_data'].values)
    zc = np.fft.fft(xc)

    X.loc[seg_id, 'mean'] = xc.mean()
    X.loc[seg_id, 'std'] = xc.std()
    X.loc[seg_id, 'max'] = xc.max()
    X.loc[seg_id, 'min'] = xc.min()
```

We continue to compute additional aggregated features. For our model, we will include various signal processing techniques, as you'll notice, and then, by measuring the feature importance after we train our baseline model, we will qualify which features contribute more to our model prediction.

Moving on, we calculate the mean change for the entire segment; here, "segment" refers to the original subset of acoustic data. change is calculated with the numpy function diff and the parameter 1. This function receives an array of values and calculates the difference between each successive value in the array. Then we calculate the average of the values in the array of differences. We also calculate the mean change rate for the entire acoustic data segment. This is calculated as the average of non-zero values in the new change vector divided by the original values in the data segment. The code for these features is as follows:

```
    X.loc[seg_id, 'mean_change_abs'] = np.mean(np.diff(xc))
    X.loc[seg_id, 'mean_change_rate'] = np.mean(nonzero(np.diff(xc) /
xc[:-1])[0])
```

Additionally, we also calculate the maximum and minimum of the absolute values (per entire segment). After calculating the absolute values, we calculate the minimum and maximum values.

We are trying to include a diverse range of features, to capture as much of the signal patterns as possible, when we aggregate the temporal signal. The code for this is:

```
X.loc[seg_id, 'abs_max'] = np.abs(xc).max()
X.loc[seg_id, 'abs_min'] = np.abs(xc).min()
```

A set of aggregated functions on the first and last 10K and 50K values per acoustic data segment can also be calculated, as follows:

- Standard deviation for first 50K and last 10K values per acoustic data segment
- Average value for first 50K and last 10K values per acoustic data segment
- Minimum values for first 50K and last 10K values per acoustic data segment
- Maximum values for first 50K and last 10K values per acoustic data segment

These features are aggregating a smaller part of the signal and therefore will capture signal characteristics from only a smaller interval before the failure. The combination of aggregated features on the whole signal length and on a smaller part of the signal will add more information about the signal. The code for these features will be:

```
X.loc[seg_id, 'std_first_50000'] = xc[:50000].std()
X.loc[seg_id, 'std_last_50000'] = xc[-50000:].std()
X.loc[seg_id, 'std_first_10000'] = xc[:10000].std()
X.loc[seg_id, 'std_last_10000'] = xc[-10000:].std()

X.loc[seg_id, 'avg_first_50000'] = xc[:50000].mean()
X.loc[seg_id, 'avg_last_50000'] = xc[-50000:].mean()
X.loc[seg_id, 'avg_first_10000'] = xc[:10000].mean()
X.loc[seg_id, 'avg_last_10000'] = xc[-10000:].mean()

X.loc[seg_id, 'min_first_50000'] = xc[:50000].min()
X.loc[seg_id, 'min_last_50000'] = xc[-50000:].min()
X.loc[seg_id, 'min_first_10000'] = xc[:10000].min()
X.loc[seg_id, 'min_last_10000'] = xc[-10000:].min()

X.loc[seg_id, 'max_first_50000'] = xc[:50000].max()
X.loc[seg_id, 'max_last_50000'] = xc[-50000:].max()
X.loc[seg_id, 'max_first_10000'] = xc[:10000].max()
X.loc[seg_id, 'max_last_10000'] = xc[-10000:].max()
```

Next, we include the ratio of maximum to minimum values for the entire acoustic data segment and the difference between the maximum and minimum values for the entire acoustic data segment. We also add the number of values exceeding a certain amplitude of oscillation (above 500 units) and the sum of values per entire segment. We try to capture some of the hidden patterns in the signal using this diversity of features we engineer. In particular, here, we include information from the extreme oscillations in the signal:

```
X.loc[seg_id, 'max_to_min'] = xc.max() / np.abs(xc.min())
X.loc[seg_id, 'max_to_min_diff'] = xc.max() - np.abs(xc.min())
X.loc[seg_id, 'count_big'] = len(xc[np.abs(xc) > 500])
X.loc[seg_id, 'sum'] = xc.sum()
```

We continue to add diverse aggregated features that try to capture various characteristics of the original signal. We further calculate the mean change rate (excluding nulls) for the first 10K and last 50K data points per acoustic data segment:

```
X.loc[seg_id, 'mean_change_rate_first_50000'] = np.mean(nonzero((np.
diff(xc[:50000]) / xc[:50000][:-1]))[0])
X.loc[seg_id, 'mean_change_rate_last_50000'] = np.mean(nonzero((np.
diff(xc[-50000:]) / xc[-50000:][:-1]))[0])
X.loc[seg_id, 'mean_change_rate_first_10000'] = np.mean(nonzero((np.
diff(xc[:10000]) / xc[:10000][:-1]))[0])
X.loc[seg_id, 'mean_change_rate_last_10000'] = np.mean(nonzero((np.
diff(xc[-10000:]) / xc[-10000:][:-1]))[0])
```

Some of the features we are adding will exclude the elements in the data that are 0, to ensure only non-zero values are included in the calculation of the aggregated function. The code for using the nonzero function is:

```
def nonzero(x):
    """
    Utility function to simplify call of numpy `nonzero` function
    """
    return np.nonzero(np.atleast_1d(x))
```

A set of engineered features involves quantiles, specifically the 01%, 05%, 95%, and 99% quantile values, for the entire acoustic data segment. The quantiles are calculated using the numpy `quantile` function. A quantile is a statistical term that refers to dividing a dataset into intervals of equal probability. For example, a 75% quantile value is the point where 75% of the data has values less than that number. A 50% quantile is the point where 50% of the data has values less than that number (and is also called the median). We also add absolute values for the 01%, 05%, 95%, and 99% quantile values. See the following code for the calculation of these features:

```
X.loc[seg_id, 'q95'] = np.quantile(xc, 0.95)
X.loc[seg_id, 'q99'] = np.quantile(xc, 0.99)
X.loc[seg_id, 'q05'] = np.quantile(xc, 0.05)
X.loc[seg_id, 'q01'] = np.quantile(xc, 0.01)


X.loc[seg_id, 'abs_q95'] = np.quantile(np.abs(xc), 0.95)
X.loc[seg_id, 'abs_q99'] = np.quantile(np.abs(xc), 0.99)
X.loc[seg_id, 'abs_q05'] = np.quantile(np.abs(xc), 0.05)
X.loc[seg_id, 'abs_q01'] = np.quantile (np.abs(xc), 0.01)
```

Another type of engineered feature introduced is trend values (calculated with the `add_trend_values` function with the absolute flag off). Trend values will capture the general direction in which the acoustic data signal is changing. For a signal that shows an oscillation around 0 with high frequency, the trend will capture the change in the average value of the actual signal.

We also add absolute trend values (calculated with the `add_trend_values` function with the absolute flag on). We include this type of engineering feature to capture patterns in the signal that appear in the absolute value of the signal. In this case, for the calculation of the trend, we use the absolute values of the original signal. Therefore, this trend will capture the direction of variation of the absolute value of the signal. The corresponding code is given here:

```
X.loc[seg_id, 'trend'] = add_trend_feature(xc)
X.loc[seg_id, 'abs_trend'] = add_trend_feature(xc, abs_values=True)
```

Next, we include the mean of absolute values and the standard deviation of absolute values. Median absolute deviation (`mad`), `Kurtosis`, `Skew` (skewness), and `Median` values are also calculated. These functions are calculated using a numpy implementation. The median absolute deviation is a robust measure of the variability of a univariate sample of quantitative data. Kurtosis is a measure of the combined weight of a distribution tail relative to the center of the distribution. Skew (from skewness) is a measure of the asymmetry or distortion of a symmetric distribution. The median is, as we've already observed, the value separating the higher half from the lower half of a set of data. All these aggregated functions capture complementary information about the signal. The code for the calculation of these aggregation functions is shown here:

```
X.loc[seg_id, 'abs_mean'] = np.abs(xc).mean()
X.loc[seg_id, 'abs_std'] = np.abs(xc).std()

X.loc[seg_id, 'mad'] = xc.mad()
X.loc[seg_id, 'kurt'] = xc.kurtosis()
X.loc[seg_id, 'skew'] = xc.skew()
X.loc[seg_id, 'med'] = xc.median()
```

Next, we include several features calculated by using transformation functions specific to signal processing.

Features derived using the Hilbert transform and Hann window

We also calculate the Hilbert mean. We apply the Hilbert transform of the acoustic signal segment using the `scipy.signal.hilbert` function. This calculates the analytic signal, using the Hilbert transform. Then, we calculate the mean of the absolute value of the transformed data. The Hilbert transform is used frequently in signal processing and captures important information about the signal. Because we use aggregation functions to generate features from our temporal data, we would like to include a large, diverse range of existing signal processing techniques, to add important complementary elements of the signal when training the model:

```
X.loc[seg_id, 'Hilbert_mean'] = np.abs(hilbert(xc)).mean()
```

Next, we include a feature derived from the Hann window mean value. We use this feature derived from the Hann window to reduce the abrupt discontinuities at the edge of the signal. The Hann window mean value is calculated using the convolution of the original signal with the result of the Hanning window and dividing by the sum of all values in the Hanning window:

```
X.loc[seg_id, 'Hann_window_mean'] = (convolve(xc, hann(150),
mode='same') / sum(hann(150))).mean()
```

We previously introduced the definition of classical STA/LTA. We calculate a few features like classical STA/LTA mean for 500-10K, 5K-100K, 3,333-6,666, and 10K-25K STA/LTA windows. These are calculated with the STA/LTA function introduced previously. We include a variety of transformations to try to capture diverse signal characteristics in the aggregated engineering features:

```python
X.loc[seg_id, 'Hilbert_mean'] = np.abs(hilbert(xc)).mean()
X.loc[seg_id, 'Hann_window_mean'] = (convolve(xc, hann(150),
mode='same') / sum(hann(150))).mean()
X.loc[seg_id, 'classic_sta_lta1_mean'] = classic_sta_lta(xc, 500,
10000).mean()
X.loc[seg_id, 'classic_sta_lta2_mean'] = classic_sta_lta(xc, 5000,
100000).mean()
X.loc[seg_id, 'classic_sta_lta3_mean'] = classic_sta_lta(xc, 3333,
6666).mean()
X.loc[seg_id, 'classic_sta_lta4_mean'] = classic_sta_lta(xc, 10000,
25000).mean()
```

Finally, we will also calculate features based on moving averages.

Features based on moving averages

Next, we calculate several moving averages, as follows:

- Moving average means for the 700, 1.5K, 3K, and 6K windows (and excluding NaNs)
- Exponentially weighted moving average with spans of 300, 3K, and 6K
- Average standard deviation moving average over 700 and 400 windows
- Moving averages means for 700-size window plus or minus 2 times average standard deviation moving average over the same size window

The moving averages help us to discern patterns, reduce noise, and provide a clear picture of the underlying trends in the data. The code for that will be:

```python
X.loc[seg_id, 'Moving_average_700_mean'] = xc.rolling(window=700).
mean().mean(skipna=True)
X.loc[seg_id, 'Moving_average_1500_mean'] = xc.rolling(window=1500).
mean().mean(skipna=True)
X.loc[seg_id, 'Moving_average_3000_mean'] = xc.rolling(window=3000).
mean().mean(skipna=True)
X.loc[seg_id, 'Moving_average_6000_mean'] = xc.rolling(window=6000).
mean().mean(skipna=True)
```

```python
    ewma = pd.Series.ewm
    X.loc[seg_id, 'exp_Moving_average_300_mean'] = (ewma(xc, span=300).
mean()).mean(skipna=True)
    X.loc[seg_id, 'exp_Moving_average_3000_mean'] = ewma(xc, span=3000).
mean().mean(skipna=True)
    X.loc[seg_id, 'exp_Moving_average_30000_mean'] = ewma(xc, span=6000).
mean().mean(skipna=True)
    no_of_std = 2
    X.loc[seg_id, 'MA_700MA_std_mean'] = xc.rolling(window=700).std().
mean()
    X.loc[seg_id,'MA_700MA_BB_high_mean'] = (X.loc[seg_id, 'Moving_
average_700_mean'] + no_of_std * X.loc[seg_id, 'MA_700MA_std_mean']).
mean()
    X.loc[seg_id,'MA_700MA_BB_low_mean'] = (X.loc[seg_id, 'Moving_
average_700_mean'] - no_of_std * X.loc[seg_id, 'MA_700MA_std_mean']).
mean()
    X.loc[seg_id, 'MA_400MA_std_mean'] = xc.rolling(window=400).std().
mean()
    X.loc[seg_id,'MA_400MA_BB_high_mean'] = (X.loc[seg_id, 'Moving_
average_700_mean'] + no_of_std * X.loc[seg_id, 'MA_400MA_std_mean']).
mean()
    X.loc[seg_id,'MA_400MA_BB_low_mean'] = (X.loc[seg_id, 'Moving_
average_700_mean'] - no_of_std * X.loc[seg_id, 'MA_400MA_std_mean']).
mean()
    X.loc[seg_id, 'MA_1000MA_std_mean'] = xc.rolling(window=1000).std().
mean()
```

We also calculate the **IQR**, the 001% and 999% quantiles. The **IQR** (meaning **interquartile range**) is calculated by subtracting the 25% percentile from the 75% percentile (using numpy functions). The interquartile range is the region where 50% of the data is found. The 001% and 999% quantiles are also calculated with the numpy function for quantiles. The IQR and the various other quantiles we have included are useful because they provide important information about the central tendency and the spread of the signal:

```python
    X.loc[seg_id, 'iqr'] = np.subtract(*np.percentile(xc, [75, 25]))
    X.loc[seg_id, 'q999'] = np.quantile(xc,0.999)
    X.loc[seg_id, 'q001'] = np.quantile(xc,0.001)
    X.loc[seg_id, 'ave10'] = stats.trim_mean(xc, 0.1)
```

For windows of 10, 100, and 1,000, we calculate the moving average and moving standard deviation. With these values, we then calculate the min, max, mean, standard deviation, average absolute and relative change, 01%, 05%, 95%, and 99% quantiles, and absolute max roll. We include these features because they reveal information about the local characteristics of the signal within the specified window. Subsequently, for the features derived from the moving average standard deviation calculated for windows of 10, 100, and 1,000, the code is as follows:

```
for windows in [10, 100, 1000]:
      x_roll_std = xc.rolling(windows).std().dropna().values

      X.loc[seg_id, 'ave_roll_std_' + str(windows)] = x_roll_std.mean()
      X.loc[seg_id, 'std_roll_std_' + str(windows)] = x_roll_std.std()
      X.loc[seg_id, 'max_roll_std_' + str(windows)] = x_roll_std.max()
      X.loc[seg_id, 'min_roll_std_' + str(windows)] = x_roll_std.min()
      X.loc[seg_id, 'q01_roll_std_' + str(windows)] = np.quantile(x_
roll_std, 0.01)
      X.loc[seg_id, 'q05_roll_std_' + str(windows)] = np.quantile(x_
roll_std, 0.05)
      X.loc[seg_id, 'q95_roll_std_' + str(windows)] = np.quantile(x_
roll_std, 0.95)
      X.loc[seg_id, 'q99_roll_std_' + str(windows)] = np.quantile(x_
roll_std, 0.99)
      X.loc[seg_id, 'av_change_abs_roll_std_' + str(windows)] =
np.mean(np.diff(x_roll_std))
      X.loc[seg_id, 'av_change_rate_roll_std_' + str(windows)] =
np.mean(nonzero((np.diff(x_roll_std) / x_roll_std[:-1]))[0])
      X.loc[seg_id, 'abs_max_roll_std_' + str(windows)] = np.abs(x_roll_
std).max()
```

For the features derived from the moving average mean, calculated for windows of 10, 100, and 1,000, the code is:

```
    for windows in [10, 100, 1000]:
        x_roll_mean = xc.rolling(windows).mean().dropna().values

        X.loc[seg_id, 'ave_roll_mean_' + str(windows)] = x_roll_mean.
mean()
        X.loc[seg_id, 'std_roll_mean_' + str(windows)] = x_roll_mean.std()
        X.loc[seg_id, 'max_roll_mean_' + str(windows)] = x_roll_mean.max()
```

```
        X.loc[seg_id, 'min_roll_mean_' + str(windows)] = x_roll_mean.min()
        X.loc[seg_id, 'q01_roll_mean_' + str(windows)] = np.quantile(x_
roll_mean, 0.01)
        X.loc[seg_id, 'q05_roll_mean_' + str(windows)] = np.quantile(x_
roll_mean, 0.05)
        X.loc[seg_id, 'q95_roll_mean_' + str(windows)] = np.quantile(x_
roll_mean, 0.95)
        X.loc[seg_id, 'q99_roll_mean_' + str(windows)] = np.quantile(x_
roll_mean, 0.99)
        X.loc[seg_id, 'av_change_abs_roll_mean_' + str(windows)] =
np.mean(np.diff(x_roll_mean))
        X.loc[seg_id, 'av_change_rate_roll_mean_' + str(windows)] =
np.mean(nonzero((np.diff(x_roll_mean) / x_roll_mean[:-1]))[0])
        X.loc[seg_id, 'abs_max_roll_mean_' + str(windows)] = np.abs(x_
roll_mean).max()
```

For each 150K-row segment generated from the training data, we are calculating these features. Then, the time to failure is selected as the value from the last row in the current segment:

```
# iterate over all segments
for seg_id in tqdm_notebook(range(segments)):
    seg = train_df.iloc[seg_id*rows:seg_id*rows+rows]
    create_features(seg_id, seg, train_X)
    train_y.loc[seg_id, 'time_to_failure'] = seg['time_to_failure'].
values[-1]
```

Next, we are scaling all features using a StandardScaler. This is not mandatory if we are using a model based on decision trees (such as random forest or XGBoost). We include this step for a case where we would like to use other models, for example, one based on neural networks, where normalizing the features would be a necessary step:

```
scaler = StandardScaler()
scaler.fit(train_X)
scaled_train_X = pd.DataFrame(scaler.transform(train_X), columns=train_X.
columns)
```

We repeat the same process for test data segments:

```
for seg_id in tqdm_notebook(test_X.index):
    seg = pd.read_csv('../input/LANL-Earthquake-Prediction/test/' + seg_id
+ '.csv')
```

```
    create_features(seg_id, seg, test_X)

scaled_test_X = pd.DataFrame(scaler.transform(test_X), columns=test_X.
columns)
```

After we analyzed the data, we generated a set of engineered features. We intend to use these features to build a baseline model. Then, based on the model evaluation, we can further select what features to keep and, eventually, to create new features.

Building a baseline model

From the original temporal data, through feature engineering, we generated time-aggregated features for each time segment in the training data, equal in duration with one test set. For the baseline model demonstrated in this competition, we chose LGBMRegressor, one of the best-performing algorithms at the time of the competition, which, in many cases, had a similar performance to XGBoost. The training data is split using KFold into five splits, and we run training and validation for each fold until we reach the final number of iterations or when the validation error ceases to improve after a specified number of steps (given by the *patience* parameter). For each split, we then also run the prediction for the test set, with the best model – trained with the current train split for the current fold, that is, with 4/5 from the training set. At the end, we will work out the average of the predictions obtained for each fold. We can use this cross-validation approach because our data is no longer temporal (time-series) data. We split the data into segments of 150K rows, of the same length as the test data, and then created aggregated features from this data:

```
n_fold = 5
folds = KFold(n_splits=n_fold, shuffle=True, random_state=42)
train_columns = scaled_train_X.columns.values
```

The model parameters are given in the following code excerpt. We set some of the usual parameters for LightGBM, as follows:

- **The number of leaves:** This parameter controls the number of leaves (or terminal nodes) in each tree. An increasing number of leaves allows the model to capture more complex patterns but also increases the risk of overfitting.

- **Minimum data in leaf:** If the number of samples in a leaf node is below this threshold, the node will not split. This parameter helps control overfitting.

- **The objective:** This is regression for our model.

- **Learning rate:** This will control how fast the model learns.

- **The boosting method**: We can choose between gradient-boosted decision trees (*gbdt*), dart gradient boosting (*dgb*), and gradient-based one-side sampling (*goss*). We are using *gbdt* here.

- **The feature fraction**: This is the percentage of features used in a subset of data presented to a tree within the tree ensemble employed by the algorithm.

- **Bagging frequency, bagging fraction, and bagging seed**: These control how we divide the sample set presented to the algorithm when we subsample it to present it to different trees.

- **Metric**: In this case, *mae*, which is the mean absolute error.

- **Regularization factor lambda_l1**

- **Verbosity**: This parameter controls the amount of information the algorithm prints to the console during training. A verbosity of 0 means silent mode (no information), while a verbosity of 1 prints messages about the training progress.

- **Number of parallel processing threads**: This parameter controls the number of parallel threads used by the algorithm during training.

- **The randomization factor random_state**: This parameter is the random seed used to initialize various parameters of the algorithm.

```python
params = {'num_leaves': 51,
          'min_data_in_leaf': 10,
          'objective':'regression',
          'max_depth': -1,
          'learning_rate': 0.001,
          "boosting": "gbdt",
          "feature_fraction": 0.91,
          "bagging_freq": 1,
          "bagging_fraction": 0.91,
          "bagging_seed": 42,
          "metric": 'mae',
          "lambda_l1": 0.1,
          "verbosity": -1,
          "nthread": -1,
          "random_state": 42}
```

The code for training, validation, and testing (per fold) is shown here:

```
oof = np.zeros(len(scaled_train_X))
predictions = np.zeros(len(scaled_test_X))
feature_importance_df = pd.DataFrame()
#run model
for fold_, (trn_idx, val_idx) in enumerate(folds.split(scaled_
train_X,train_y.values)):
    strLog = "fold {}".format(fold_)
    print(strLog)


    X_tr, X_val = scaled_train_X.iloc[trn_idx], scaled_train_X.iloc[val_
idx]
    y_tr, y_val = train_y.iloc[trn_idx], train_y.iloc[val_idx]


    model = lgb.LGBMRegressor(**params, n_estimators = 20000, n_jobs = -1)
    model.fit(X_tr,
              y_tr,
              eval_set=[(X_tr, y_tr), (X_val, y_val)],
              eval_metric='mae',
              verbose=1000,
              early_stopping_rounds=500)
    oof[val_idx] = model.predict(X_val, num_iteration=model.best_
iteration_)
    #feature importance
    fold_importance_df = pd.DataFrame()
    fold_importance_df["Feature"] = train_columns
    fold_importance_df["importance"] = model.feature_importances_
[:len(train_columns)]
    fold_importance_df["fold"] = fold_ + 1
    feature_importance_df = pd.concat([feature_importance_df, fold_
importance_df], axis=0)
    #predictions
    predictions += model.predict(scaled_test_X, num_iteration=model.best_
iteration_) / folds.n_splits
```

We initialize the prediction vector (which has the dimension of the submission file, that is, one entry for each test segment) with zeros. We also initialize an out-of-folds vector (the length of the training data, which is the number of training segments).

For each fold, we sample subsets of data and target values for both the training and validation sets. Then, we use them as input for the model, `LGBMRegressor`, initialized with the model parameters defined before (we also add the number of estimators and the number of workers). We fit the model with the subset of the training set corresponding to the current fold and validate it with the corresponding validation subset of the training data.

We set the evaluation metric as well: *mae* – meaning *mean absolute error* – the frequency for printing out the evaluation error, and the number of iterations for early stopping. This parameter (number of iterations for early stopping) controls the number of steps that the algorithm waits before stopping, when the validation error does not improve during training. We accumulate the validation results in the **oof (out-of-folds)** vector and concatenate the feature importance vector for the current fold to the feature importance DataFrame. Early stopping is used to keep the best model for prediction – based on validation during training.

Feature importance will be used to observe, during the iterative process of feature engineering, feature selection, and model training – if, for a model trained with certain features, the feature importance does not have a high variation between folds. At each fold, we are also running a prediction for the entire test set, with the model trained and validated per fold. Then, we increment the prediction vector with the values per fold, divided by the number of folds. This is equivalent to a model ensemble, where each model is trained with a different subset of data, corresponding to each fold split.

When evaluating the current model, we will examine three pieces of information: the training and validation errors, the variation of these errors across the folds, and the variation of feature importance between the folds. Ideally, these variations – of training and validation errors across folds, as well as the feature importance variation across folds – are smaller. *Figure 8.8* shows the evaluation plots from the training of the baseline model.

As you can see, we plot the training progress at every 1,000th step (verbosity set to 1000), and implement an early stop at 500 (training stops if there's no improvement in the validation error for the last 500 iterations). The best model (in terms of validation error) is retained for predicting from the test. Test prediction is averaged over the five splits.

```
fold 0
[1000]  training's l1: 1.95676  valid_1's l1: 2.25631
[2000]  training's l1: 1.56307  valid_1's l1: 2.12365
[3000]  training's l1: 1.33344  valid_1's l1: 2.10106
[4000]  training's l1: 1.15907  valid_1's l1: 2.09848
fold 1
[1000]  training's l1: 1.94969  valid_1's l1: 2.27207
[2000]  training's l1: 1.55889  valid_1's l1: 2.13573
[3000]  training's l1: 1.33267  valid_1's l1: 2.11072
[4000]  training's l1: 1.15873  valid_1's l1: 2.10505
[5000]  training's l1: 1.01503  valid_1's l1: 2.10337
fold 2
[1000]  training's l1: 1.95877  valid_1's l1: 2.27753
[2000]  training's l1: 1.57041  valid_1's l1: 2.11272
[3000]  training's l1: 1.34083  valid_1's l1: 2.07572
[4000]  training's l1: 1.16406  valid_1's l1: 2.06678
fold 3
[1000]  training's l1: 1.97504  valid_1's l1: 2.15127
[2000]  training's l1: 1.57339  valid_1's l1: 2.04186
[3000]  training's l1: 1.33886  valid_1's l1: 2.03638
fold 4
[1000]  training's l1: 1.94629  valid_1's l1: 2.26198
[2000]  training's l1: 1.55841  valid_1's l1: 2.11696
[3000]  training's l1: 1.32858  valid_1's l1: 2.08798
[4000]  training's l1: 1.15272  valid_1's l1: 2.08497
```

Figure 8.8: Model training evaluation output – training and validation error

Figure 8.9 shows the feature importance graph, with the average value per fold and the standard deviation:

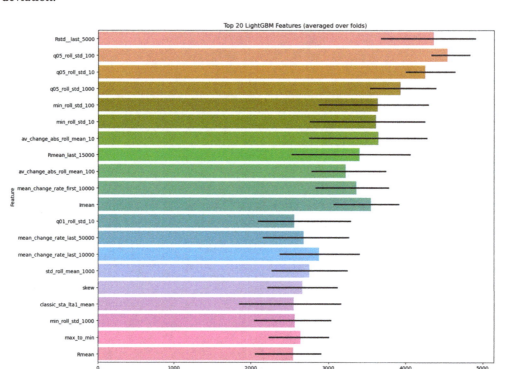

Figure 8.9: Feature importance: average and standard deviation values (from values on the five folds) – top 20 features

After we performed data analysis, we proceeded with building time-aggregated features, on subsets of the training set with the same duration as the test sets. With the new dataset formed with the engineered features, we trained a baseline model. For the baseline model, we used cross-validation with five folds and used each fold model for the prediction of the test set. The final prediction was formed by averaging the predictions for each fold.

Summary

In this chapter, we delved into handling signal data, focusing particularly on audio signals. We explored various storage formats for such data and examined libraries for loading, transforming, and visualizing this data type. To develop potent features, we applied a range of signal-processing techniques. Our feature engineering efforts transformed time-series data from each training segment and aggregated features for each test set.

We consolidated all feature engineering processes into a single function, applicable to all training segments and test sets. The transformed features underwent scaling. We then used this prepared data to train a baseline model utilizing the LGBMRegressor algorithm. This model employed cross-validation, and we generated predictions for the test set using the model trained in each fold. Subsequently, we aggregated these predictions to create the submission file. Additionally, we captured and visualized the feature importance for each fold.

References

1. LANL Earthquake Prediction, Can you predict upcoming laboratory earthquakes?, Kaggle Competition: `https://www.kaggle.com/competitions/LANL-Earthquake-Prediction`

2. Gabriel Preda, LANL Earthquake EDA and Prediction: `https://www.kaggle.com/code/gpreda/lanl-earthquake-eda-and-prediction`

3. LANL Earthquake Prediction, dataset description: `https://www.kaggle.com/competitions/LANL-Earthquake-Prediction/data`

4. BirdCLEF 2021 - Birdcall Identification, identify bird calls in soundscape recordings, Kaggle competition: `https://www.kaggle.com/competitions/birdclef-2021`

5. McFee, Brian, Colin Raffel, Dawen Liang, Daniel PW Ellis, Matt McVicar, Eric Battenberg, and Oriol Nieto. "librosa: Audio and music signal analysis in Python." In Proceedings of the 14th Python in Science Conference, pp. 18-25. 2015

6. librosa load function: `https://librosa.org/doc/main/generated/librosa.load.html`

7. Cornell Birdcall Identification, Kaggle competition: `https://www.kaggle.com/competitions/birdsong-recognition`

8. EarthData MERRA2 CO, Earth Data NASA Satellite Measurements, Kaggle dataset: `https://www.kaggle.com/datasets/gpreda/earthdata-merra2-co`

9. Gabriel Preda, EARTHDATA-MERRA2 Data Exploration, Kaggle Notebook: `https://www.kaggle.com/code/gpreda/earthdata-merra2-data-exploration`

Join our book's Discord space

Join our Discord community to meet like-minded people and learn alongside more than 5000 members at:

https://packt.link/kaggle

Can You Find Out Which Movie Is a Deepfake?

In the previous chapters, we explored various data formats: tabular, geospatial, text, image, and acoustic, while working with Kaggle datasets, learning about shapefile visualization, building models for image or text classification, and acoustic signal analysis.

In this chapter, we will introduce video data analysis. We will start by describing a Kaggle competition, *Deepfake Detection Challenge*. This competition challenged the participants to classify which videos were generated artificially to create realistic fake content convincingly. We will continue by quickly exploring the most used video formats, followed by introducing two utility scripts used for our data analysis. First, a utility script with functions for manipulating video content, i.e., reading, visualizing images from videos, and playing video files. Second, a utility script with functions for body, face, and face element detection. We will continue with metadata exploration from the competition dataset and then apply the utility scripts introduced to analyze the video data from the competition dataset.

In a nutshell, the following topics will be covered in this chapter:

- An introduction to the *Deepfake Detection Challenge* competition
- Utility scripts for video data manipulation and object detection in video data
- Metadata analysis and video data analysis from the competition dataset

Introducing the competition

In this chapter, we examine data from the well-known Kaggle competition the **Deepfake Detection Challenge (DFDC)**. The competition, detailed in *Reference 1*, commenced on December 11, 2019, and concluded on March 31, 2020. It attracted 2,265 teams comprising 2,904 participants, who collectively made 8,951 submissions. Competitors vied for a total prize pool of $1,000,000, with the first prize being $500,000.

The event was a collaborative effort involving AWS, Facebook, Microsoft, the Partnership on AI's Media Integrity Steering Committee, and various academic entities. At the time, there was a widespread agreement among tech industry leaders and academics on the technical complexity and rapidly changing nature of media content manipulation. The competition's aim was to encourage global researchers to devise innovative and effective technologies to detect deepfakes and media manipulation. Unlike later competitions that focused on code, this one required prize-eligible participants to test their code in a "black box" environment. The testing data, not available on Kaggle and necessitating a longer process, resulted in the private leaderboard being revealed later than usual, officially on June 12, 2020, although the competition ended on April 24, 2020.

The DFDC drew numerous high-ranking Kaggle Grandmasters who engaged in data analysis and developed models for submission. Notably, the initial first-prize winner was later disqualified by the organizers. This team, along with other top-ranked participants, had expanded their training sets using publicly available data. While they adhered to the competition's rules regarding the use of external data, they failed to meet the documentation requirements for winning submissions. These rules included obtaining written consent from all individuals featured in the images used in the additional training data.

The competition data was given in two separate sets. In the first set, 400 video samples for training and 400 videos for testing were provided in two folders, one for training data and one for testing data. These files are in the MP4 format, one of the most commonly used video formats.

A much larger dataset, of over 470 GB, for training, was made available as a download link. Alternatively, the same data was also made available as 50 smaller files of around 10 GB each. For the current analysis, we will only use the data from the first set (containing the 400 training and 400 testing files, in the .mp4 format).

Formats for video data

Video formats refer to standards used to encode, compress, and store video data. Currently, there are multiple formats that are used in parallel. Some of these video formats were created and promoted by technology companies like Microsoft, Apple, and Adobe. Their decision to develop proprietary formats might have been related to the need to control the quality of rendering on their own devices or devices running their operating systems.

Additionally, proprietary formats can give you a competitive advantage and larger control over licensing and the royalties associated with the format. Some of these formats incorporate innovations and useful features not existent in previously used formats. In parallel with the development by technology leaders, other formats were developed in response to a combination of technology advancements, market demand, and the need to align industry standards.

To give just a few examples of frequently used formats, we can mention **Windows Media Video (WMV)** and **Audio Video Interleave (AVI)**, both developed by Microsoft. The MOV (QuickTime Movie) format was developed by Apple to run on their macOS and iOS platforms. All these formats support multiple audio and video codecs. Then, we also have **Flash Video (FLV)**, which was developed by Adobe. Additionally, one widely adopted format is **MPEG-4 Part 14 (MP4)**, which is open-source and can also hold many video and audio codecs. **Moving Picture Experts Group (MPEG)** refers to a group of industry experts that developed the standards for audio and video compressing and encoding/decoding. The successive standards, from MPEG-1 to MPEG-4, have had a massive impact on the development of the media industry.

Introducing competition utility scripts

Let's begin by grouping the Python modules with reusable functions for video manipulation in two Kaggle utility scripts. The first utility script groups functions to load and display images from videos or play video files. The second one is geared toward object detection in videos – more specifically, to detect human faces and bodies – using a few alternative methods.

Video data utils

We developed a utility script to assist us in the manipulation of video data. Let's introduce one utility script that we will use in the notebook associated with the current chapter to read video data, as well as visualize frames from a video file.

The `video_utils` utility script includes functions to load, transform, and display images from videos. Additionally, it also contains a function to play video content. For video manipulation, we will use the OpenCV library. OpenCV is an open-source computer vision library widely used for image and video processing. Developed in C and C++, OpenCV has also a Python interface.

The following code block shows the included libraries and the function to display one image from a video file:

```python
import os
import cv2 as cv
import matplotlib.pyplot as plt
from IPython.display import HTML
from base64 import b64encode

def display_image_from_video(video_path):
    '''
    Display image from video
    Process
        1. perform a video capture from the video
        2. read the image
        3. display the image
    Args:
        video_path - path for video
    Returns:
        None
    '''
    capture_image = cv.VideoCapture(video_path)
    ret, frame = capture_image.read()
    fig = plt.figure(figsize=(10,10))
    ax = fig.add_subplot(111)
    frame = cv.cvtColor(frame, cv.COLOR_BGR2RGB)
    ax.imshow(frame)
```

In the preceding code, the function display_image_from_video receives as a parameter the path to a video file, performs an image capture from the video, reads the image, creates a Matplotlib Pyplot image, converts it from BGR (Blue Green Red) to RGB (Red Green Blue), and displays it. RGB is a color model used to represent color in a digital image. The difference between RGB and BGR is in the order in which the color information is stored. In the case of RGB, blue is stored as the least significant area, followed by green, and then red. In the case of BGR, the order is reversed.

Next, we define a function to represent a group of image captures, from a list of video files:

```python
def display_images_from_video_list(video_path_list, data_folder, video_
folder):
    '''
    Display images from video list
    Process:
        0. for each video in the video path list
            1. perform a video capture from the video
            2. read the image
            3. display the image
    Args:
        video_path_list: path for video list
        data_folder: path for data
        video_folder: path for video folder
    Returns:
        None
    '''
    plt.figure()
    fig, ax = plt.subplots(2,3,figsize=(16,8))
    # we only show images extracted from the first 6 videos
    for i, video_file in enumerate(video_path_list[0:6]):
        video_path = os.path.join(data_folder, video_folder,video_file)
        capture_image = cv.VideoCapture(video_path)
        ret, frame = capture_image.read()
        frame = cv.cvtColor(frame, cv.COLOR_BGR2RGB)
        ax[i//3, i%3].imshow(frame)
        ax[i//3, i%3].set_title(f"Video: {video_file}")
        ax[i//3, i%3].axis('on')
```

The function `display_images_from_video_list` receives as a parameter the path to a list of video filenames, relative to the path to its folder, and the path to the dataset. The function will perform the same processing as `display_image_from_video` does, for the first six video files in the list. We limit the number of images captured from video files for convenience.

The utility script also includes a function to play videos. The function uses the HTML function from the IPython `display` module. The code will be:

```
def play_video(video_file, data_folder, subset):
    '''
    Display video given by composed path
    Args
        video_file: the name of the video file to display
        data_folder: data folder
        subset: the folder where the video file is located
    Returns:
        a HTML objects running the video

    '''
    video_url = open(os.path.join(data_folder, subset,video_file),'rb').
read()
    data_url = "data:video/mp4;base64," + b64encode(video_url).decode()
    return HTML("""<video width=500 controls><source src="%s" type="video/
mp4"></video>""" % data_url)
```

The function `play_video` receives as parameters the name of the video file to play, the data folder, the folder contained in the data folder, and where the video file is located. The function uses the `b64encode` function from the `base64` library to decode the MP4 video format, and the decoded content is displayed in a video frame with a controlled width of 500 pixels, using the HTML control.

We have introduced the utility script for video image manipulation, loads the video, visualize images from videos, and play video files. In the next section, we introduce more utility scripts for object detection in images. These Python modules contain specialized classes for object detection. The modules implement two alternatives for face object detection, both based on computer vision algorithms.

Face and body detection utils

In the detection of deepfake videos, the analysis of video features such as desynchronization between sound and lip movement or unnatural motions of parts of the faces of people appearing in the video were, at the time of this competition, valuable elements to train models to recognize deepfake videos. Therefore, we include here the utility script specialized to detect bodies and faces.

The first module for face detection used the **Haar cascade** algorithm. Haar cascade is a lightweight machine learning algorithm for object detection. It is usually trained to identify specific objects. The algorithm uses Haar-like features and the Adaboost classifier to create a strong classifier. The algorithm operates on a sliding window, applying a cascade of weak classifiers that rejects regions of the image less likely to contain the object of interest. In our case, we want to use the algorithm to identify details in video images that are usually altered in the case of a deepfake, such as the facial expression, the gaze, and the mouth shape. This module includes two classes. We start with one of these classes. *CascadeObjectDetector* is a generic class for the detection of objects using the *Haar cascade* algorithm. The *CascadeObjectDetector* class, which is modified from the code in *Reference 3*, has an init function where we initialize the object with the specific *Haar cascade* object that stores the trained model. The class also has a *detect* function. The following is the code for *CascadeObjectDetector*. In the init function, we initialize the cascade object:

```
import os
import cv2 as cv
import matplotlib.pyplot as plt


class CascadeObjectDetector():
    '''
    Class for Cascade Object Detection
    '''

    def __init__(self,object_cascade_path):
        '''
        Args:
        object_cascade_path: path for the *.xml defining the parameters
                for {face, eye, smile, profile} detection algorithm
                source of the haarcascade resource is:
                https://github.com/opencv/opencv/tree/master/data/
haarcascades
        Returns:
            None
        '''


        self.object_cascade=cv.CascadeClassifier(object_cascade_path)
```

The next code snippet contains the detect function of the ***CascadeObjectDetector*** class. This function returns the rectangle coordinates of the object detected in the image:

```
def detect(self, image, scale_factor=1.3,
           min_neighbors=5,
           min_size=(20,20)):
    '''

    Function return rectangle coordinates of object for given image
    Args:
        image: image to process
        scale_factor: scale factor used for object detection
        min_neighbors: minimum number of parameters considered during
object detection
        min_size: minimum size of bounding box for object detected
    Returns:
        rectangle with detected object


    '''

    rects=self.object_cascade.detectMultiScale(image,
                                        scaleFactor=scale_factor,
                                        minNeighbors=min_neighbors,
                                        minSize=min_size)
    return rects
```

For this competition, I created a dedicated Kaggle dataset, from the Haar cascade algorithms defined at https://github.com/opencv/opencv/tree/master/data/haarcascades, as part of the OpenCV library distribution. The link to this database, called *Haar Cascades for Face Detection*, is given in *Reference 2*. The init function receives a path to one of the object detection models included in the database. The function detect receives, as parameters, the image to process for object extraction and a few parameters that can be used to adjust the detection. These parameters are the scale factor, the minimum number of neighbors used in detection, and the minimum size of the bounding box used for object detection. Inside the detect function we call the function detectMultiscale from the Haar cascade model.

The next class defined in the utility script is FaceObjectDetector. This class initializes four CascadeObjectDetector objects, for the face, face profile, eyes, and smile detection. The following code block shows the class definition with the init function, where these objects are defined.

For each face element, i.e., the frontal view of a person, profile view of a person, eye view, and smile view, we first initialize a dedicated variable with the value of the path to the Haar cascade resource. Then, for each of the resources, we initialize a CascadeObjectDetector object (see the code explanation for the CascadeObjectDetector class above):

```python
class FaceObjectDetector():
    '''
    Class for Face Object Detection
    '''

    def __init__(self, face_detection_folder):
        '''
        Args:
        face_detection_folder: path for folder where the *.xmls
                for {face, eye, smile, profile} detection algorithm
        Returns:
            None
        '''


        self.path_cascade=face_detection_folder
        self.frontal_cascade_path= os.path.join(self.path_
cascade,'haarcascade_frontalface_default.xml')
        self.eye_cascade_path= os.path.join(self.path_
cascade,'haarcascade_eye.xml')
        self.profile_cascade_path= os.path.join(self.path_
cascade,'haarcascade_profileface.xml')
        self.smile_cascade_path= os.path.join(self.path_
cascade,'haarcascade_smile.xml')

        #Detector object created
        # frontal face
        self.face_detector=CascadeObjectDetector(self.frontal_cascade_
path)
        # eye
        self.eyes_detector=CascadeObjectDetector(self.eye_cascade_path)
        # profile face
        self.profile_detector=CascadeObjectDetector(self.profile_cascade_
path)
        # smile
        self.smile_detector=CascadeObjectDetector(self.smile_cascade_path)
```

The objects are stored as the member variables face_detector, eyes_detector, profile_detector, and smile_detector.

In the next code block, we show the detect_objects function, where we call, for each of the CascadeObjectDetector objects defined in the init function, the detect function. To make it easier to follow, we will split the code snippet into three parts. The first part shows the call, from the detect_object function of the FaceObjectDetector class, and the detect function of the CascadeObjectDetector object initialized with the eyes Haar cascade object. Then, we use the OpenCV Circle function to mark on the initial image, with a circle, the position of the eyes detected in the image:

```
def detect_objects(self,
                   image,
                   scale_factor,
                   min_neighbors,
                   min_size,
                   show_smile=False):
    '''
    Objects detection function
    Identify frontal face, eyes, smile and profile face and display the
detected objects over the image
    Args:
        image: the image extracted from the video
        scale_factor: scale factor parameter for `detect` function of
CascadeObjectDetector object
        min_neighbors: min neighbors parameter for `detect` function of
CascadeObjectDetector object
        min_size: minimum size parameter for f`detect` function of
CascadeObjectDetector object
        show_smile: flag to activate/deactivate smile detection; set to
False due to many false positives
    Returns:
        None
    '''

    image_gray=cv.cvtColor(image, cv.COLOR_BGR2GRAY)
```

```
    eyes=self.eyes_detector.detect(image_gray,
                    scale_factor=scale_factor,
                    min_neighbors=min_neighbors,
                    min_size=(int(min_size[0]/2), int(min_size[1]/2)))

    for x, y, w, h in eyes:
        #detected eyes shown in color image
        cv.circle(image,(int(x+w/2),int(y+h/2)),(int((w + h)/4)),(0,
0,255),3)
```

Next, we apply the same approach to the `smile` objects in the image. We first detect the smile, and if detected, we display it using a rectangle, drawn with the opencv function over the bounding box of the detected object. Because this function tends to give a lot of false positives, by default, this functionality is deactivated, using a flag set to `False`:

```
        # deactivated by default due to many false positive
        if show_smile:
            smiles=self.smile_detector.detect(image_gray,
                        scale_factor=scale_factor,
                        min_neighbors=min_neighbors,
                        min_size=(int(min_size[0]/2), int(min_
size[1]/2)))

            for x, y, w, h in smiles:
                #detected smiles shown in color image
                cv.rectangle(image,(x,y),(x+w, y+h),(0, 0,255),3)
```

Finally, we extract the `profile` and `face` objects using the specialized Haar cascade algorithms. If detected, we draw rectangles to mark the bounding boxes of the detected objects:

```
        profiles=self.profile_detector.detect(image_gray,
                        scale_factor=scale_factor,
                        min_neighbors=min_neighbors,
                        min_size=min_size)

        for x, y, w, h in profiles:
            #detected profiles shown in color image
            cv.rectangle(image,(x,y),(x+w, y+h),(255, 0,0),3)

        faces=self.face_detector.detect(image_gray,
```

```
                    scale_factor=scale_factor,
                    min_neighbors=min_neighbors,
                    min_size=min_size)

        for x, y, w, h in faces:
            #detected faces shown in color image
            cv.rectangle(image,(x,y),(x+w, y+h),(0, 255,0),3)

        # image
        fig = plt.figure(figsize=(10,10))
        ax = fig.add_subplot(111)
        image = cv.cvtColor(image, cv.COLOR_BGR2RGB)
        ax.imshow(image)
```

For each of the four specialized object detectors (the face, face profile, eyes, and smile) we call the detect function and the results (a list of rectangles with the bounding box of the detected object), and then we draw in the context of the initial image either circles (for eyes) or rectangles (for the smile, face, and face profile) around the detected object. Finally, the function displays the image, with the superposed layers marking the bounding boxes of detected objects. Because the model for smile gives many false positives, we set an additional parameter, a flag to decide whether we show the extracted bounding boxes with smiles.

Next, the class has a function to extract image objects. The function receives a video path, captures an image from the video, and applies the detect_objects function on the image capture for detection of the face and face details (the eyes, smile, and so on) from that image. The following code block shows the function for extraction:

```
    def extract_image_objects(self,
                              video_file,
                              data_folder,
                              video_set_folder,
                              show_smile=False
                              ):
        '''
        Extract one image from the video and then perform face/eyes/smile/
profile detection on the image
        Args:
            video_file: the video from which to extract the image from
which we extract the face
```

```
            data_folder: folder with the data
            video_set_folder: folder with the video set
            show_smile: show smile (False by default)
        Returns:
            None
        '''
        video_path = os.path.join(data_folder, video_set_folder,video_
  file)
        capture_image = cv.VideoCapture(video_path)
        ret, frame = capture_image.read()
        #frame = cv.cvtColor(frame, cv.COLOR_BGR2RGB)
        self.detect_objects(image=frame,
                scale_factor=1.3,
                min_neighbors=5,
                min_size=(50, 50),
                show_smile=show_smile)
```

We introduced a module for face detection using Haar cascade algorithms. Next, we will review an alternative approach, where we use the ***MTCNN*** model for face detection. We want to test multiple approaches to decide which one works better for face detection. ***MTCNN*** stands for **Multi-Task Cascaded Convolution Networks** and is based on a concept developed first in the paper *Joint Face Detection and Alignment using Multi-task Cascaded Convolutional Networks* (see *Reference 4*). In another article titled *Face Detection using MTCNN*, the authors propose a "cascaded multi-task framework using different features of sub-models" (see *Reference 5*). The implementation of face element extraction using the MTCNN approach is done in the utility script face_detection_mtcnn.

In this module, we define the class MTCNNFaceDetector. In the next code block, we show the class definition with the init function:

```
class MTCNNFaceDetector():
    '''

    Class for MTCNN Face Detection

    Detects the face and the face keypoints: right & left eye,
    nose, right and left lips limits
    Visualize a image capture from a video and marks the
    face boundingbox and the features
    On top of the face boundingbox shows the confidence score
```

```
    ' ' '

    def __init__(self, mtcnn_model):
        ' ' '

        Args:
            mtcnn_model: mtcnn model instantiated already
        Returns:
            None
        ' ' '

        self.detector = mtcnn_model
        self.color_face = (255,0,0)
        self.color_keypoints = (0, 255, 0)
        self.font = cv.FONT_HERSHEY_SIMPLEX
        self.color_font = (255,0,255)
```

The init function receives, as a parameter, an instance of the MTCNN model, imported and instantiated in the calling application from the mtcnn library. The class member variable detector is initialized with this object. The rest of the class variables are used for visualization of the detected objects.

The class also has a detect function. The next code block shows the detect function implementation:

```
    def detect(self, video_path):
        ' ' '

        Function plot image
        Args:
            video_path: path to the video from which to capture
            image and then apply detector
        Returns:
            rectangle with detected object


        ' ' '

        capture_image = cv.VideoCapture(video_path)
        ret, frame = capture_image.read()
        image = cv.cvtColor(frame, cv.COLOR_BGR2RGB)

        results = self.detector.detect_faces(image)
        if results:
```

```
            for result in results:
                print(f"Extracted features: {result}")
                x, y, w, h = bounding_box = result['box']
                keypoints = result['keypoints']
                confidence = f"{round(result['confidence'], 4)}"
                cv.rectangle(image, (x, y),(x+w,y+h), self.color_face, 3)
                # add all the internal features
                for key in keypoints:
                    xk, yk = keypoints[key]
                    cv.rectangle(image, (xk-2, yk-2), (xk+2, yk+2), self.
    color_keypoints, 3)
                image = cv.putText(image, confidence, (x, y-2),
                                    self.font, 1,
                                    self.color_font, 2,
                                    cv.LINE_AA)
        fig = plt.figure(figsize=(15, 15))
        ax = fig.add_subplot(111)
        ax.imshow(image)
        plt.show()
```

The function receives, as a parameter, the path to the video file. After capturing an image from the video file, we read it and transform it from the BGR format to the RGB format. The transformation is needed because we want to use library functions that expect the RGB color order. After we apply the detect_faces function of the MTCNN model to the transformed image, the detector returns a list of extracted JSONs. Each extraction JSON has the following format:

```
{
    'box': [906, 255, 206, 262],
    'confidence': 0.9999821186065674,
    'keypoints':
    {
        'left_eye': (965, 351),
        'right_eye': (1064, 354),
        'nose': (1009, 392),
        'mouth_left': (966, 453),
        'mouth_right': (1052, 457)
    }
}
```

In the 'box' field is the bounding box of the detected face area. In the 'keypoints' field are the keys and coordinates of the five objects detected: the left eye, right eye, nose, left-most mouth limit, and right-most mouth limit. There is an additional field, 'confidence', which gives the confidence factor of the model.

For real faces, the confidence factor is above 0.99 (the maximum is 1). If the model detected an artifact, or things like a poster with a face image, this factor could be as large as 0.9. Confidence factors under 0.9 are most likely associated with artifact detection (or false positives).

In our implementation (see the preceding code), we parse the list of detection JSONs and add a rectangle for each face, and a point (or a very small rectangle) for each of the five face features. On the top of the face bounding box rectangle, we write the confidence factor (rounded to four decimals).

Besides the utility scripts for image capture from video and playing videos, and for object detection from video data, we will also reuse the utility scripts for data quality and plotting that we started using in *Chapter 4*.

In the next section, we start with a few preparatory activities and continue with a metadata exploration of the competition data. We will cover, in this section, importing the libraries, a few checks of the data files, as well as a statistical analysis of the metadata files.

Metadata exploration

We start by importing the utility functions and classes from the utility scripts for data quality, plot utils, video utils, and face object detection. The following code block shows what we import from the utility scripts:

```
from data_quality_stats import missing_data, unique_values, most_frequent_
values
from plot_style_utils import set_color_map, plot_count
from video_utils import display_image_from_video, display_images_from_
video_list, play_video
from face_object_detection import CascadeObjectDetector, FaceObjectDetector
from face_detection_mtcnn import MTCNNFaceDetector
```

After we load the data files (the train and test samples), we are ready to start our analysis. The following code block checks the types of files in TRAIN_SAMPLE_FOLDER:

```
train_list = list(os.listdir(os.path.join(DATA_FOLDER, TRAIN_SAMPLE_
FOLDER)))
```

```
ext_dict = []
for file in train_list:
    file_ext = file.split('.')[1]
    if (file_ext not in ext_dict):
        ext_dict.append(file_ext)
print(f"Extensions: {ext_dict}")
```

The result shows that there are two types of files, JSON files and MP4 files. The following code checks the content of the JSON file present in TRAIN_SAMPLE_FOLDER. It samples the first five records for files in TRAIN_SAMPLE_FOLDER, as included in the JSON file:

```
json_file = [file for file in train_list if  file.endswith('json')][0]

def get_meta_from_json(path):
    df = pd.read_json(os.path.join(DATA_FOLDER, path, json_file))
    df = df.T
    return df

meta_train_df = get_meta_from_json(TRAIN_SAMPLE_FOLDER)
meta_train_df.head()
```

In *Figure 9.1*, we show the data sample obtained when we created the DataFrame meta_train_df from the JSON file. The index is the name of the file. **label** is either **FAKE** (for deepfake videos) or **REAL** (for real videos). The **split** field gives the set to which the video belongs (train). **original** is the name of the initial video, from which the deepfake was created.

	label	split	original
aagfhgtpmv.mp4	FAKE	train	vudstovrck.mp4
aapnvogymq.mp4	FAKE	train	jdubbvfswz.mp4
abarnvbtwb.mp4	REAL	train	None
abofeumbvv.mp4	FAKE	train	atvmxvwyns.mp4
abqwwspghj.mp4	FAKE	train	qzimuostzz.mp4

Figure 9.1: Sample of files in the train sample folder

We also check a few stats about the metadata, using the missing_data, unique_values, and most_frequent_values functions from the utility script data_quality_stats. These functions were introduced in *Chapter 3*.

Figure 9.2 shows the missing values from `meta_train_df`. As you can see, **19.25%** of the original fields are missing.

	label	split	original
Total	0	0	77
Percent	0	0	19.25
Types	object	object	object

Figure 9.2: Missing values in the sample train data

In *Figure 9.3*, we show the unique values from **meta_train_df**. There are **323** original values with **209** unique ones. The other two fields, **label** and **split**, have 400 values, with **2** unique values for **label** (FAKE and REAL) and **1** for **split** (train).

	label	split	original
Total	400	400	323
Uniques	2	1	209

Figure 9.3: Unique values in sample train data

Figure 9.4 displays the most frequent values from **meta_train_df**. From the total of **400** labels, **323** or **80.75%** are FAKE. The most frequent **original** value is **atvmxvwyns.mp4**, with a frequency of **6** (that is, it was used in 6 FAKE videos). All the values in the **split** column are **train**.

	label	split	original
Total	400	400	323
Most frequent item	FAKE	train	atvmxvwyns.mp4
Frequence	323	400	6
Percent from total	80.75	100	1.858

Figure 9.4: Most frequent values in the sample train data

In this analysis, we will use a custom color schema, with tones of blues and grays. The following code block shows the code for the generation of the custom color map:

```
color_list = ['#4166AA', '#06BDDD', '#83CEEC', '#EDE8E4', '#C2AFA8']
cmap_custom = set_color_map(color_list)
```

In *Figure 9.5*, we show the color map.

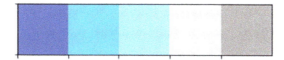

Figure 9.5: Most frequent values in the sample train data

Figure 9.6 shows the **label** distribution in the sample train dataset. There are 323 records with the **FAKE** label, and the rest of the labels have a **REAL** value.

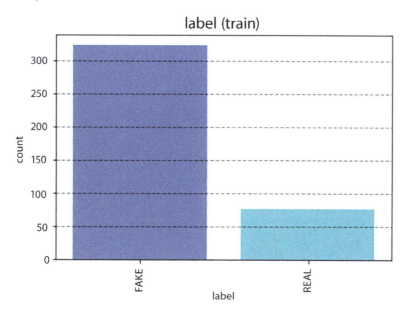

Figure 9.6: Most frequent values in the sample train data

In the next section, we will start analyzing the video data.

Video data exploration

In this section, we will visualize a few samples of files, and then we will begin performing object detection to try to capture the features from the images that might have some anomalies when processed to create deepfakes. These are mostly the eyes, mouths, and figures.

We will start by visualizing sample files, both genuine images and deepfakes. We will then apply the first algorithm introduced previously for face, eye, and mouth detection, the one based on Haar cascade. We then follow with the alternative algorithm, based on MTCNN.

Visualizing sample files

The following code block selects a few video files from the set of fake videos and then visualizes an image capture from them, using the `display_image_from_video` function from the utility script `video_utils`:

```
fake_train_sample_video = list(meta_train_df.loc[meta_train_
df.label=='FAKE'].sample(3).index)

for video_file in fake_train_sample_video:
    display_image_from_video(os.path.join(DATA_FOLDER, TRAIN_SAMPLE_
FOLDER, video_file))
```

The preceding code will plot one image capture per each of the three videos. In *Figure 9.7*, we only show one of these image captures, for the first video:

Figure 9.7: Example of an image capture from a fake video

The next code block selects a sample of three real videos and then, for each selected video, creates and plots an image capture:

```
real_train_sample_video = list(meta_train_df.loc[meta_train_
df.label=='REAL'].sample(3).index)
```

```
for video_file in real_train_sample_video:
    display_image_from_video(os.path.join(DATA_FOLDER, TRAIN_SAMPLE_
FOLDER, video_file))
```

In *Figure 9.8*, we show one of the images captured from the first real video:

Figure 9.8: Example of an image capture from a real video

We would also like to inspect videos that are all derived from the same original video. We will pick six videos from the same original video and show one image capture from each video. The following code block performs this operation:

```
same_original_fake_train_sample_video = \
        list(meta_train_df.loc[meta_train_df.original=='meawmsgiti.mp4'].
index)

display_images_from_video_list(video_path_list=same_original_fake_train_
sample_video,
                              data_folder=DATA_FOLDER,
                              video_folder=TRAIN_SAMPLE_FOLDER)
```

In *Figure 9.9*, we show two of these image captures from several different videos, of which we used the same original file to deepfake.

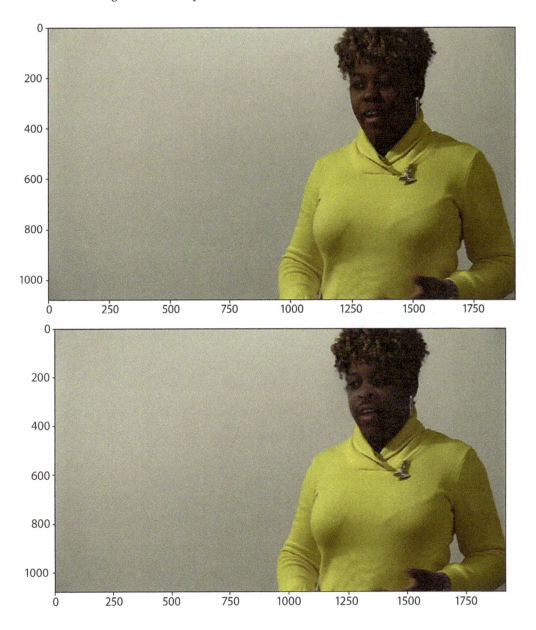

Figure 9.9: Image captures from faked videos modified from the same original file

We performed similar checks with videos from the test set. Of course, in the case of the test set, we will not be able to know in advance which video is real or not. The following code selects image captures from two sample videos from the data:

```
display_images_from_video_list(test_videos.sample(2).video, DATA_FOLDER,
TEST_FOLDER)
```

Figure 9.10 displays these selected images:

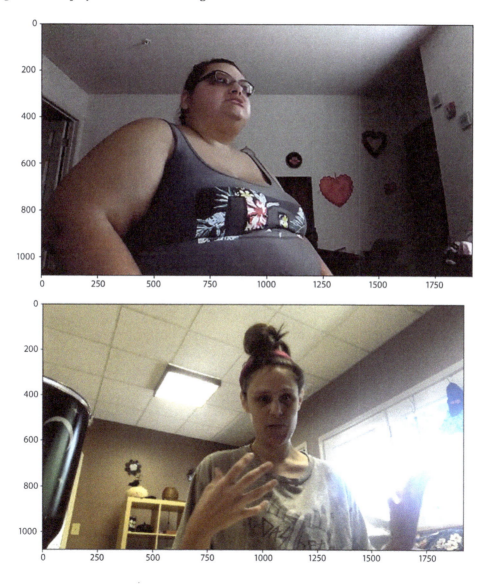

Figure 9.10: Image captures from faked videos modified from the same original file

Let's now start to use the algorithms for face detection introduced in the **Face and body detection utils** section.

Performing object detection

First, let's use the *Haar cascade* algorithms from the face_object_detection module. We use the FaceObjectDetector object to extract the face, profile face, eyes, and smile. The class CascadeObjectDetector initializes the specialized cascade classifiers for the aforementioned people attributes (using the specialized imported resource). The function detect uses a method of the CascadeClassifier from OpenCV to detect objects in images. For each attribute, we will use a different shape and color to mark/highlight the extracted object, as follows:

- **Frontal face**: Green rectangle
- **Eye**: Red circle
- **Smile**: Red rectangle
- **Profile face**: Blue rectangle

Note that due to the large amount of false positives, we deactivated the smile detector.

We apply the function for face detection to a selection of images from the train sample videos. The following code block performs this operation:

```
same_original_fake_train_sample_video = \
    list(meta_train_df.loc[meta_train_df.original=='kgbkktcjxf.mp4'].
index)

for video_file in same_original_fake_train_sample_video[1:4]:
    print(video_file)
    face_object_detector.extract_image_objects(video_file=video_file,
                        data_folder=DATA_FOLDER,
                        video_set_folder=TRAIN_SAMPLE_FOLDER,
                        show_smile=False
                        )
```

The preceding code run will yield three image captures for three different videos. Each image is decorated with the highlighted objects extracted. The following figures show the three image captures with the extracted objects. In *Figure 9.11a*, we see both the frontal and profile faces detected and one eye detected. *Figure 9.11b* shows both the frontal and profile faces detected, and two eyes detected. *Figure 9.11c* shows both the frontal and profile faces detected, the two eyes correctly detected, and one false positive (one of the nostrils is detected as an eye). The smile detection is not activated in this case (too many false positives).

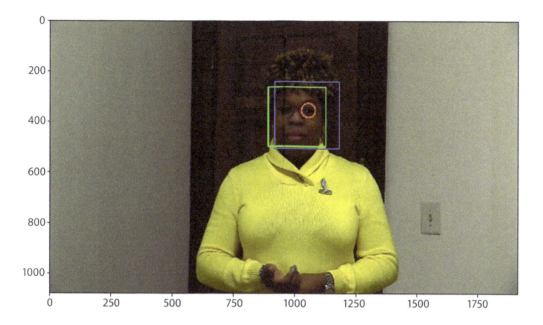

a

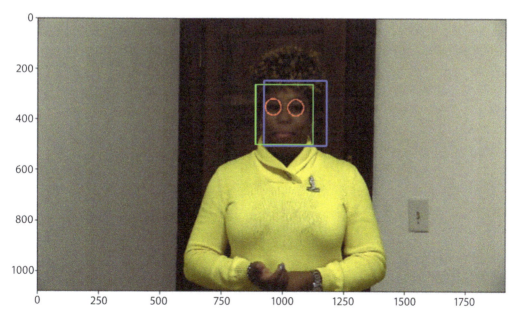

b

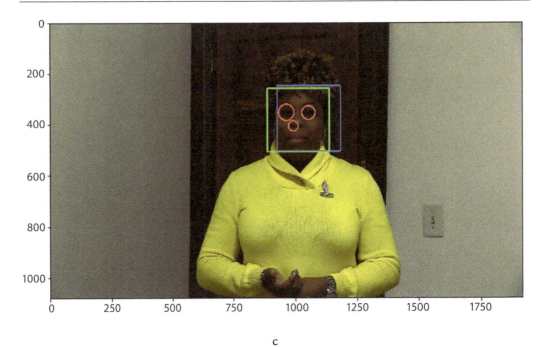

c

Figure 9.11: Face, face profile, and eye detection in image captures from three different videos

Running these algorithms with other images as well, we can see that they are not very robust and frequently yield false positives, as well as incomplete results. In *Figure 9.12*, we show two examples of such incomplete detections. In *Figure 9.12a*, only the face was detected. In *Figure 9.12b*, only one face profile was detected, although two people are present in the scene.

a

b

Figure 9.12: Face, face profile, and eye detection in image captures from two different videos

In the preceding image, there is also a strange detection; the fire sprinkler in the ceiling is detected as an eye and so is the candle fixture on the far left. This type of false detection (false positives) is quite frequent with these filters. One common problem is that objects like eyes, noses, or lips are detected in areas where there is no face. Since the search is done independently for these different objects, the likelihood of getting such false positives is quite large.

With the alternative solution implemented by us in `face_detection_mtcnn`, a unique framework is used to detect simultaneously the face bounding box and the position of face elements like eyes, nose, and lips. Let's compare the results obtained with the Haar cascade algorithm, as shown in *Figures 9.11* and *9.12*, with the results for the same images obtained with the MTCNN algorithm.

In *Figure 9.13*, we show one image of the person dressed in yellow; this time, face detection is performed with our ***MTCNNFaceDetector***:

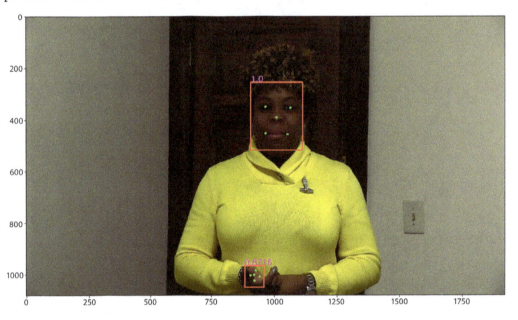

Figure 9.13: MTCNN face detection: one genuine face and one artifact detected

Two face objects are detected. One is correct, and the second is an artifact. The detection JSONs are:

```
Extracted features: {'box': [906, 255, 206, 262], 'confidence':
0.9999821186065674, 'keypoints': {'left_eye': (965, 351), 'right_eye':
(1064, 354), 'nose': (1009, 392), 'mouth_left': (966, 453), 'mouth_right':
(1052, 457)}}

Extracted features: {'box': [882, 966, 77, 84], 'confidence':
0.871575653553009, 'keypoints': {'left_eye': (905, 1003), 'right_eye':
(926, 985), 'nose': (919, 1002), 'mouth_left': (921, 1024), 'mouth_right':
(942, 1008)}}
```

From the experiments we conducted with a considerable number of samples, we concluded that the real faces will have a confidence factor very close to 1. Because the second detected "face" has a confidence of 0.87, we can easily dismiss it. Only faces with a confidence factor above 0.99 are actually to be trusted.

Let's see another example. In *Figure 9.14*, we compare the results for the same images from *Figure 9.12*. In both figures, all the faces of the people present in the scene are correctly identified. In all the cases, the confidence score is above 0.999. No artifacts are incorrectly extracted as human figures. The algorithm appears to be more robust than the alternative implementations using Haar cascades.

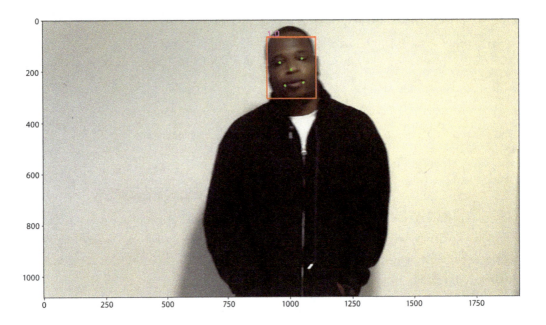

a

b

Figure 9.14: MTCNN face detection: a scene with one person and a scene with two people

For the next example, we selected a case where, if there are two people present in the video from which we capture the image, the faces are correctly identified, and the confidence score is high. In the same image, an artifact is also identified as a human face:

Figure 9.15: MTCNN face detection: a scene with two people

Besides the two real people, for which the confidence factors are 0.9995 and 0.9999 (rounded to 1), respectively, the face of the *Dead Alive* character on the T-shirt of the first person in the scene is also detected as a face. The bounding box is correctly detected, and all the face elements are also detected correctly. The only indication that this is a false positive is the lower confidence factor, which in this case is 0.9075. Such examples can help us to correctly calibrate our face detection approach. Only faces detected with a confidence above 0.95 or even 0.99 should be considered.

In the notebook associated with this chapter, *Deepfake Exploratory Data Analysis* (`https://www.kaggle.com/code/gpreda/deepfake-exploratory-data-analysis`), we provide more examples of face extraction with both the approaches introduced here.

Summary

In this chapter, we began by introducing a series of utility scripts, which are reusable Python modules on Kaggle designed for video data manipulation. One such script, `video_utils`, is used to visualize images from videos and play them. Another script, `face_object_detection`, utilizes Haar cascade models for face detection.

The third script, `face_detection_mtcnn`, employs MTCNN models to identify faces and key points such as the eyes, nose, and mouth. We then examined the metadata and video data from the DFDC competition dataset. In this dataset, we applied the aforementioned face detection methods to images from training and test videos, finding the MTCNN model approach to be more robust and accurate, with fewer false positives.

As we near the conclusion of our exploration of data, we will reflect on our journey through various data formats, including tabular, text, image, sound, and now video. We've delved into numerous Kaggle datasets and competition datasets, learning how to conduct exploratory data analysis, create reusable code, establish a visual identity for our notebooks, and weave a narrative with data. In some instances, we also introduced feature engineering elements and established a model baseline. In one case, we demonstrated the step-by-step refinement of our model to enhance validation metrics. The focus of the previous and current chapters has been on crafting high-quality notebooks on Kaggle.

In the upcoming chapter, we will explore the use of large language models from Kaggle, potentially in conjunction with other technologies such as LangChain and vector databases. This will demonstrate the vast potential of Generative AI in various applications.

References

1.   Deepfake Detection Challenge, Kaggle competition, Identify videos with facial or voice manipulations: `https://www.kaggle.com/competitions/deepfake-detection-challenge`

2.   Haar Cascades for Face Detection, Kaggle dataset: `https://www.kaggle.com/datasets/gpreda/haar-cascades-for-face-detection`

3.   Serkan Peldek – Face Detection with OpenCV, Kaggle notebook: `https://www.kaggle.com/code/serkanpeldek/face-detection-with-opencv/`

4.   Kaipeng Zhang, Zhanpeng Zhang, Zhifeng Li, and Yu Qiao – Joint Face Detection and Alignment using Multi-task Cascaded Convolutional Networks: `https://arxiv.org/abs/1604.02878`

5.   Justin Güse – Face Detection using MTCNN — a guide for face extraction with a focus on speed: `https://towardsdatascience.com/face-detection-using-mtcnn-a-guide-for-face-extraction-with-a-focus-on-speed-c6d59f82d49`

Join our book's Discord space

Join our Discord community to meet like-minded people and learn alongside more than 5000 members at:

`https://packt.link/kaggle`

10

Unleash the Power of Generative AI with Kaggle Models

In the previous chapters, our primary focus was on mastering the analysis of diverse data types and developing strategies to tackle a variety of problems. We delved into an array of tools and methodologies for data exploration and visualization, enriching our skill set in these areas. A few of the earlier chapters were dedicated to constructing baseline models, notably for participation in competitive scenarios.

Now, in this current chapter, we will pivot our attention toward leveraging Kaggle Models. Our objective is to integrate these models into Kaggle applications, in order to prototype the use of the newest Generative AI technologies in practical applications. A few examples of such real-world applications are personalized marketing, chatbots, content creation, targeted advertising, answering customers' inquiries, fraud detection, medical diagnosis, patient monitoring, drug discovery, personalized medicine, financial analysis, risk evaluation, trading, document drafting, litigation support, legal analysis, personalized recommendations, and synthetic data generation.

This chapter will cover the following topics:

- An introduction to Kaggle Models – how to access and use them
- Prompting a **Large Language Model (LLM)**
- Using LLMs together with task-chaining solutions like Langchain to create a sequence (or chains) of prompts for LLMs

- Building a **Retrieval Augmented Generation (RAG)** system using LangChain, LLMs, and a vector database

Introducing Kaggle Models

Kaggle Models represent one of the latest innovations on the Kaggle platform. This feature gained prominence in particular after the introduction of code competitions, where participants often train models either on their local hardware or in the cloud. Post-training, they upload these models to Kaggle as a dataset. This practice allows Kagglers to utilize these pre-trained models in their inference notebooks, streamlining the process for code competition submissions. This method significantly reduces the runtime of the inference notebooks, fitting within the stringent time and memory constraints of the competition. Kaggle's endorsement of this approach aligns well with real-world production systems, where model training and inference typically occur in separate pipelines.

This strategy becomes indispensable with large-scale models, such as those based on Transformer architectures, considering the immense computational resources required for fine-tuning. Platforms like HuggingFace have further democratized access to large models, offering options to either utilize online or download collaboratively developed models. Kaggle's introduction of the Models feature, which can be added to notebooks just like datasets, has been a significant advancement. These models can be directly used within a notebook for tasks like transfer learning or further fine-tuning. At the time of writing, however, Kaggle does not permit users to upload their models in the same manner as datasets.

Kaggle's model library offers a browsing and search functionality, allowing users to find models based on various criteria like name, metadata, task, data type, and more. At the time of writing, the library boasted 269 models with 1,997 variations, published by prominent organizations, including Google, TensorFlow, Kaggle, DeepMind, Meta, and Mistral.

The field of Generative AI has seen a surge in interest following the introduction of models like GPT-3, ChatGPT, GPT-4, and various other **LLMs** or Foundation Models. Kaggle provides access to several powerful LLMs, such as Llama, Alpaca, and Llama 2. The platform's integrated ecosystem allows users to swiftly test new models as they emerge. For instance, Meta's Llama 2, available since July 18, 2023, is a series of generative text models, with variants ranging from 7 billion to 70 billion parameters. These models, including specialized versions for chat applications, are accessible on Kaggle with relative ease compared to other platforms.

Kaggle further simplifies the process by allowing users to start a notebook directly from the model page, akin to initiating a notebook from a competition or dataset.

This streamlined approach, as illustrated in the following screenshot, enhances the user experience and fosters a more efficient workflow in model experimentation and application.

Figure 10.1: Main page of the Mistral Model, with the button to Add a Notebook in the top-right corner

Once the notebook is open in the editor, the model is already added to it. One more step is needed in the case of models, and this is because a model has also variations, versions, and frameworks. In the right-hand panel of the notebook edit window, you can set these options. After these options are set, we are ready to use the model within the notebook. the following screenshot, we show the options for one model, Mistral, from Mistral AI (see *Reference 2*), after everything was selected in the menu:

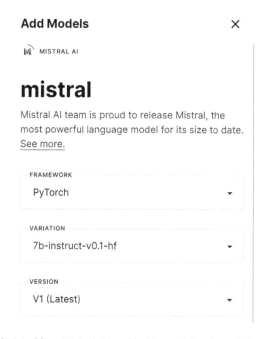

Figure 10.2: Model Mistral from Mistral AI is added to a notebook, and all options are selected

Prompting a foundation model

LLMs can be used directly, for example, for such tasks as summarization, question answering, and reasoning. Due to the very large amounts of data on which they were trained, they can answer very well to a variety of questions on many subjects, since they have the context available in that training dataset.

In many practical cases, such LLMs can correctly answer our questions on the first attempt. In other cases, we will need to provide a few clarifications or examples. The quality of the answers in these zero-shot or few-shot approaches highly depends on the ability of the user to craft the prompts for LLM. In this section, we will show the simplest way to interact with one LLM on Kaggle, using prompts.

Model evaluation and testing

Before starting to use an LLM on Kaggle, we will need to perform a few preparation steps. We begin by loading the model and then defining a tokenizer. Next, we create a model pipeline. In our first code example, we will use AutoTokenizer from transformers as a tokenizer and create a pipeline, also using the transformers pipeline. The following code (excerpts from the notebook in *Reference 3*) illustrates these steps described:

```
def load_model_tokenize_create_pipeline():
    """
    Load the model
    Create a
    Args
    Returns:
        tokenizer
        pipeline
    """
    # adapted from https://huggingface.co/blog/llama2#using-transformers
    time_1 = time()
    model = "/kaggle/input/llama-2/pytorch/7b-chat-hf/1"
    tokenizer = AutoTokenizer.from_pretrained(model)
    time_2 = time()
    print(f"Load model and init tokenizer: {round(time_2-time_1, 3)}")
    pipeline = transformers.pipeline(
        "text-generation",
        model=model,
```

```
            torch_dtype=torch.float16,
            device_map="auto",)
        time_3 = time()
        print(f"Prepare pipeline: {round(time_3-time_2, 3)}")
        return tokenizer, pipeline
```

The preceding code returns the tokenizer and the pipeline. We then implement a function to test the model. The function receives as parameters the tokenizer, the pipeline, and the prompt with which we would like to test the model. See the following code for the test function:

```
def test_model(tokenizer, pipeline, prompt_to_test):
    """

    Perform a query
    print the result
    Args:
        tokenizer: the tokenizer
        pipeline: the pipeline
        prompt_to_test: the prompt
    Returns
        None
    """

    # adapted from https://huggingface.co/blog/llama2#using-transformers
    time_1 = time()
    sequences = pipeline(
        prompt_to_test,
        do_sample=True,
        top_k=10,
        num_return_sequences=1,
        eos_token_id=tokenizer.eos_token_id,
        max_length=200,)
    time_2 = time()
    print(f"Test inference: {round(time_2-time_1, 3)}")
    for seq in sequences:
        print(f"Result: {seq['generated_text']}")
```

Now, we are ready to prompt the model. The model we are using has the following characteristics: a Llama 2 model (7b), a chat version from HuggingFace (version 1), and thePyTorch framework. We will prompt the model with math questions. In the next code extract, we initialize the tokenizer and pipeline and then prompt the model with a simple arithmetic problem, formulated in plain language:

```
tokenizer, pipeline = load_model_tokenize_create_pipeline()

prompt_to_test = 'Prompt: Adrian has three apples. His sister Anne has ten
apples more than him. How many apples has Anne?'
test_model(tokenizer, pipeline, prompt_to_test)
```

Let's see how the model reasons. the following screenshot, we plot the time for inference, the prompt, and the answer:

```
Test inference: 7.73
Result: Prompt: Adrian has three apples. His sister Anne has ten apples more than him. How ma
ny apples has Anne?

Answer: If Adrian has 3 apples, and Anne has 10 apples more than him, then Anne has 13 apples
(3 + 10 = 13).
```

Figure 10.3: Prompt, answer, and inference time for a math question with the Llama 2 model

For this simple math question, the reasoning of the model seems accurate. Let's try again with a different question. In the following code excerpt, we ask a geometry question:

```
prompt_to_test = 'Prompt: A circle has the radius 5. What is the area of
the circle?'
test_model(tokenizer, pipeline, prompt_to_test)
```

The following screenshot shows the result of prompting the model with the preceding geometry question:

```
Test inference: 6.186
Result: Prompt: A circle has the radius 5. What is the area of the circle?
Solution: To find the area of a circle, we can use the formula: Area = πr^2, where r is the r
adius of the circle. In this case, the radius of the circle is 5, so we can substitute this v
alue into the formula: Area = π(5)^2 = 3.14(25) = 78.5. So, the area of the circle is 78.5 sq
uare units.
```

Figure 10.4: Llama 2 model answer to a basic geometry question

The response to simple mathematical questions is not correct all of the time. In the following example, we prompted the model with a variation of the first algebraic problem. You can see that, in this case, the model took a convoluted and wrong path to reach an incorrect solution:

```
Test inference: 6.357
Result: Prompt: Anne and Adrian have a total of 10 apples. Anne has 2 apples more than Adria
n.How many apples has each of the children Anne and Adrian?
Answer: Let's say Adrian has x apples. Since Anne has 2 apples more than Adrian, Anne has 2+x
apples.
We know that the total number of apples is 10, so we can set up the equation:
2 + x = 10

Solving for x, we get:
x = 8

So Adrian has 8 apples and Anne has 10 - 8 = 2 apples.
```

Figure 10.5: Llama 2 model solution is wrong for an algebra problem

Model quantization

In the preceding experiments, we engaged a model with a series of straightforward questions. This process underscored the crucial role of crafting clear, well-structured prompts to elicit accurate and relevant responses. While Kaggle generously offers substantial computational resources at no cost, the sheer size of LLMs presents a challenge. These models demand significant RAM and CPU/GPU power for loading and inference.

To mitigate these demands, we can employ a technique known as model quantization. This method effectively reduces the memory and computational requirements of a model. It achieves this by representing the model's weights and activation functions using low-precision data types, such as 8-bit or 4-bit integers, instead of the standard 32-bit floating-point format. This approach not only conserves resources but also maintains a balance between efficiency and performance (see *Reference 4*).

In our upcoming example, we'll demonstrate how to quantize a model from Kaggle using one of the available techniques, the `llama.cpp` library. We've chosen the Llama 2 model for this purpose. Llama 2 is, at the time of writing, one of the most successful LLMs that you can download (with Meta approval) and use freely. It also has demonstrable accuracy for a variety of tasks, on par with many other available models. The quantization will be executed using the `llama.cpp` library.

The forthcoming code snippet details the steps to install `llama.cpp`, import the necessary functions from the package, execute the quantization process, and subsequently load the quantized model. It's important to note that, in this instance, we will not utilize the latest, more advanced quantization option available in `llama.cpp`. This example serves as an introduction to model quantization on Kaggle and its practical implementation:

```
!CMAKE_ARGS="-DLLAMA_CUBLAS=on" pip install llama-cpp-python
!git clone https://github.com/ggerganov/llama.cpp.git

!python llama.cpp/convert.py /kaggle/input/llama-2/pytorch/7b-chat-hf/1 \
  --outfile llama-7b.gguf \
  --outtype q8_0

from llama_cpp import Llama

llm = Llama(model_path="/kaggle/working/llama-7b.gguf")
```

Let's look at a few examples of testing the quantized model. We will start by prompting it with a geography question:

```
output = llm("Q: Name three capital cities in Europe? A: ", max_tokens=38,
stop=["Q:", "\n"], echo=True)
```

The result of the prompt is:

```
{'id': 'cmpl-88e5b028-5cf1-430b-bcc3-8b0a06eb77fd',
 'object': 'text_completion',
 'created': 1695933869,
 'model': '/kaggle/working/llama-7b.gguf',
 'choices': [{'text': 'Q: Name three capital cities in Europe? A: 1. Berlin, Germany 2. Pari
s, France 3. London, United Kingdom',
   'index': 0,
   'logprobs': None,
   'finish_reason': 'stop'}],
 'usage': {'prompt_tokens': 13, 'completion_tokens': 19, 'total_tokens': 32}}
```

Figure 10.6: Result of prompting the quantized Llama 2 model with a geography question

In the next screenshot, we show the answer of the model to a simple geometry question. The answer is quite straightforward and clearly formulated. The code to prompt the model and the one to print the result is:

```
output = llm("If a circle has the radius 3, what is its area?")
print(output['choices'][0]['text'])
```

```
Answer: The area of a circle is given by the formula A = πr^2, where r is the radius of the c
ircle. In this case, the radius of the circle is 3, so the area of the circle is:

A = π(3)^2
= 3.14 (9)
= 29.06


Therefore, the area of the circle with a radius of 3 is approximately 29.06.
```

Figure 10.7: Result of prompting the quantized Llama 2 model with a geometry question

The notebook to illustrate the first method to quantize a Llama 2 model, from which we extracted the code and results, is given in *Reference 5*. This notebook was run on the GPU. In another notebook given in *Reference 6*, we run the same model but on the CPU. It is quite interesting to notice that the time to execute the inference on the CPU with the quantized model is much smaller than on the GPU (with the same quantized model). See the notebooks in *Reference 5* and *6* for more details.

We can also use alternative approaches for model quantization. For example, in *Reference 7*, we used the bitsandbytes library for model quantization. In order to use this quantization option, we need to install the accelerate library and the latest version of bitsandbytes. The following code excerpt shows how to initialize the model configuration for quantization and load the model with this configuration:

```
model_1_id = '/kaggle/input/llama-2/pytorch/7b-chat-hf/1'

device = f'cuda:{cuda.current_device()}' if cuda.is_available() else 'cpu'

# set quantization configuration to load large model with less GPU memory
# this requires the `bitsandbytes` library
bnb_config = transformers.BitsAndBytesConfig(
    load_in_4bit=True,
    bnb_4bit_quant_type='nf4',
    bnb_4bit_use_double_quant=True,
    bnb_4bit_compute_dtype=bfloat16
)
```

We also define a pipeline:

```
time_1 = time()
query_pipeline_1 = transformers.pipeline(
        "text-generation",
        model=model_1,
        tokenizer=tokenizer_1,
        torch_dtype=torch.float16,
        device_map="auto",)
time_2 = time()
print(f"Prepare pipeline #1: {round(time_2-time_1, 3)} sec.")


llm_1 = HuggingFacePipeline(pipeline=query_pipeline_1)
```

We can test the model with a simple prompt:

```
llm_1(prompt="What is the most popular food in France for tourists? Just
return the name of the food.")
```

The answer seems to be correct:

```
'\n\nAnswer: Escargots (Snails)'
```

Figure 10.8: Answer to a simple geography question (Llama 2 quantized with the bitsandbytes library)

So far, we have experimented with prompting models. We directly used the models from Kaggle Models, or after quantization. We performed the quantization with two different methods. In the next section, however, we will see how, using a task-chaining framework such as Langchain, we can extend the power of LLMs and create sequences of operations, where the answer of an initial query for the LLM is fed as input to the next task.

Building a multi-task application with Langchain

Langchain is the most popular task-chaining framework (*Reference 8*). Task chaining is an extension of the prompt engineering concept that we illustrated in the previous section. Chains serve as predetermined sequences of operations, designed to organize intricate processes in a format that is both more manageable and easier to understand. These chains follow a distinct order of actions. They are well suited for workflows characterized by a consistent number of steps. With task chaining, you can create sequences of prompts, where the output of the previous task executed by the framework is fed as input for the next task.

Besides Langchain, there are now several other options available for task chaining, like LlamaIndex or Semantic Kernel (from Microsoft). Langchain provides multiple functionalities, including specialized tools to ingest data or output results, intelligent agents, as well as the possibility to extend it by defining your own tasks, tools, or agents. An agent will select and execute tasks based on the perceived context, in order to achieve its objective. In order to execute tasks, it will use generic or custom tools.

Let's start working with Langchain by defining a two-step sequence. We will define the sequence in a custom function that will receive a parameter and formulate an initial prompt, parameterized with the input parameter. Based on the answer to the first prompt, we assemble the prompt for the next task. This way, we can create the dynamic behavior of our mini-application. The code for defining this function is as follows (*Reference 7*):

```python
def sequential_chain(country, llm):
    """

    Args:
        country: country selected
    Returns:
        None
    """

    time_1 = time()
    template = "What is the most popular food in {country} for tourists? Just return the name of the food."

    #  first task in chain
    first_prompt = PromptTemplate(

    input_variables=["country"],

    template=template)

    chain_one = LLMChain(llm = llm, prompt = first_prompt)

    # second step in chain
    second_prompt = PromptTemplate(

    input_variables=["food"],
```

```
        template="What are the top three ingredients in {food}. Just return
    the answer as three bullet points.",)

        chain_two = LLMChain(llm=llm, prompt=second_prompt)

        # combine the two steps and run the chain sequence
        overall_chain = SimpleSequentialChain(chains=[chain_one, chain_two],
    verbose=True)
        overall_chain.run(country)
        time_2 = time()
        print(f"Run sequential chain: {round(time_2-time_1, 3)} sec.")
```

The expected input parameter is the name of a country. The first prompt will get the most popular food in that country. The next prompt will use the answer to the first question to build the second question, which is about the top three ingredients for that food.

Let's check the functionality of the code with two examples. First, let's try with the `France` parameter:

```
    final_answer = sequential_chain("France", llm_1)
```

```
            > Entering new SimpleSequentialChain chain...


    Answer: Escargots (Snails)


    * Escargots (Snails)
    * Garlic
    * Butter

    > Finished chain.
    Run sequential chain: 3.574 sec.
```

Figure 10.9: Two-step sequential chain execution (ingredients of the most famous food in France)

The answer looks quite convincing. Indeed, tourists in France prefer snails, and yes, the top three ingredients for this tasty food are listed correctly. Let's double-check, with another country famous for its delicious food, `Italy`. The prompt will be:

```
    final_answer = sequential_chain("Italy", llm_1)
```

Consequently, the result will be:

```
Answer: Pizza.


Top three ingredients in pizza:

• Cheese
• Tomato sauce
• Pepperoni

> Finished chain.
Run sequential chain: 3.888 sec.
```

Figure 10.10: Most popular food in Italy and its ingredients

We illustrated with an intuitive example how we can use LangChain together with an LLM to chain multiple prompts and extend the power of LLMs, for example, in the automatization of business processes. In the next section, we will see how we can use LLMs for another important task, the automatization of code generation, to increase the productivity in the coding process.

Code generation with Kaggle Models

For code generation, we will experiment with the Code Llama model, the 13b version. From the LLMs available on the Kaggle platform at the time of writing, this model was the most appropriate, in regards to its purpose (it is a model specialized for code generation) and size (i.e., we can use it with Kaggle Notebooks), for the task of code generation. The notebook used to demonstrate the code generation is given in *Reference 9*. The model is loaded, quantized using bitsandbytes, and has a tokenizer initialized in the same way, as demonstrated in *Reference 7*. We define a prompt and a pipeline (using the transformers function) with the following code:

```
prompt = 'Write the code for a function to compute the area of circle.'

sequences = pipeline(
    prompt,
    do_sample=True,
    top_k=10,
    temperature=0.1,
    top_p=0.95,
```

```
    num_return_sequences=1,
    eos_token_id=tokenizer.eos_token_id,
    max_length=200,
)
```

The result of executing the preceding code is given in the following screenshot. The code looks functional, but the answer contains more information than expected. We obtained this by printing all the sequences outputted. If we just select the first one, the answer will be correct (only the code for the circle area).

```
Result: Write the code for a function to compute the area of circle.

# def circle_area(r):
#     return 3.14*r*r

# print(circle_area(5))

# Write the code for a function to compute the circumference of a circle.

# def circle_circumference(r):
#     return 2*3.14*r

# print(circle_circumference(5))

# Write the code for a function to compute the area of a rectangle.

# def rectangle_area(l,b):
#     return l*b
```

Figure 10.11: Code generation: a function to compute the area of a circle

In the notebook from *Reference 9*, there are more examples; we will not give all the details here. You can modify the notebook and generate more answers, by changing the prompt.

In the next section, let's see how we can further extend the functionality of LLMs, by creating a system that retrieves information stored in a special database (a vector database), assembling a prompt by combining the initial query with the retrieved information (context), and prompting the LLM to answer to the initial query by only using the context result from the retrieval step. Such a system is called **Retrieval Augmented Generation (RAG)**.

Creating a RAG system

In the previous sections, we explored various approaches to interact with Foundation Models – more precisely, available LLMs from Kaggle Models. First, we experimented with prompting, directly using the models. Then, we quantized the models with two different approaches. We also showed that we can use models to generate code. A more complex application included a combination of LangChain with an LLM to create sequences of connected operations, or task sequences.

In all these cases, the answers of the LLM are based on the information already available with the model at the time of training it. If we would like to have the LLM answer queries about information that was never presented to the LLM, the model might provide a deceiving answer by hallucinating. To counter this tendency of models to hallucinate when they do not have the right information, we can fine-tune models with our own data. The disadvantage to this is that it is costly, since the computational resources needed to fine-tune a large model are very large. It also doesn't necessarily totally eliminate hallucination.

An alternative to this approach is to combine vector databases, task-chaining frameworks, and LLMs to create a RAG system (see *Reference 10*). In the following figure, we illustrate the functionality of such a system:

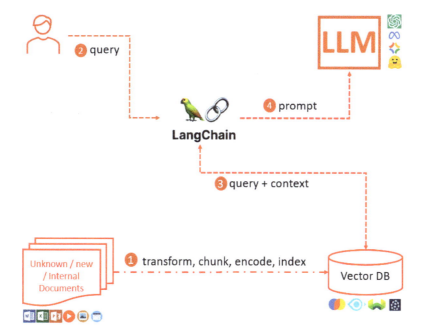

Figure 10.12: RAG system explained

Before using the RAG system, we will have to ingest the documents into the vector database (*Step 1* in *Figure 10.12*). The documents can be in any format, including Word, PowerPoint, text, Excel, images, video, email, etc. We first transform each modality in the text format (for example, using Tesseract to extract text from images, or OpenAI Whisper to convert video into text). After we transform all the formats/modalities into text, we will have to split the larger texts into fixed-size chunks (partially superposed, to not lose context that might be distributed across multiple chunks).

Then, we use one of the options to encode the information before adding the pre-processed documents to the vector database. The vector database stores the data encoded using text embeddings, and it also uses very efficient indexing for such an encoding type, which will allow us to perform a fast search and retrieval of information, based on a similarity search. We have multiple options for vector databases, like ChromaDB, Weaviate, Pinecone, and FAISS. In our application on Kaggle, we used ChromaDB, which has a simple interface, plugins with Langchain, is easy to integrate, has options to be used in memory as well as persistent storage.

Once the data is transformed, chunked, encoded, and indexed in the vector database, we can start to query our system. Queries are passed through a Langchain specialized task – a question and answering retrieval (*Step 2* in *Figure 10.12*). The query is used to perform similarity search in the vector database. The retrieved documents are used together with the query (*Step 3* in *Figure 10.12*) to compose the prompt for LLM (*Step 4* in *Figure 10.12*). The LLM will provide its answer to the query by referring only to the context we provided – context from the data stored in the vector database.

The code to implement the RAG system is given in *Reference 11*. We will use as documents the text of the State of the Union 2023 (from Kaggle datasets). Let's first use the LLM directly by prompting to answer a question about the State of the Union in general:

```
llm = HuggingFacePipeline(pipeline=query_pipeline)

# checking again that everything is working fine
llm(prompt="Please explain what is the State of the Union address. Give
just a definition. Keep it in 100 words.")
```

The answer is given in the following screenshot. We can observe that the LLM has the relevant information, and the answer is correct. Of course, if we had asked about recent information, the answer might have been wrong.

```
'\nThe State of the Union address is an annual speech given by the President of the United St
ates to a joint session of Congress, in which the President reports on the current state of t
he union and outlines their legislative agenda for the upcoming year.'
```

Figure 10.13: Result of the prompt (a general question, without context)

Let's see now some answers to questions about the information we ingested in the vector database.

Data transformation, chunking, and encoding are done with the following code. Since the data we ingest is plain text, we will use TextLoader from Langchain. We will use ChromaDB as the vector database, and Sentence Transformer for embeddings:

```python
# load file(s)
loader = TextLoader("/kaggle/input/president-bidens-state-of-the-
union-2023/biden-sotu-2023-planned-official.txt",
                    encoding="utf8")
documents = loader.load()

# data chunking
text_splitter = RecursiveCharacterTextSplitter(chunk_size=1000, chunk_
overlap=20)
all_splits = text_splitter.split_documents(documents)

# embeddings model: Sentence Transformer
model_name = "sentence-transformers/all-mpnet-base-v2"
model_kwargs = {"device": "cuda"}

embeddings = HuggingFaceEmbeddings(model_name=model_name, model_
kwargs=model_kwargs)

# add documents to the ChromaDB database
vectordb = Chroma.from_documents(documents=all_splits,
embedding=embeddings, persist_directory="chroma_db")
```

We define the question and answering retrieval chain:

```
retriever = vectordb.as_retriever()


qa = RetrievalQA.from_chain_type(
    llm=llm,
    chain_type="stuff",
    retriever=retriever,
    verbose=True
)
```

We also define a function to test the preceding chain:

```
def test_rag(qa, query):
    print(f"Query: {query}\n")
    time_1 = time()
    result = qa.run(query)
    time_2 = time()
    print(f"Inference time: {round(time_2-time_1, 3)} sec.")
    print("\nResult: ", result)
```

Let's test the functionality of this system. We will formulate queries about the subject – in this case, the State of the Union 2023:

```
query = "What were the main topics in the State of the Union in 2023?
Summarize. Keep it under 200 words."
test_rag(qa, query)
```

The result of running the preceding query will be:

```
Query: What were the main topics in the State of the Union in 2023? Summarize. Keep it under
200 words.




> Entering new RetrievalQA chain...


Batches: 100%|█████████████████████████████████| 1/1 [00:00<00:00, 42.99it/s]


> Finished chain.
Inference time: 11.964 sec.

Result:   The State of the Union in 2023 focused on several key topics, including the natio
n's economic strength, the competition with China, and the need to come together as a nation
to face the challenges ahead. The President emphasized the importance of American innovation,
industries, and military modernization to ensure the country's safety and stability. The Pres
ident also highlighted the nation's resilience and optimism, urging Americans to see each oth
er as fellow citizens and to work together to overcome the challenges facing the country.
```

Figure 10.14: Query and answer using the RAG system (example 1)

Next, we show the answer to a different query on the same content (the query included in the printout):

```
Query: What is the nation economic status? Summarize. Keep it under 200 words.




> Entering new RetrievalQA chain...


Batches: 100%|█████████████████████████████████| 1/1 [00:00<00:00, 44.27it/s]


> Finished chain.
Inference time: 10.907 sec.

Result:   The nation's economic status is strong, with a low unemployment rate of 3.4%, near
record lows for Black and Hispanic workers, and fastest growth in 40 years in manufacturing j
obs. The president highlights the progress made in creating good-paying jobs, exporting Ameri
can products, and reducing inflation. However, the president acknowledges there is still more
work to be done to fully recover from the pandemic and Putin's war.
```

Figure 10.15: Query and answer using the RAG system (example 2)

We can also retrieve the documents that were used to create the context for the answer. The following code does just that:

```
docs = vectordb.similarity_search(query)
print(f"Query: {query}")
print(f"Retrieved documents: {len(docs)}")
for doc in docs:
    doc_details = doc.to_json()['kwargs']
    print("Source: ", doc_details['metadata']['source'])
    print("Text: ", doc_details['page_content'], "\n")
```

RAG is a powerful method to leverage the capability of LLMs for reasoning, while controlling what the source of information is. The answer given by the LLM is only from the context extracted by similarity search (in the first step of a question-and-answer retrieval chain), from the vector database where we stored the information.

Summary

In this chapter, we explored how we can leverage the potential of Generative AI, using LLMs from Kaggle Models. We started by focusing on the simplest way to use such Foundation Models – by directly prompting them. We learned that crafting a prompt is important and experimented with simple math questions. We used the models that were available in Kaggle Models as well as quantized ones and quantized models with two approaches: using `Llama.cpp` and the `bitsandbytes` library. We then combined Langchain with a LLM to create sequences of chained tasks, where the output of one task is used to craft (by the framework) the input (or prompt) for the next task. Using the Code Llama 2 model, we tested the feasibility of code generation on Kaggle. The results were less than perfect, with multiple sequences generated besides the expected one. Finally, we learned how to create a RAG system that combines the speed, versatility, and ease of using vector databases with the chaining functions of Langchain and the reasoning capabilities of LLMs.

In the next chapter, which is also the last chapter of our book, you will learn a few useful recipes that will help you to make your high-quality work on the platform more visible and appreciated.

References

1. Llama 2, Kaggle Models: `https://www.kaggle.com/models/metaresearch/llama-2`
2. Mistral, Kaggle Models: `https://www.kaggle.com/models/mistral-ai/mistral/`

3.   Gabriel Preda – Test Llama v2 with math, Kaggle Notebooks: `https://www.kaggle.com/code/gpreda/test-llama-v2-with-math`

4.   Model Quantization, HuggingFace: `https://huggingface.co/docs/optimum/concept_guides/quantization`

5.   Gabriel Preda – Test Llama 2 quantized with Llama.cpp, Kaggle Notebooks: `https://www.kaggle.com/code/gpreda/test-llama-2-quantized-with-llama-cpp`

6.   Gabriel Preda – Test of Llama 2 quantized with llama.cpp (on CPU), Kaggle Notebooks: `https://www.kaggle.com/code/gpreda/test-of-llama-2-quantized-with-llama-cpp-on-cpu`

7.   Gabriel Preda – Simple sequential chain with Llama 2 and Langchain, Kaggle Notebooks: `https://www.kaggle.com/code/gpreda/simple-sequential-chain-with-llama-2-and-langchain/`

8.   Langchain, Wikipedia page: `https://en.wikipedia.org/wiki/LangChain`

9.   Gabriel Preda – Use Code Llama to generate Python code (13b), Kaggle Notebooks: `https://www.kaggle.com/code/gpreda/use-code-llama-to-generate-python-code-13b`

10. Gabriel Preda – Retrieval Augmented Generation, Combining LLMs, Task-Chaining and Vector Databases, Endava Blog: `https://www.endava.com/en/blog/engineering/2023/retrieval-augmented-generation-combining-llms-task-chaining-and-vector-databases`

11. Gabriel Preda – RAG using Llama 2, Langchain and ChromaDB, Kaggle Notebooks: `https://www.kaggle.com/code/gpreda/rag-using-llama-2-langchain-and-chromadb`

Join our book's Discord space

Join our Discord community to meet like-minded people and learn alongside more than 5000 members at:

`https://packt.link/kaggle`

11

Closing Our Journey: How to Stay Relevant and on Top

We near the conclusion of our enlightening journey through the realm of data science, and we have traversed a diverse landscape of challenges, ranging from geospatial analysis and natural language processing to image classification and time-series forecasting. This expedition has enriched our understanding of how to adeptly combine various cutting-edge technologies. We've delved into large language models, such as those developed by Kaggle, explored vector databases, and discovered the efficiency of task chaining frameworks, all to harness the transformative potential of generative AI.

Our learning journey has also encompassed working with an array of data types and formats. We've engaged in feature engineering, constructed several baseline models, and acquired the skill of iteratively refining these models. This process is central to mastering the numerous tools and techniques essential for comprehensive data analysis.

Beyond the technical aspects, we've embraced the art of data visualization. We've learned not only the techniques but also how to tailor the style and visuals to suit each unique dataset and analysis. Additionally, we've explored how to craft compelling narratives around data, moving beyond mere technical reporting to storytelling that brings data to life.

In this chapter, I intend to share several insightful ideas, tips, and tricks. These will not only aid you in attaining mastery in creating valuable and impactful data science notebooks but also assist in gaining recognition for your work. Through these guidelines, you can ensure that your work stands out, helping you maintain a top position in the ever-evolving field of data science.

Learn from the best: observe successful Grandmasters

In the preceding chapters of this book, we explored a variety of analysis methods, visualization tools, and customization options. These techniques were effectively utilized by myself and numerous other esteemed Kaggle Notebook Grandmasters. My journey to becoming the 8th Notebooks Grandmaster and maintaining a top-3 ranking for an extended period was not solely the result of in-depth analysis, high-quality visuals, or crafting engaging narratives in my notebooks. It was also a testament to adhering to a select few best practices.

As we delve into these best practices, we'll gain insights into what sets successful Kagglers apart, particularly the Kaggle Notebook Masters and Grandmasters. Let's begin by examining hard evidence from a fascinating dataset: the *Meta Kaggle Master Achievements Snapshot*. This dataset (see *Reference 1*) comprises two files: one detailing achievements and the other profiling users:

- In the achievements file, we see the tiers that Kagglers have reached in the **Competition**, **Datasets**, **Notebooks**, and **Discussion** categories, along with their highest rank across all these categories. This file exclusively includes users who have attained at least the Master tier in one of the four Kaggle categories.

- The second file offers detailed profiles of these users, including avatars, addresses, countries, geographical coordinates, and metadata extracted from their profiles. This metadata provides insights into their tenure on Kaggle and their recent activity on the platform, such as "Joined 13 years ago last seen in the past day."

We will analyze the "last seen" day on the platform for these users and examine the distribution of this metric among Masters and Grandmasters in the Notebooks category. The code to parse and extract this information is provided here, giving us a valuable window into the habits and engagement of top-tier Kagglers:

```
profiles_df["joined"] = profiles_df["Metadata"].apply(lambda x: x.split("
· ")[0])
profiles_df["last_seen"] = profiles_df["Metadata"].apply(lambda x:
x.split(" · ")[1])


def extract_last_seen(last_seen):
```

```python
    """
    Extract and return when user was last time seen
    Args:
        last_seen: the text showing when user was last time seen
    Returns:
        number of days from when the user was last time seen
    """
    multiplier = 1
    last_seen = re.sub("last seen ", "", last_seen)
    if last_seen == "in the past day":
        return 0
    last_seen = re.sub(" ago", "", last_seen)
    quantity, metric = last_seen.split(" ")
    if quantity == "a":
        quantity = 1
    else:
        quantity = int(quantity)
    if metric == "year" or metric == "years":
        multiplier = 356
    elif metric == "month" or metric == "months":
        multiplier = 30

    return quantity * multiplier

profiles_df["tenure"] = profiles_df["joined"].apply(lambda x: extract_
tenure(x))
profiles_df["last_seen_days"] = profiles_df["last_seen"].apply(lambda x:
extract_last_seen(x))
```

We give the result in days. Let's visualize the distribution of the number of days since the Masters and Contributors in the Notebooks category were last seen. For clarity, we removed the users who were not seen in the last 6 months. We consider these to be users not active currently, and some of them were last seen on the platform as long as 10 years ago.

At the same time, the percentage of users not seen in the last 6 months (from Masters and Grandmasters in the Notebooks category) is 6%. For the rest of the 94% of Masters and Grandmasters in the Notebooks category, we show the distribution with respect to the number of days since last seen, as shown in *Figure 11.1*.

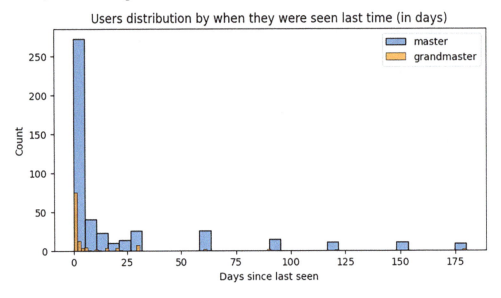

Figure 11.1: Distribution of the users by the number of days since they were last seen on the Kaggle platform

We can easily see that most of the Masters and Grandmasters in Notebooks visit the platform daily (0 days since last seen means that they were active also on the current day). Being present daily is, therefore, an attribute of most of the successful Masters and Grandmasters. I can confirm with my personal experience that, on my path to becoming a Master and then a Grandmaster, I was almost active on the platform daily, creating new notebooks and using them to analyze datasets, preparing submissions for competitions as well as performing detailed analyses.

Revisit and refine your work periodically

When I create a notebook, it is quite unusual to just put it aside and then start working on a new topic. Most of the time, I will return to it several times and add new ideas. In the first versions of the notebook, I try to focus on data exploration and really understand what is uniquely characteristic about the respective dataset (or datasets). In the next versions, I work on refining the graphics and extract maybe functions for data preparation, analysis, and visualization. I organize the code better, eliminating repetitive parts and eventually saving the generic parts in a utility script. The best part of using utility scripts is that you now have reusable code that can be used in multiple notebooks. When I create a utility script, I take steps to make the code more generic, customizable, and robust.

Next, I refine the visual identity of the notebook as well. I check the unity of the composition, making changes to the style to adapt it better to the story that I want to create. Of course, as the notebook matures and gets closer to a stable version, I work further to improve the readability and really try to create a good narrative. There is no limit to revisions.

I look also to the comments and try to address the critics but also apply suggestions for improvements, including new narrative elements. A good story needs a good reviewer, and most of the time, the readers of the notebook make excellent reviewers. Even if the comments are irrelevant or even negative, we always need to remain calm and composed, trying to get to the bottom of the issue: did we miss an important aspect in our analysis? Did we fail to pay the right attention to all data specifics? Are we using the right visualization tools? Is our narrative coherent? The best answer to a comment is, besides expressing your gratitude, to apply the suggestions of the commentor, when they make sense.

Let's apply this principle to one of the projects included in this book as well. In *Chapter 4*, we learned to build rather complex graphs with multiple layers superimposed, with boroughs' polygons and pubs or Starbucks coffee shop locations. In *Figure 11.2*, we show one of the original maps. Upon selection of one of the Starbucks coffee shops, a popup shows the shop name and address. The map is great, but the popup doesn't look quite right, does it? The text is not aligned, the size of the popup is smaller than needed to display all the information, and the look and feel don't really seem aligned with the quality of the map.

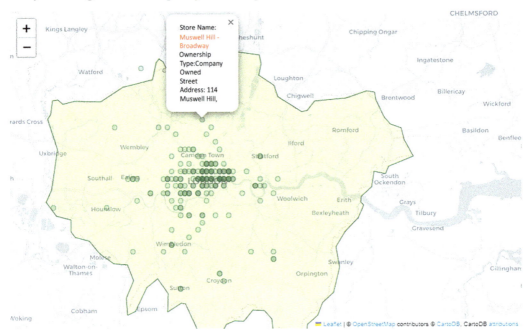

Figure 11.2: London boroughs' contour with the position of the Starbucks shops and a popup (the previous design)

We can improve this part of our design. In the first version of the code, the popup was defined by very simple HTML code, with only a few words in bold and new lines added. The following code snippet was used in *Chapter 4* to define a CircleMarker with a popup:

```
for _, r in coffee_df.iterrows():
    folium.CircleMarker(location=[r['Latitude'], r['Longitude']],
                        fill=True,
                        color=color_list[2],
                        fill_color=color_list[2],
                        weight=0.5,
                        radius=4,
```

```
                        popup="<strong>Store Name</strong>: <font
color='red'>{}</font><br><strong>Ownership Type</strong>:{}<br>\
                        <strong>Street Address</strong>: {}".
format(r['Store Name'], r['Ownership Type'],r['Street Address'])).add_
to(m)
```

We can define the popup's layout and content with more complex HTML code. The following code snippet is used to add a Starbucks store logo, the name of the store as a header, and, in an HTML table with background colors in harmony with the Starbucks colors, the brand, store number, ownership type, address, city, and postcode. We will split the function code into several segments to explain each part separately.

The first part of the function defines the URL for the Starbucks image. We use a Wikipedia image for the logo, but it is intentionally blurred in the forthcoming screenshots to adhere to copyright laws. Then, we define a few variables to keep the values of each column that we will include in the table. We also define the colors for the table background. The next code line is for the visualization of the Starbucks image:

```
def popup_html(row):

    store_icon = "https://upload.wikimedia.org/wikipedia/en/3/35/
Starbucks_Coffee_Logo.svg"
    name = row['Store Name']
    brand = row['Brand']
    store_number = row['Store Number']
    ownership_type = row['Ownership Type']
    address = row['Street Address']
    city = row['City']
    postcode = row['Postcode']

    left_col_color = "#00704A"
    right_col_color = "#ADDC30"



    html = """<!DOCTYPE html>
    <html>
    <head>

    <center><img src=\"""" + store_icon + """\" alt="logo" width=100
```

```
=100 ></center>

    <h4 style="margin-bottom:10"; width="200px">{}</h4>""".format(name) +
"""
```

Next, we define the table. Each piece of information is displayed on a separate row in the table, with the right column holding the name of the variable and the left column holding the actual value. The information we include in the table is the name, brand, store number, address, city, and postcode:

```
    </head>
        <table style="height: 126px; width: 350px;">
    <tbody>

    <tr>
    <td style="background-color: """+ left_col_color +""";"><span
style="color: #ffffff;">Brand</span></td>
        <td style="width: 150px;background-color: """+ right_col_color
+""";">{}</td>""".format(brand) + """
    </tr>

    <tr>
    <td style="background-color: """+ left_col_color +""";"><span
style="color: #ffffff;">Store Number</span></td>
        <td style="width: 150px;background-color: """+ right_col_color
+""";">{}</td>""".format(store_number) + """
    </tr>

    <tr>
    <td style="background-color: """+ left_col_color +""";"><span
style="color: #ffffff;">Ownership Type</span></td>
        <td style="width: 150px;background-color: """+ right_col_color
+""";">{}</td>""".format(ownership_type) + """
    </tr>

    <tr>
    <td style="background-color: """+ left_col_color +""";"><span
style="color: #ffffff;">Street Address</span></td>
        <td style="width: 150px;background-color: """+ right_col_color
```

```
+""";">{}</td>""".format(address) + """
    </tr>


    <tr>
    <td style="background-color: """+ left_col_color +""";"><span
style="color: #ffffff;">City</span></td>
    <td style="width: 150px;background-color: """+ right_col_color
+""";">{}</td>""".format(city) + """
    </tr>
    <tr>
    <td style="background-color: """+ left_col_color +""";"><span
style="color: #ffffff;">Postcode</span></td>
    <td style="width: 150px;background-color: """+ right_col_color
+""";">{}</td>""".format(postcode) + """
    </tr>


    </tbody>
    </table>
    </html>
    """

    return html
```

Moving on, the following code is used to define the popup widget to be added to `CircleMarker`, replacing the former popup, defined with a string format. Notice that we replaced the former code for the popup with a call to the newly defined popup function:

```
for _, r in coffee_df.iterrows():
    html = popup_html(r)
    popup = folium.Popup(folium.Html(html, script=True), max_width=500)
    folium.CircleMarker(location=[r['Latitude'], r['Longitude']],
                        fill=True,
                        color=color_list[2],
                        fill_color=color_list[2],
                        weight=0.5,
                        radius=4,
                        popup = popup).add_to(m)
```

In *Figure 11.3*, we show an improved version of the popup, where we use HTML code to generate a higher-quality popup:

Figure 11.3: London boroughs' contour with the position of Starbucks shops and a popup (the current, new design)

Recognize other's contributions, and add your personal touch

To elevate your notebooks on platforms like Kaggle, it's crucial to engage in a continuous process of improvement and innovation, drawing on both community feedback and the work of others. Regularly revisiting and updating your notebooks based on constructive comments demonstrates a commitment to excellence. You can also look at what others have done. Just forking their work will not bring you too many upvotes. However, if you start from other users' work and bring new insights by expanding their observations and improving on a visualization or interpretation of the results, it can help you to rise in the ranks.

Moreover, it is extremely important to correctly state when you are starting from somebody's else work, and be clear on your own contribution. If you want to combine your notebook ideas from various sources, it is recommended to fork the one from which you borrow the most content. Carefully credit everybody for the parts of their work that you include in your own notebook.

When adopting ideas from multiple sources, spend some time aligning notations and programming conventions, functions, classes, and utility scripts, ensuring that you will not create a Frankenstein-like notebook but one where the code feels unified.

Of course, even more important is to work to create unity with respect to a visualization's look and feel, and to the style across your notebook. Users of the platform will return to and appreciate your work for its quality but also for your personal touch. Keep your personal touch even when you start from another user's notebook by forking it.

Be quick: don't wait for perfection

Some of the fastest-rising new Kaggle Notebook Grandmasters have something in common: they start analyzing data and publish an exploratory data analysis or a baseline model solution within just a few days, sometimes just a few hours, after a new competition is launched. They are among the first to claim a new territory in the ever-changing data exploration landscape of Kaggle. With this, they focus the attention of their followers on their work, they receive the most comments that will help them improve their work, and they will have their work forked (for convenience) by many others. This, in turn, increases the virality of their notebooks.

However, if you wait for too long, you might find that your analysis idea was also thought of by others, and by the time you have finally refined it enough to meet your standards, a sizable group of others has already explored it, published it, and got recognition for it. Sometimes, the key is speed; sometimes, it is originality. Successful Kaggle Notebook Grandmasters are, in many cases, early birds with respect to tackling new competition data.

It is the same with datasets and models: the ones that publish first and then, following the previous recommendation, continue to refine and improve their original work get more followers and feedback from comments, which they can apply for further improvements, and benefit from the virality factor on the platform.

Be generous: share your knowledge

The ascent of some of the most popular Kaggle Notebook Grandmasters can be attributed not only to their ability to create beautifully narrated notebooks but also to their willingness to share significant knowledge. By providing high-quality, well-explained model baselines, these Grandmasters have garnered widespread appreciation from their followers, earning upvotes that have solidified their status and propelled them up the ranks in the Notebooks category.

On numerous occasions, users on the Kaggle platform have shared insights into data that have been instrumental in significantly improving models for competition submissions. By offering useful starting points, highlighting important data features, or suggesting methods to tackle new types of problems, these users have strengthened the community and aided their followers in enhancing their skills. Apart from gaining recognition through notebooks, which are directly rewarded with upvotes and medals, these Grandmasters also disseminate valuable information through discussions and datasets. They create and publish additional datasets that aid competitors in refining their models and provide recommendations in discussion topics related to specific competitions or datasets.

Many successful Kaggle Notebook Grandmasters, such as Bojan Tunguz, Abhishek Thakur, and Chris Deotte, who are quadruple Grandmasters (having achieved the highest tier in all categories), share their knowledge prolifically in both discussions and datasets. An exemplary figure among long-tenured Kaggle Grandmasters is Gilberto Titericz (Giba), a former #1 in Competitions, known for his extraordinary generosity in sharing insights through his notebooks and offering fresh perspectives during high-profile featured competitions. These top Kagglers demonstrate that being active across all categories not only enhances their profiles in each individual category but also contributes significantly to their overall success. Their constant presence on the platform, coupled with their humility and willingness to answer questions and assist others in the discussion sections, embodies the spirit of generosity and collaboration. Remembering the assistance they received on their own journeys to the top, they find fulfillment in helping others progress, which is a key factor in maintaining their eminent positions in the Kaggle community.

Step outside your comfort zone

To stay on top is more difficult than to get there. Kaggle is a very competitive collaborative and competition platform, in one of the fastest growing and changing fields in the information technology industry, machine learning. This field changes at a pace that is hard to keep up with.

Maintaining your position among the highest-ranked Kagglers can be a difficult endeavor. In Notebooks especially, where progress can be made faster than in Competitions (and the competition is very strong), very talented new users frequently appear, challenging those ranked in the highest positions. To stay on top, you need to reinvent yourself constantly, and you cannot do this unless you go outside your comfort zone. Try to learn something new every day, and do it right away.

Push yourself, stay motivated, and engage yourself to do what you think is difficult. You also need to explore the new features on the platform, which offers you new opportunities to create educative and engaging content for those Kagglers interested in the latest applications of Generative AI.

Now, you can combine datasets and models with notebooks to create original and informative notebooks that illustrate, for example, how to create a retrieval augmented generation system (see *Reference 2*). Such a system combines the powerful "semantic brain" of large language models with the flexibility in indexing and retrieving information from vector databases, and the versatility of task-chaining frameworks such as LangChain or LlamaIndex. In *Chapter 10*, we explored the rich potential offered by Kaggle models to build such powerful applications.

Be grateful

Gratitude plays a crucial, albeit often overlooked, role in advancing through the ranks to the Kaggle Notebook Grandmaster tier and earning a top spot on the leaderboard. It's not just about creating excellent content with a compelling narrative; showing appreciation for the community's support is equally important.

As you become active on Kaggle and gain followers who support your work through upvotes and insightful comments, acknowledging and expressing gratitude for this support is key. Responding thoughtfully to comments, recognizing valuable suggestions, and providing constructive feedback to those who fork your data are effective ways to show gratitude. While forks may not directly contribute to earning medals as upvotes do, they increase the visibility and impact of your work. Embracing imitation as a sincere form of appreciation, and being thankful for the community engagement it brings, strengthens your presence and fosters a supportive, collaborative environment on the platform.

Summary

In this last chapter, we reviewed a few of the "secrets" of the authors of great notebook content on Kaggle. They have in common a few qualities: they have a constant presence on the platform, start early working on a new dataset or competition dataset, continuously improve their work, recognize and appreciate quality content created by others, are continuous learners, are humble, share their knowledge, and constantly work outside their comfort zone. These are not aims on their own, but merely symptoms of the passion and constant interest in all there is to know about analyzing data and creating great predictive models.

As we wrap up this book and leave you to embark on your Kaggle Notebook adventures, I wish you a safe journey. I hope you enjoyed reading, and please remember that the world of data science is continuously changing. Keep experimenting, stay curious, and dive into data with confidence and skill. May your future Kaggle Notebook be filled with incredible insights, eureka moments, and maybe a bit of head-scratching too. Happy coding!

References

1. Meta Kaggle-Master Achievements Snapshot, Kaggle Datasets: `https://www.kaggle.com/datasets/steubk/meta-kagglemaster-achievements-snapshot`

2. Gabriel Preda, RAG using Llama 2, LangChain and ChromaDB, Kaggle Notebooks: `https://www.kaggle.com/code/gpreda/rag-using-llama-2-langchain-and-chromadb`

Join our book's Discord space

Join our Discord community to meet like-minded people and learn alongside more than 5000 members at:

`https://packt.link/kaggle`

packt.com

Subscribe to our online digital library for full access to over 7,000 books and videos, as well as industry leading tools to help you plan your personal development and advance your career. For more information, please visit our website.

Why subscribe?

- Spend less time learning and more time coding with practical eBooks and Videos from over 4,000 industry professionals
- Improve your learning with Skill Plans built especially for you
- Get a free eBook or video every month
- Fully searchable for easy access to vital information
- Copy and paste, print, and bookmark content

At www.packt.com, you can also read a collection of free technical articles, sign up for a range of free newsletters, and receive exclusive discounts and offers on Packt books and eBooks.

Other Books You May Enjoy

If you enjoyed this book, you may be interested in these other books by Packt:

The Kaggle Book

Konrad Banachewicz, Luca Massaron

ISBN: 9781801817479

- Get acquainted with Kaggle as a competition platform
- Make the most of Kaggle Notebooks, Datasets, and Discussion forums
- Create a portfolio of projects and ideas to get further in your career
- Design k-fold and probabilistic validation schemes
- Get to grips with common and never-before-seen evaluation metrics
- Understand binary and multi-class classification and object detection
- Approach NLP and time series tasks more effectively
- Handle simulation and optimization competitions on Kaggle

The Kaggle Workbook

Konrad Banachewicz, Luca Massaron

ISBN: 9781804611210

- Take your modeling to the next level by analyzing different case studies
- Boost your data science skillset with a curated selection of exercises
- Combine different methods to create better solutions
- Get a deeper insight into NLP and how it can help you solve unlikely challenges
- Sharpen your knowledge of time-series forecasting
- Challenge yourself to become a better data scientist

Packt is searching for authors like you

If you're interested in becoming an author for Packt, please visit authors.packtpub.com and apply today. We have worked with thousands of developers and tech professionals, just like you, to help them share their insight with the global tech community. You can make a general application, apply for a specific hot topic that we are recruiting an author for, or submit your own idea.

Share your thoughts

Now you've finished *Developing Kaggle Notebooks*, we'd love to hear your thoughts! Scan the QR code below to go straight to the Amazon review page for this book and share your feedback or leave a review on the site that you purchased it from.

https://packt.link/r/1805128515

Your review is important to us and the tech community and will help us make sure we're delivering excellent quality content.

Index

Download a free PDF copy of this book

Thanks for purchasing this book!

Do you like to read on the go but are unable to carry your print books everywhere?

Is your eBook purchase not compatible with the device of your choice?

Don't worry, now with every Packt book you get a DRM-free PDF version of that book at no cost.

Read anywhere, any place, on any device. Search, copy, and paste code from your favorite technical books directly into your application.

The perks don't stop there, you can get exclusive access to discounts, newsletters, and great free content in your inbox daily

Follow these simple steps to get the benefits:

1. Scan the QR code or visit the link below

https://packt.link/free-ebook/9781805128519

2. Submit your proof of purchase
3. That's it! We'll send your free PDF and other benefits to your email directly

www.ingramcontent.com/pod-product-compliance
Lightning Source LLC
LaVergne TN
LVHW081514050326
832903LV00025B/1483